The Beacon on the Hill

THE
BEACON
ON THE HILL

The Story of Christ Church, Swindon,
and the Community it Serves

MARK BRIDGEMAN

ISBN: 978 1 8381882 1 4

British Library Cataloguing in Publication Data
A catalogue record for this book is available from the
British Library

Printed and bound in Great Britain by
Bell & Bain Ltd, Glasgow

CONTENTS

*'On Hearing the Full Peal of Ten Bells from
Christ Church, Swindon, Wilts.'*, by John Betjeman.

THE BEACON ON THE HILL

On Hearing the Full Peal of Ten Bells
from Christ Church, Swindon, Wilts.

Your peal of ten ring over then this town,
Ring on my men nor ever ring them down.
This winter chill, let sunset spill cold fire
On villa'd hill and on Sir Gilbert's spire,
So new, so high, so pure, so broach'd, so tall.
Long run the thunder of these bells through all!

Oh still white headstones on these fields of sound
Hear you the wedding joybells wheeling round!
Oh brick-built breeding boxes of new souls,
Hear how the pealing through the louvres rolls!
Now birth and death-reminding bells ring clear,
Loud under 'planes and over changing gear.

John Betjeman

Reproduced from the *Collected Poems of John Betjeman* (1958) with
the kind permission of John Murray (Publishers) Ltd.

Sir John Betjeman CBE was an English poet, writer, and broadcaster. Born in London, and educated at Magdalen College, Oxford, Betjeman had a passion for poetry and for Victorian architecture, which inspired him to write the above poem, on a visit to Swindon. He came to Swindon again in 1962 to record a television documentary about the town; and was made (a popular) Poet Laureate of the United Kingdom from 1972 until his death in 1984, at the age of 77.

Foreword
to the Original Edition of
The Old Lady On The Hill

The year 2001 is a momentous point in the history of the Anglican Church in Old Town, Swindon. We celebrate the 150th Anniversary of Christ Church in November and only a month before that, the 75th Anniversary of the daughter church St Mary-in-the-Mall. I am delighted to have the opportunity of writing this foreword for the history of the parish. It tells the human story of Christ Church, its joys and sorrows, but above all the story of God's faithfulness and Grace toward the Christian community over generations, past & present.

It is a privilege being called by God to serve Him and the people of Old Town as Vicar of Christ Church. I have so much appreciated the wise counsel and friendship of my two immediate predecessors, Canon Derek Palmer and Canon Owen Barraclough. It is a great encouragement to know that long before any of us ever came to Swindon people were praying here, and long after we leave people will continue praying here. Our task is to play a small part in the continuing work and mission of the Christian church in Swindon.

Some of you will remember much of the history recorded here as you have been associated with Christ Church for many years. Others will have joined God's family in Swindon much more recently. Many of you will associate Christ Church with landmarks of your own family history through Baptisms, Weddings and Funerals. Whoever we are and whatever our reasons for reading this splendid book there is something here for us all.

In May 1999 in time for our Pentecost celebrations a new noticeboard for the front of Christ Church was designed and donated by a local Graphic Designer, Robert Dixon who had just been confirmed in the Ecumenical Parish of Old Town. The picture shows the sun shining through the clouds, a particularly evocative image with these words superimposed:

The Beacon on the Hill

Christ Church, Swindon
Jesus Christ is the same yesterday, today and forever
An Anglican church open daily for friendship, worship,
prayer and support
Jesus is Lord

These words are a constant reminder of why we are here and that we are part of Christ's church. I pray that our involvement with Christ Church and St Mary's will be a great blessing to us and to others. May God continue to guide His people here as we move into the third Christian Millennium with all its challenges and opportunities. May we pass on the Christian faith, 'Jesus Christ, the same yesterday, today and forever' and our historic Church buildings to the next generation as faithfully as possible; and may we all be true Christian ambassadors and friends of Christ Church.

Reverend Simon Stevenette
Vicar of Christ Church, Swindon
November 2001

The Revd. Simon Stevenette (right) during his induction at
Christ Church. Pictured with his father, Revd. John Stevenette.

Foreword to the 2020 Edition of
The Beacon On The Hill

Thank you for supporting the publication of this special book and for reading the continuing story of Christ Church.

I was born on the 21st July 1962 in Brighton, on the same day as Brian and Pam Bridgeman were married in St Barnabas Church, Swindon. I have a vivid memory of 7th November 2001, our 150th anniversary celebration service when Brian Bridgeman walked down the aisle, with his co-writer Teresa Squires, and we launched the book *The Old Lady on the Hill*, with a prayer of blessing. It is very special, now twenty years later Pam Bridgeman is now one of our Church Wardens and Lay Chair; and also that Pam and Brian's son Mark is writing this new book. God bless you and your family.

As I thank God, my family and all those who have worked with us as teammates over these years, I am aware that much has changed which I will reflect briefly upon. Praise God that some things never change, His faithfulness, compassion, grace and mercy for instance. Personally, I praise God for his continuing call, blessing and equipping for the challenges implicit in my ordination service when I was given a copy of the New Testament with the words:

'Simon, proclaim the Gospel in each and every generation'.

Nicola and I were married in 1986 at St Edward's Leek by my father John Stevenette. Nicola and I share Christian ministry together. We have been blessed with 5 sons; Thomas born in 1991, Robert in 1993, Edward in 1995, William in 1998 and Hugo in 2004. We were a young family when we moved to Swindon in September 1998. Nicola and I are grateful to the people of Swindon and so many friends at Christ Church with St Mary's in the Old Town Partnership of Churches who have supported us, loved us, and prayed for us as a family.

As a husband, Dad, son, brother, Vicar and human being I have learnt a huge amount over these last 22 years, I trust that I have matured spiritually and become wiser. Running is one of my passions and on April 25th 2002 I ran the London Marathon in my 40th year raising money for local charities including the Friends of Christ Church Skyline Appeal. My usual run three times a week takes me through the Lawns into the Polo Ground, through the Arboretum and twice around Coate Water. It is a special time of prayer, recreation when I focus my body, mind and spirit on what is important. I run in all seasons so enjoy or endure different weathers. The run takes me close to the Great Western Hospital where my life was saved life twice; in 2003/04 from Hodgkin's Lymphoma cancer necessitating a Stem Cell transplant in September 2004, after I had relapsed following the birth of our 5th son Hugo in May 2004. In September 2016 I contracted Sepsis, most likely developed from cutting back thorny trees in the church yard. These were life-changing experiences for me and us as a family.

We have seen the Swindon Community, the physical Christ Church with St Mary's site and above all people's lives transformed by God's grace and generosity. The fruit of this has been in celebrating the Christian faith each year when men and women, boys and girls of all ages are baptised and confirmed in our Partnership Confirmations in one of our three churches, Bath Road Methodist, Immanuel United Reformed Church or Christ Church.

I have been changed by meeting so many fascinating people throughout our community as Vicar, friend, Chaplain, school Governor, and Rotarian colleague. I have loved working in our Swindon Deanery as Area Dean for six years 2011-17 and across the Bristol Diocese becoming Honorary Canon at Bristol Cathedral in October 2015.

I have been changed by international visits to Westborough USA and Uganda linked to the Bristol Diocese. We have, together, developed new plans and projects to share the love of God in Jesus Christ in the power of his Holy spirit with the great people of our Old Town parish. This has been seen in worship, prayer, preaching, teaching and maintaining and developing our buildings. We have worked with other partners in running an outstanding Community Centre to combat loneliness; to support mental health and well-being through the award winning Mindful Employer Network, to support Asylum Seekers moving as guests to our town through The Harbour Project, to support children and young people through our Sunday club, toddler groups, schools work and our Partnership Messy Church. Above all I have learnt that every person I meet is a gift from God, unique, special, deeply loved and very gifted. As I listen to the stories and encourage their spiritual growth I am continually surprised by God by his provision and presence.

Thank you for your partnership in the Gospel, for all we have shared and celebrated together as a church family. Let us look to the future with joy and expectation thanking God and our sisters and brothers who have gone before us and for the solid foundation on which we build.

I love the Park Run movement, which is a voluntary initiative for people of all ages and abilities to run 5kms at 9am each Saturday, ours is at Lydiard Park. I love the rounds of applause cheering people on as they complete the course in whatever time. Friends, please be aware of the Saints who are cheering us on and praying that we might be faithful and keep the faith until the end. To God be the Glory, Great things he has done.

Reverend Canon Simon Stevenette
Vicar of Christ Church, Swindon
June 2020

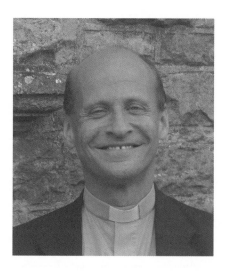

Introduction

The Historian H.S.Tallamy, in his *Studies in the History of Swindon 1950*, lamented that Swindon was '*always just off the map of history*'. The great national events of the centuries seemed to leave little impression on the town. Perhaps this book can go some way to redressing that balance, with an updated, expanded and revised history of Christ Church and its enduring influence on, and within, the town it looks majestically over.

There has been much interest from the community in Swindon in learning more about the history of Christ Church, and about its predecessor Holy Rood in the Lawns. Sadly the two books written on those magnificent buildings are long out of print and the authors (Brian Bridgeman and Denis Bird) passed away. I was approached by The Friends of Christ Church in 2019 to discuss the opportunity to update my father's book *The Old Lady on the Hill*, published in 2001, shortly before his death. I seized the opportunity. However, *The Beacon on the Hill*, is much more than just an update on the previous book. I decided very early on in the process that this was, perhaps, a once in a lifetime opportunity to produce a book that would not only include all of *The Old Lady on the Hill* and *The Story of Holy Rood*, by Denis Bird (of which copyright has passed to me), but to revise, enhance and update the complete story of almost 1,000 years of worship in Old Town. The narrative has been much added to and I hope the extra stories, information and pictures will be of interest to everyone.

This new book provides a welcome opportunity for the reader to access the complete story of both churches, but also that of Old Town, and the growth of Swindon. Modern research techniques have also enabled me to delve much deeper than was possible for either my father or Denis Bird – and the results are very interesting indeed!

To begin the story of Christ Church, however, we must travel much further back in time to the era before Sir Gilbert Scott's masterpiece sat proudly as the highest point in the town.

I hope your enjoyment of the book reflects my pride in being able to write it.

Mark Bridgeman

1

Holy Rood:
The Old Parish Church Of Swindon

The Early History of Swindon

People have lived in the area we now call Swindon for a very long time, leaving us many clues to their whereabouts. One of the most enduring images seen from the present town is the copse of trees (Four Mile Clump) on the top of Liddington Hill, which was the site of an Iron Age hillfort. Along with its near neighbour, Barbury Castle, this was positioned on the ancient strategic route of the Ridgeway, which strode across the Downs; the Neolithic equivalent of the M4. The Romans too left their mark in the arrow straight route of Ermin Street, passing villa settlements at a site to the east of the current town near Wanborough, and a temple complex to the north at what is now Abbey Meads.

Holy Rood 2020.

The hilltop now occupied by Old Town may have originally been known as 'Thanesland' (perhaps of Viking origin?). However, the name Swindon is of a later Saxon origin, and is taken to mean *Swine-Dun* or place of the pigs – perhaps a reference to pigs or wild boar that roamed the hillside. Another less well known theory is that the name Swindon derives from *Sweyn Forkbeard*, the Danish King of England and father of Canute who recognised the strategic importance of the hill, claiming it for his own while en route to a battle against a Saxon army at Bath in 1013. The area then becoming known as Sweyn's Hill or Sweyn-Dun.

There was certainly a settlement here by the time of the Domesday Survey. When William-the-Conqueror's clerks arrived here in 1086, to complete their inventory of the land for their king, the name 'Suindune' was officially recorded and is inscribed half -a -dozen times in Medieval Latin within the pages of The Domesday Book. Their

Holy Rood 2020.

16

entries recorded the presence of two mills, indicative of a reasonably sized agricultural population, and three rich landowners. Miles Crispin, the Lord of Wootton, Odin The Chamberlain, and Wadard the Knight (who was immortalised on the Bayeux Tapestry, thus becoming perhaps the first Swindonian whose image was recorded). All three had, no doubt, acquired their slice of 'Suindune' as a reward for helping to vanquish King Harold in 1066.

It was also noted that the hill gave good defensive advantage in times of trouble; and was well served by natural springs which ensured a continual fresh water supply.

Wadard the Knight as he appeared on the Bayeux Tapestry

Britain had been a Christian province of the later Roman Empire, and there were certainly British bishops in existence by AD 314. Christianity was, at first, mainly a religion of the towns and cities, with paganism still existing in rural areas, particularly following the disintegration of Roman civilisation and the Anglo-Saxon invasions of the 5th and 6th centuries. The conversion of the British was achieved from AD 597 onwards by the missions of St Augustine and his followers, and a parish system appears to have been well developed by the 10th century. So, we can imagine Christians worshipping in the Swindon area for certainly the last millennium, and possibly for several centuries before that. During the Victorian era a coin was discovered close to the site of Holy Rood in the Lawns. The inscribed Gaul gold coin featured a head on the obverse and a horse on the reverse, and was provisionally dated to the first century B.C.

Earliest reference to the Parish Church

It is tempting to imagine that a late Saxon wooden church existed in Swindon at the time of the Norman conquest, although no records survive to verify this. At a meeting of the Swindon Local History Study Group in March, 1963, Norwegian-born PR Broderstad, a retired grocer from Prospect Place, asserted that Odin the Chamberlain had begun the construction of Holy Rood, shortly after being gifted land there by William-the-Conqueror in 1066. Mr Broderstad, a Swindon resident since 1914, claimed that Odin, who owned around 1,500 acres on the hillside, built the church to *'make amends for his Viking sins, but was unable to complete the job after being recalled by William to help quell a Saxon rebellion.'*

However, there are no known references to a church building until 1154, a century later. This reference occurs in documents relating to a dispute over a grant made by the incumbent Lord of the Manor, William Pont-de-l'Arche (or possibly by his son Robert), in which he made a gift of the church and land to Southwick Priory in Hampshire.

Incidentally, this event explains why a Vicar and not a Rector serves Swindon parish. In the Middle Ages a substantial number of parish churches in England were gifted by lay 'owners' to a suitable monastery, which was then responsible for the upkeep of the chancel (while the congregation retained responsibility for the nave). In addition, the monastery also acquired lands to help finance the appointment of a parish priest or Vicar. The tithes, the important 'tenth' of the community produce, also accrued to the monastery. If the church remained under lay patronage, however, the priest would hold the lands and receive tithes in his own right; and was known as the Rector. Southwick Priory no longer holds the *'living'* of Swindon, having been a victim of the Dissolution of the Monasteries during the reign of Henry VIII, but Vicars have remained in Swindon in the 850 years since the original grant was made (see Appendix A).

Major building phases

No trace remains today of the building mentioned in 1154, although parts may have been incorporated into later work. The earliest extant structure is the chancel, which was rebuilt by craftsmen from Southwick Priory between 1280 and 1300, and still features a fine chancel arch with the stone-carved heads of a king and queen, possibly Edward I and Eleanor of Castile (now sadly much weathered). The chancel was the most sacred part of the building; and was separated from the congregation by a carved wooden screen depicting the Crucifixion – the Rood from which the church took its name.

William de Valence 1st Earl of Pembroke

At first, the arch still opened into the old Norman nave, which was not rebuilt until some years after the chancel, but probably well before 1350. Considering that the parishioners were expected to pay for the nave they were quite ambitious in both the design and quality of construction. The nave was double-aisled with 6 pillars and 8 arches, and a clerestory above. Contemporary with the chancel, a small north chapel was built to one side, and was probably the work of the owner of the local manor, at this time William de Valence, Earl of Pembroke, whose family would have retained this part for their own private use. Tradition continued many centuries later when this section of the church was used by the Goddard family.

The name Holy Rood (not to be confused with the more modern Roman Catholic Holy Rood church in Swindon) is probably derived from the old Saxon word 'roda' meaning cross or rod. When combined with the prefix 'Holy' its meaning becomes the 'True Cross' (referring to the original wooden cross used in Christ's crucifixion). The use of the word 'Rood' also seems to confirm the origins of the church as a Saxon one.

The building work undertaken in the fourteenth century represented a high point in the history of Holy Rood. Although a century later, the nave aisles were rebuilt slightly wider, and a south door and porch added, the greater prosperity brought to the rest of the country by the wool trade of the late Middle Ages seems to have passed Swindon by. It remained a small market town, of no local, and certainly no national importance. The church would have been the most obvious and important public building in the small settlement on the top of the hill, but of no greater significance to the surrounding area than Wootton Bassett, Highworth, or Marlborough.

Despite an increasing number in the congregation (572 communicants are recorded in 1672), the next major building phase at Holy Rood did not occur until the 18th century. In 1736 John Vilett, local landowner and the Lay Rector (a position bought by the Vilett family along with church lands after the dissolution of Southwick Priory in the 16th century), undertook extensive restoration of the church. He was responsible for rebuilding the south wall of the chancel, unfortunately losing the original windows and priest's door in the process. A new round-headed east window was inserted, and a small vestry added between the chapel and chancel on the north side. The roof inside the chancel was reconstructed, re-using the original medieval timbers where possible. A small bell-cote was added to the existing tower on the south side of the church[1]. In 1741, five new bells, cast by Abraham Rudhall, were hung in the tower to replace the previous four that were known to exist (from an inventory dated 1556).

In the list of Vicars of Swindon, the incumbent in 1527 was John Unthanke (listed in the appendix at the end of this book), who remained in the post until his death in 1560. These dates are significant in English history, particularly with regard to those who practised their religion with any conviction. John Unthanke took up his position

---

1   Although the early history of the tower is difficult to piece together with certainty, Denis Bird has conjectured that the tower was in fact a very old structure, even pre-dating the nave. This seems more likely than the local anecdotal evidence that the tower was an 18th century structure.

during the reign of Henry VIII, who declared the Church of England separate from the Church of Rome, and ordered the dissolution of the monasteries. In 1547, Henry was succeeded by his son Edward VI, who in his short-lived reign promised to be a more reforming Protestant than his father. 1553 saw the succession of his sister, Mary I, better known to history as Bloody Mary for the zeal with which she enforced Catholicism on the country and burnt Protestant martyrs at the stake. Not until 1558, and the reign of Elizabeth I, was religious toleration at last restored to England. Church services at Holy Rood changed from English to Latin, and then back again! It appears remarkable that Unthanke was able to remain as Vicar during these turbulent years without attracting undue attention from the Church authorities. Perhaps the relative importance of parishes at that time may offer a clue. His salary of £15 and 7 shillings was half that of the richer parish of Burford.

A similar scenario was played out a century later, when William Gallimore was Vicar for 29 years from 1623 to 1662 (spanning the reign of James I, who died in 1625), Charles I (executed in 1649), the Commonwealth under Oliver Cromwell, and the Restoration of Charles II in 1660. Perhaps the incumbent who received the most renown beyond the parish was Narcissus Marsh (vicar from 1662 to 1663). He would go on to become a respected mathematician, Provost of Trinity College, Dublin, and eventually Archbishop of Armagh. Henry Thompson, his successor, (Vicar from 1663 to 1703), served under James II (the last Catholic king of England), William and Mary (after the Glorious Revolution of 1688 returned the throne to a Protestant), and Queen Anne. His staying power not quite the equal of 'the Vicar of Bray'[2], but not far behind!

Revd. Narcissus Marsh

2   The story of The Vicar of Bray is recounted in an 18th century song, in which a parson boasts of having kept his benefice from the reign of Charles II to George I (i.e. from 1660 to 1714) by changing his beliefs to suit the times. The song is apparently based on a certain Simon Aleyn, who was Vicar of Bray in Berkshire.

Swindonians appeared to be survivors. Not only did the Vicars keep their livings (and their heads), but in 1580, John Alexander was born and subsequently set what must have certainly been a record for the town at the time. He passed away on 18 May 1697, aged an incredible 117 years. His wife Ann, who died after him in March 1698 did not quite live up to her husband's longevity, being a mere 98 when she passed away. John had lived through the reigns of 6 monarchs, plus the Commonwealth period under Oliver Cromwell. He had seen some of the most stirring and formative periods of his country's history, including the Civil War and the execution of Charles I.[3]

One of the events possibly observed by John Alexander during the Civil War was the only time prior to the nineteenth century when Swindon appears to have been mentioned in the context of national, rather than local, history. After relieving the siege at Gloucester in September 1643, Cromwell's General, Robert Devereux, Earl of Essex, was travelling back east with his army. During their journey, they came to Swindon, and camped in the Old Town Square. Holy Rood was the nearest place of worship, and the Earl took communion there, using his own chaplain rather than the local Vicar (William Gallimore).

Robert Devereux
3rd Earl of Essex

In 1603 John Alexander may also have witnessed the, then, Vicar Milo Kendall assault Elizabeth Villet in the rector's pew at Holy Rood. Apparently Kendall did not approve of her husband Nicholas Villet being appointed Rector; and disputed

---

3   William Morris believes that John Alexander's tombstone is not original, and the details of his longevity based on hearsay. He bases this on the fact that the inscription was added to a later tomb, which contained three other panels : 'Francis Barnes, Saddler, died Nov 17 1780, aged 63 years and Elizabeth his wife, who died Feb 27 1795, aged 67 years'; 'Henry Lubbock, saddler, died May 10 1816' and 'Susan Alexander, died April 23 1820, aged 60'. Morris surmises that Elizabeth Barnes was the granddaughter or great-granddaughter of John Alexander, and Susan her daughter (and wife of Henry Lubbock). Susan was the last of the descendants of John Alexander, and the famous inscription commemorated family oral tradition about their illustrious ancestor.

her right to seat in the chancel! Perhaps this rather unfitting scene was witnessed enviously by some of the '*Swindon Poor*' who were forced to scramble for one of the 93 seats in church specifically allocated as '*Poor Seats*'?

Nevertheless, the church did take its responsibilities to the poor and disadvantaged seriously. Records from 1692 show payments of 1 shilling made to '*two women whose husbands were taken by the French.*' Payments of 9d were made to '*two seaman that had been taken by the French.*' The scope of payments included '*4 maimed Dutchmen 1s 0d*', and 2 shillings paid to a '*poor man whose house was lost by fire.*' In 1692, following the naval victory over the French at the Battle of La Hogue, a payment of 14 shillings was '*paid wide for beer expended*' (a payment especially to be used on beer for the purposes of celebrating the victory).

The remnants of the nave contain an interesting plaque to the above-mentioned John Alexander. Sadly, however, many of the other memorials have become indecipherable through age and corrosion. Some were restored in 1977 by Swindon's master stonemason Ron Packer, who reported that some of the 18th century memorials were '*so well done, so graceful and well-proportioned that they wouldn't disgrace Westminster Abbey.*'

Other significant and fine memorials inside the remains of the church, now unseen by the public, include those of Elenor Huchens died 1610, Revd. John Neate died 1719, Mrs Millicent Neate, died

Memorial to Richard Tuckey

1764, Mary Wayt died 1724, and William Horne, died 1730.

Churchwardens accounts

Paradoxically, by the time Vilett undertook his remodelling in the 1730's, church attendance at Holy Rood had declined since the previous century. Communion was celebrated only seven times a year, and there were a total of 50-60 communicants at Easter. Nevertheless, Churchwardens accounts surviving from this time present a lively picture of the life of the church and parish.

An almost complete set of Churchwardens Accounts survive from 1770 to 1825. In 1770, the churchwardens of Holy Rood, Mr John Goolding and William Heath, paid two shillings and fourpence for a stout, leather-bound book, in which the accounts were kept for the next 55 years. The affairs of the outside world do not merit a mention. What is contained in the pages gives illuminating detail of a world long lost to us.

There were two principal accounts maintained during the period in question – The Church Account and the Poor Account. In addition, there is mention of a third account between 1772 and 1779 – known as the Church Rate. This was a rate levied by the Churchwardens on all parish occupiers, towards the maintenance of the church fabric. This was, not surprisingly, an unpopular rate, and although it remained legal until 1868, fell into abeyance at Holy Rood in 1779, when the credit balance of 7s 3d was transferred to the Church Account. Despite the fact that an average of £10 was raised each year (today's equivalent of approximately £1,700), only one item of expenditure is recorded in 7 years. That was the payment of one shilling to a certain Isaac Law, *'for mending the Churchyard Gatts'* (gates).

Income for the Church Account and Poor Account was raised mainly by rents from property and land owned by the Church. The rents could vary in amount, but necessarily always upwards. External events such as the Enclosure Awards or general economic depression affected monetary values, but there was little year-on-year inflation as we are used to in our modern economy.

Items in the accounts are not kept in a particularly orderly manner. Frequently, no annual balance was made, and mistakes are apparent in account details. The literacy level of the Churchwardens seems to have varied considerably, and rarely do we find a clerk as methodical as John Gosling, who kept the accounts from 1798. Most Churchwardens are not named in the accounts until the early 1800's.

The descriptions of expenditure recorded in the accounts provide the most interest for the modern reader. In 1771, for example, John Lester was paid six shillings for *'whipping dogs'*. By 1812 the paid office of Dog Whipper seemed to have been incorporated with that of 'Door Shutter'. By 1817, dog whipping was obsolete, but door shutting continued to attract an annual salary. A 'Dog Whipper' was a church official employed to remove unruly dogs from the church grounds, or even from the building itself during services. It was common practice for members of the congregation to bring their animals with them to church, rather than risk the valuable asset 'disappearing' during their absence!

On a positive note, sermons must have been stimulating as there is no record of the church hiring a *'Sluggard Waker'* – another common appointment in parishes during the 18th century. The role entailed a

Dog Whippers And Sluggard Wakers
(18th century illustration)

person being employed during services to poke or hit drowsy members of the congregation on the head with a long pole!

During the tenure of William Nichols (sometimes spelt Nicholls) as Vicar, from 1737-1758, expenditure on the fabric of Holy Rood reached impressive levels. Although it appears not without a struggle on the part of the Vicar. Following his appointment in 1737 Nichols quickly resigned his post, it appears due to the poor condition of the church. He was re-nominated, reappointed and money was miraculously found for several projects that required urgent attention.

A tower, bell chamber and five bells were added in 1741. The method used to build the floor of the bell chamber, in the upper storey of the tower, must have been unique. Four large yew trees that had been planted in a square outside the original entrance porch were topped. Their trunks were then used as four corner pillars to hold in place cross beams, on which was laid the floor of the bell chamber. The remainder of the tower was then built around them! Newport Street School was started with an expenditure of £57 11s per annum. This was helped with endowments of £5 per annum from Thomas Goddard and William Nash. In 1748 the churchwardens spent a staggering £487 on the restoration of Holy Rood – the equivalent of more than £100,000 today.

Another common expense was the provision of refreshment when any tenant paid his rent, or a new tenancy was taken out. In April 1771, Samuel Edwards was paid 6d for 'beer as usual' on such an occasion. In 1794, the letting of church ground merited 10s 6d at the Bell Inn. The last such payment was recorded in 1813.

The bellringers were rewarded with a payment once a year for their annual dinner. For forty years, they dined out for the sum of one guinea (one pound and one shilling), but by 1810 they gained an extra four shillings, when they dined at the Masons Arms. In 1816, they ate at the King of Prussia public house.

Expenditure on repairs to the church (in addition to the Church Rate mentioned above) was mentioned in the Church Accounts, but fairly small sums were involved before 1800. For example, in October 1771, Walter Taylor was paid 4s 6d for 'Mending the Tower', Joseph Woodhams 7s for '*Mending the Church*', Isaac Laws 2s 2d for '*Mending the Bells*' and Thomas Davis 3s 0d for the Treble Bell rope. One of the more notable items was £2 12s 4d (£350 today) to Robert Jones in May 1790 '*for a Font*'.

After the turn of the century, spending on repairs became more significant. Whitewashing the church cost £3 6s 3d in May 1805; it cost 4s less (by another workman) in 1812. The Church Walk and the Church Yard Wall were repaired in 1813; the Vestry was added in 1820, and a new Gallery in 1823. The bells needed attention too, costing £21 between 1801 and 1825. After a Vestry Meeting in 1805, an annual sum of 12s was voted for '*Exercising the Engine three times a year namely Lady-day, Midsummer and Michaelmas the same to be paid by the Churchwardens and carried to the Church Account.'* The engine in question appears to be a fire-engine, which was housed at a rent of £1 a year (it is not known where), but there is no mention of the fire-engine's origin. The Churchwardens of the early 19th century were obviously a prudent group of men; not only did they buy and maintain a fire engine to safeguard church property, they also insured the property, the first premiums being paid from 1820.

In 1810 the prolific artist John Buckler sketched Holy Rood, as part of a commission by Richard Colt Hoare of Stourhead to produce ten volumes of drawings of churches and other historic buildings in Wiltshire. His drawing provides, perhaps, the most detailed illustration of how Holy Rood would have appeared in its heyday.

In the early part of the 19th century the interior of Holy Rood presented a cluttered appearance. The church was filled with pews, which had been present from the 16th century onwards. The Vilett

Holy Rood 1810 by John Buckler.

family, as Lay Rectors, were entitled to a pew in the chancel, and the Goddards, as Lords of the Manor, had a traditional right to a seat in the North Chapel. Other principal families could rent large box pews, which were almost like small enclosed rooms. According to William Morris, the box pews were of many different heights and sizes. They were arranged in four rows; two in the nave and one in each of the

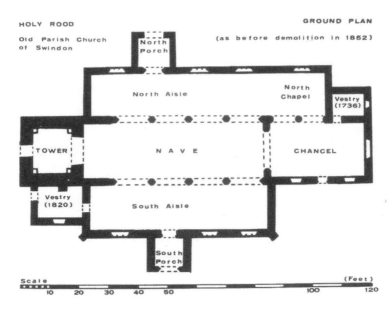

HOLY ROOD

Old Parish Church of Swindon

GROUND PLAN

(as before demolition in 1852)

Ground Plan of Holy Rood, prior to demolition in 1852

two aisles. Other parishioners could be accommodated in the galleries over the north and south aisles, while a further gallery in the tower at the west end was for the use of the choir and organ. It appears that the Curate and Lay Rectors were fully employed during the tenure of Matthew Surtees (1809–23). The Revd. Surtess did not reside at the vicarage at all during his incumbency, spending the majority of his time working elsewhere. Throughout his 14 year stay in Swindon

Holy Rood Interior 1847 (Denis Bird)

a curate lived in the vicarage house, taking the majority of services, along with the Lay staff.

The pulpit was of carved oak of 17th century design. It was two-storied; the Vicar delivered his sermon from the top, while the Clerk read the lessons below. The Font stood in the North Chapel, and was apparently painted to resemble marble, with a porcelain basin. The walls, pillars and arches were whitewashed to offset the amount of dark oak woodwork, and above the chancel arch hung a board painted with the words of the Lord's Prayer, the Creed and the Ten Commandments. Overall, Holy Rood had the characteristics, not of a major town church, but of a country parish.

The more recent history of Holy Rood

In the 1840's, events took place which would change the nature of Swindon forever – Isambard Kingdom Brunel chose the low-lying land below Swindon Hill as the site of the engine repair works for his Great Western Railway, which connected London Paddington to Bristol Temple Meads. The GWR became one of the most famous of the nineteenth and early twentieth century railway companies, and the subsequent development of the Swindon Works as its principal factory meant that the town enjoyed an economic boom and unrivalled expansion which continues to this day.

At the time of the GWR's arrival, the population of Old Swindon was less than 2,000 inhabitants. This was soon outstripped by the New Town, where the focus of industry ensured almost constant immigration for several decades. The new town workers were well-

The Lawns Mansion with Holy Rood to the right.

served by their railway bosses, for not only did they enjoy purpose-built housing (in what is now known as the Railway Village), they were also served with their own market, public houses, cricket ground, hospital, and not least a magnificent new church. This was St Mark's, which was built on land donated by Colonel Vilett. The architect was George Gilbert Scott, and the dedication ceremony took place in 1845.

Old Swindon, by contrast, was left out of this new economic activity. It was not until 1900 that both the old and new Swindons were merged to form the new corporation. However even without the activity taking place just one mile away down the hill, by 1840 Holy Rood was

A Lithograph from a drawing by
John Luckett Jefferies 1850.

starting to become woefully small for the size of congregation it served. Baptisms, weddings and funerals occupied a huge proportion of church time. In 1849 the well known Swindon born author Richard Jefferies was one of the last people to be baptized at Holy Rood.

William Morris, who knew Holy Rood well and founded the Swindon Advertiser in 1854, described the church just after its closure as:

'the most insignificant ecclesiastical building in the whole neighbourhood and is, moreover, hopelessly out of condition. At the time of its abandonment it consisted of a nave with clerestory and steep pitched roof, side aisles, chancel with a north aisle and vestry,

north and south porches, and a somewhat stunted west tower rising in two stages and surmounted by a small bell-cote. The nave was separated from its north aisle by an arcade of two bays with double-chamfered arches of the later 13th century. The arches sprang from a short round pier adorned with either dogtooth or 'nailhead' decoration. The pointed chancel arch sprang from corbels carved with a male and a female head. The 14th-century nave arcades of four pointed arches were supported on octagonal piers without capitals. The exterior, apart from the chancel, appears to have been of 15th-century date.'

With the appointment of Henry Baily as Vicar in 1847, a new phase in the church's history commenced, and subscriptions were opened to raise money for a completely new church to be built. The full story begins in the next chapter.

So, what did happen to Holy Rood once it was abandoned in favour of Christ Church? In 1852, a year after the consecration of the new church, an agreement was reached to demolish the old church. Apart, that is, from the chancel, which was to be kept standing for *'any pious uses to which it may thereafter be applied'* (*Faculty for the demolition of Holy Rood*).

The chancel and the remains of the rest of the church remain much as the Victorians left them, apart from the inevitable decay of 170 years. The chancel itself was walled up, leaving only one door and one window, but the work was finished off neatly. The tower and nave were demolished, leaving only the nave arcades standing. The bells and clock were removed to Christ Church.

In the churchyard, burials continued for about another decade, although only into existing family plots. The great Goddard Vault was built on the site of the North Chapel in 1852, and over the next century the site became in practice almost exclusively a Goddard family preserve. The ruins were still cared for however, and it appears that an annual service was held there for some years during the latter Victorian era.

The first half of the twentieth century was not an entirely happy time for Holy Rood, as it gradually fell further into decay, particularly during and after the Second World War. In 1949, responsibility for

Circa 1900

Circa 1900

Holy Rood 1905.

the building was taken over by the Borough of Swindon (as it was then), and necessary repairs were initiated. When workmen entered the chancel they discovered it littered with broken monuments and crumbling masonry. Its sorry state featuring in the *Evening Advertiser* of November 25, 1954.

'*I cannot put out of my mind the appalling present state of the churchyard,*' complained the Chancellor of the Bristol Diocese. Unfortunately, the immediate efforts of the workmen did not seem to placate the local paper, who added the following withering editorial:

'*The font in which many Swindonians of past generations were baptised is being used by workmen as a block for sawing wood! It is a picture of neglect and desolation.*'

As part of the Diamond Jubilee of the Borough of Swindon in 1960, the council also carried out some restoration work on the old chancel. After the work had been completed, a pilgrimage was made to the old church for an evening service in June 1962, this being the first time for some twenty years.

Sadly, petty vandalism has played its part throughout the past 50 years. The gradual erosion of many of the features, such as pillars, railings and even headstones, from vandalism has led to the church being closed to public viewing. In 1990, vandals attacked the Goddard family vault, smashing the stone slabs on top of the sarcophagus, where the remains of various Goddards had been entombed for centuries. The graveyard is now permanently padlocked.

Inside, the importance to Swindon of the remaining structure is highlighted by its current Listed Grade II* status. The graveyard is bounded by a wall, constructed during the 18th century of rubble limestone with stone coping, topped with wrought iron railings. This too has Grade II* Listed recognition.

In 1969, churches in Old Town Swindon came together to form the Ecumenical Parish (see Chapter 5), and after further restoration work undertaken by the Borough Council, Holy Rood was hallowed on Whit Sunday, May 3rd 1971, as a Chapel of Unity for the Ecumenical Parish. The congregation stood outside in the ruins of the nave. The practice of an annual service was revived for some years, but again fell

Interior of Holy Rood, restored as a
Chapel of Unity 1970

The 70th Anniversary of the
Scouting Movement.

The Goddards Tomb.

Holy Rood in Winter.

Outdoor Service 1970s.

into abeyance. Despite this, Holy Rood was still occasionally used for services, festivals and event in the 1970s and '80s. The enduring importance of the building, however, has seen a regular early morning Easter Sunday service take place during the new millennium. It is a moving experience for all who attend, as the spring sun rises over a building that has stood on the site since at least 1154 and is Swindon's only surviving link to the early medieval era.

Perhaps it is fitting to end this introduction with the words of

Denis Bird (whose research and enthusiasm enabled the memory and importance of Holy Rood to live on):

> *'To say that ten thousand people may have been buried here may be no exaggeration.*
>
> *For although the population of early Swindon may have numbered no more than a few hundred souls at any one time, it was here that nearly all found their last resting place, generation after generation, for perhaps more than 700 years.'*

2

A New Church 1851-1885

Henry George Baily came to Swindon in 1847. Born on 8th December 1815, he was the son of George Baily, of Calne, where the families were the leading clothiers in the town and played a major part in local affairs. After attending school at Tilshead, Baily was admitted as a scholar at Christ's College, Cambridge, in 1839 and received his BA degree, made deacon and ordained priest at Chester in 1843. He then became Perpetual Curate of Hurdsfield, Cheshire, and also began eighteen months work on behalf of the London Jews'

Plan of Swindon in 1851

Society. Henry married Elizabeth Mignon in 1844 and they were eventually to have twelve children. He received his MA in 1845.

Baily became Vicar of Swindon at the age of thirty-one, just as the new railway town was becoming established in the valley below the old market town on the hill. In 1840 the total population of Old Swindon had been 1,742 but, with the opening of the Great Western Railway factory on 2nd January 1843, the population of the parish soon exploded to 3,000, (then 7,000 by 1864). By this time the old church of Holy Rood was proving woefully inadequate for the needs of the parish of the old town. The churchyard at Holy Rood had become so crowded that deceased members of the congregation were often buried in grounds of other denominations. The parents of one young man, whose body was unable to be interred at Holy Rood due to the overcrowding, wrote to Revd. Baily telling him; *'The Pastor to whom he looked in life for guidance, in death he was compelled to forsake.'*

A man of boundless energy and drive, Baily formed a committee to investigate ways of increasing the capacity of the old church. It was soon found, however, that the ancient building was not capable of being extended in a suitable manner. Ambrose Lethbridge Goddard, the son of the Lord of the Manor of High Swindon and M.P. for the Cricklade Division of Wiltshire (which included Swindon), then came forward and offered to contribute £1,000 towards building a new church – equivalent to some £100,000 today. His father also offered a suitable site for the new church and for a burial ground. A design for the new church was obtained from the eminent architect, George Gilbert Scott (1811-78). Gilbert Scott, who would be knighted in 1872, and who had also provided the design for the railway church of St. Mark's in Swindon (opened in 1845), and later the Albert Memorial and St. Pancras Hotel in London. Initially an attempt to raise the £8,000 cost of the new building (approaching £1 million today) by means of the Church Rate, a public levy charged at the discretion of the church, was discussed. However, this met with considerable public opposition and it was instead decided to rely on voluntary subscriptions. Revd. Baily wrote and posted over 23,000 letters asking for donations – a not inconsiderable task in the pre-computer age! The postage alone on the letters costing more than

£300. Baily himself donated £500 from his own pocket and, by the time of the laying of the foundation stone in June 1850, a sum of £5,000 had been raised. This was considered enough to justify the commencement of building of the new church. The importance, and significance, of raising this huge amount of money was not lost on the *Devizes and Wiltshire Gazette,* who noted that; *'the Church of England is the only rock amidst the ever-varying tides and currents of a restless age.'*

Commenorative Card issued by the architect c. 1850. There were subsequently slight differences to the finished building

George Gilbert Scott Architect

The Vicarage Swindon, Wilts December
1st 1849

Dear Sir,

I enclose a subscription list, and a copy
of an appeal now in circulation in order to
raise funds for the erection of a proposed
new parish church, and to provide a new
churchyard. This cause is a very painful and
trying one, in as much as the parishioners
last year, proposed building the church
by the increase of a rate spread over a
series of years; they had nearly completed
the arrangements for so doing, when the
mechanics in the employ of the Great
Western Railway Company, and who reside
in a district ecclesiastically separated
from the parish church, outnumbered the
respectable inhabitants in vestry, and by
their disgraceful proceedings, entirely
over through the project.

Sadly harrowing and revolting to the
feelings are the scenes of frequent occurrence
in our overcrowded churchyard – scenes too
sad and humiliating for repetition here,
– deeply painful to every Church Man, but
distressingly so to me as a minister of
Christ, when it happens as in the case of the
deceased young man, who had been sincerely
attached to one of our church, and anxiously
watched over me in life, but who by reason
of the state of our churchyard, had been
driven to the Dissenting Burial Ground, and
to use the parents' own words, 'the Pastor
to whom he looked in life for guidance, in
death was compelled to forsake'.

Having, therefore, no alternative, save
appealing to the liberality of a Christian

public, and feeling the deep responsibility
of doing my utmost to provide the success
of grace for those committed to my charge,
as well as a decent resting place for the
dead, I beg you to forgive this appeal
from a stranger, and I earnestly solicit a
donation from you, however small, it will be
gratifyingly received. It is not advisable
to send cash by letter, but Postal Orders
for larger sums, and postage stamps for
those under 10 shillings, will equally affect
the cause.

My Diocedent (the Lord Bishop of Gloucester
and Bristol) or the rural Dean, the Revd. Mr
Prower, Purton, near Swindon, will answer
any inquiries you may address to them.

Will you oblige by returning the enclosed
list, at your earliest convenience, as
it will save some expense in printing; a
postage stamp is enclosed for this purpose,

                              I beg to remain
              your very faithful servant
                              H.G. Baily

A reproduction of the letter written by Henry Baily requesting subscriptions for the construction of the new Parish Church. Some of the interesting subscribers are listed in Appendix D at the end of this book.

On Friday, 7th June 1850 the Foundation Stone of Christ Church was laid. The architect Gilbert Scott returned from Italy, just in time to witness the ceremony at the fourth, and last, of the buildings he had designed in Swindon. Many houses in Old Swindon were bedecked with flags and bunting, and garlands hung across the streets for the occasion. One of the churchwardens, James Bradford, displayed a forty-foot pole at his house with a huge banner pronouncing '*Church and Queen*'. Shortly after 11 a.m. the bells at Holy Rood were rung to summon people to

Divine Service. A large congregation gathered there to hear the Vicar and the Revd. Joseph Mansfield, (Vicar of St. Marks) lead the prayers and readings to bless the project. The baptism of the latest daughter for Mr. A. L. Goddard was also included in the service. After the service a procession was formed to march to the site of the new church (a human touch is provided by a note that the youngest daughter of Isaac Anne, Parish Clerk, lost a shoe in the procession from Holy Rood). On arrival at the new church site a hymn was sung, the words having been written by Mrs. Baily, and Mrs. A.L. Goddard (Charlotte) laid the foundation stone. The usual speeches followed and the proceedings ended with three cheers for the Vicar, three for Queen Victoria and three more for Mr. Goddard. A brass plate with the following inscription in old Roman letters was deposited under the corner stone together with a set of new coins denoting the current Queen's reign:

All Saints Church, Buckworth, Huntingdon, the design
on which Gilbert Scott based Christ Church

TO THE GLORY OF GOD; THIS CORNER STONE OF
THE NEW PARISH CHURCH OF SWINDON WAS LAID BY
CHARLOTTE THE LADY OF
AMBROSE LETHBRIDGE GODDARD Esq. M.P.

JUNE 7TH A.D. 1850
THE SITE WAS GIVEN BY AMBROSE GODDARD ESQ.
AND ONE THOUSAND POUNDS BY HIS SON THE
ABOVE NAMED AMBROSE LETHBRIDGE GODDARD.
THE REMAINDER OF THE COST (£7000) IS TO BE
RAISED BY VOLUNTARY SUBSCRIPTIONS, AIDED BY A
GRANT OF £200 FROM THE INCORPORATED SOCIETY
FOR BUILDING CHURCHES AND CHAPELS. HENRY
GEORGE BAILEY (sic). . . VICAR. JAMES BRADFORD &
ROBERT REYNOLDS. . . CHURCHWARDENS. GEORGE
GILBERT SCOTT ARCHITECT. GEORGE MYERS . . .
BUILDER . . .

The festivities ended with a 'Fancy Bazaar' in a large room at the Goddard Arms Hotel to raise funds for the ongoing project.

The new church was designed by Gilbert Scott in his middle-pointed (or decorated) Gothic style. The tower and broached spire (approximately 150 ft in height) are based on the thirteenth-century church of Buckworth, Huntingdonshire, according to John Betjeman, with only the proportions changed. Its elevated position enabling it to be seen for many miles around. The building contractor was George Myers of Lambeth who imported oak and fir from the Baltic, Memel, Riga, Wyberg, St. Petersburg and Christianstadt. The first load reached London for Swindon in January 1849 and the last in August 1850. Stonework was of Bath, Box, and Swindon stone as appropriate. Initially the church must have presented a very plain appearance, with the present East and North/South Transept stained glass windows only being dedicated from the mid 1850s onwards. The dimensions of the interior were approximately one hundred and eighteen feet in length, by fifty feet in width, exclusive of the transepts. Unusually for the time, the church was also warmed by heated air ducts. Near the western door stood the original font, made of Caen stone. The original pulpit, which stood on the site of the present one, was also of Caen stone. These are now housed in the chancel of Holy Rood. Originally there were pews for 926 people in the congregation (388 of these being appropriated for named persons). The first two seats on the south side of the Nave were allotted to Ambrose Lethbridge Goddard. He had twelve 'sittings' for himself and his family with another nine 'sittings' in the south Transept for his servants. The Goddards and their party also had a doorway in the south transept (still there today) and they would enter and leave by this using a private pathway to the Manor House at The Lawn. It is reported that the service could only commence when the Squire and his party entered! The Vicar's Warden was allocated six 'sittings' in the row behind the Squire, while, on the other side sat the People's Warden with five seats for his servants. In front of the People's Warden were the 'sittings' for the former Vicar of Swindon, the Revd. James Grooby (who continued to attend Christ Church until his death in 1854), complete with his family and servants. The South Transept seems to have been set apart for servants, including those of Vicar Baily, who could apparently only afford two! A well-to-do household attending church at this time was expected to fill several seats on a regular basis when accompanied by their servants (whose attendance at church was mandatory). Following the death of Revd. James Grooby a magnificent new stained glass window (the East Window) was erected in the church in 1855. Considered by many as the finest window in the county, it can still be viewed and appreciated today. Following its dedication by Mrs. Catherine Mary Grooby, widow of the late Revd. Grooby, the window was lovingly described in detail in the local newspaper:

> *'The window is in compartments, bearing drawings of Aaron and the dove; the brazen serpent; the ark of the covenant; and 15 designs from the parables—the sower, on ruby ground; the pearl on blue ground ; casting away the fish, ruby ground ; the publican and pharisee; the good shepherd, with sheep; the prodigal son receiving his father's portion of money going away on horseback, banquet, coming home to his father feeding same—among thieves; pharisees; anointing the man's arm on the donkey; and giving the man two pence. The whole the subjects are treated and drawn in the most masterly manner and reflect the highest credit upon the workmanship Messrs' Wailes of Newcastle, to whom the work was entrusted. The drawing and grouping of the various figures, are executed in the most effective manner, and produce a gorgeous*

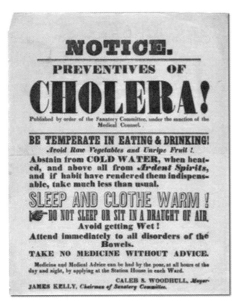

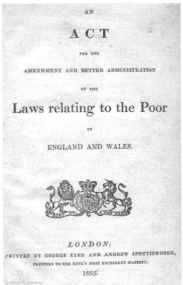

Cholera Warning Poster   *Poor Law*

effect. The window is considered to be one of the finest now erected in this county; and the reason may well be judged when Messrs. Wailes had received orders to spare no expense, and they employed upon it the first talent and workmanship of their establishment.'

Despite the opulence of the new window in the church, life for the ordinary working people of Old Town at this time was hard indeed. The average age at death in the year 1849 was just 25.7 years only. Indeed, it was noted in a Report to the General Board of Health in 1851 (in response to the recent Public Health Act and frequent outbreaks of Cholera in the town) that Swindon lacked any form of sewerage disposal other than cesspools and that the house sewage was allowed to discharge into the street gutter. It then often became mixed with the washings from slaughter-houses (butchers would kill their own animals on the premises). With meat being the staple diet in Victorian days, the effect on the environment can be imagined as well as the offensive smell always present. Drinking water was obtained usually from a well in the back yards of the cottages, often close to cesspools and where animals were kept. All this led to much ill-health resulting in Typhus fever being almost endemic. In the row of cottages in Cricklade Street, immediately south of the new church, five children had died of fever in a seven-week period. The Revd. Baily felt compelled to appear as a witness in court, defending Old Town locals who were forced to dispose of their waste into the gutters and cesspools at the back of their houses.Cholera became rife in the town during yet another outbreak. Visitors arriving at Swindon Railway Station were warned of the dangers. Newspapers published helpful advice, based on a report from *'The Lancet'*, where once again the poorer classes were blamed for the spread of the disease. Under the title *'Plain Directions For Poor People'*, the following guidance was offered:

> *'Keep the whole of your body clean, let soap and water be your friend. Cholera is fond of filth. Parents, apply this rule to your children. Live plainly and avoid all excesses. Go early to bed. Drunkenness and late nights are great friends of Cholera. Half a pound of good meat is better than a pound of bad. Let not your children stuff themselves with apples, pears, plums and sweet stuff. Rice, tapioca, barley, and oatmeal are cheap, nourishing and wholesome.'*

If a person was unfortunate enough to actually contract the disease, advice was also on hand:

> *'A mustard poultice to be placed on the pit of the stomach with castor oil to be taken every half-hour. External heat, such as warm bottles and frictions, can be applied. Flannels should be worn next to the skin and feet should be keep warm and dry. Take a small wineglass full of a tincture of compound of ginger and rhubarb. Broths and hot tea are injurious.'*

On 7th November 1851, Christ Church was consecrated, an entirely new structure, with the exception of the clock and six bells which had been transferred from the tower of Holy Rood. The striking and beautiful building would soon become a Swindon landmark, occupying its unique hillside position. It is a little-known fact, however, that 11 years later Sir Gilbert Scott would design a

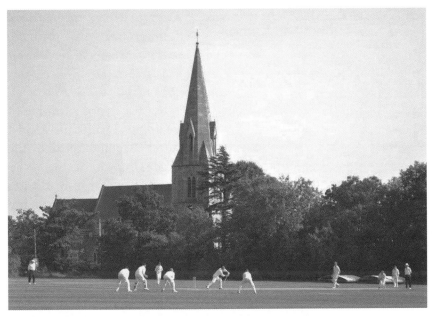

The 'other Christ Church' in Southgate

close relative to Christ Church that was so alike it could almost be mistaken for a twin! In fact, so similar were the two buildings that some uncharitable critics assumed that an assistant in Gilbert Scott's office might have merely copied the designs from the great architect's earlier efforts! That would be grossly unfair, however, on the other Christ Church, which has graced Southgate in London since 1862, and provided one of the most picturesque and quintessentially English backdrops to the adjacent Walker Cricket Ground.

The service of consecration at Christ Church in Swindon was carried out by the Right Revd. Dr. Ollivant, Bishop of Llandaff, who officiated on behalf of the Bishop of Gloucester and Bristol who was ill at the time. The sermon was preached by the Revd. Giles Daubeney, Rector of Lydiard Tregoze, to a large congregation including many local clergymen, including the Marquess of Lansdowne (the Lord Lieutenant of the county). Christ Church's new organ was played for the first time (see the later chapter on the organ and choir). After leaving the Church the Marquess of Lansdowne, the Bishop and many of the clergy with their families were entertained at the

THE NEW CHURCH AT SWINDON
WILL BE CONSECRATED (God willing),
BY THE
LORD BISHOP OF LLANDAFF,
TO-MORROW
F R I D A Y the 7th N O V E M B E R.
THE Doors will be open, for admission by tickets only, from ten till half-past ten o'clock; and for admission generally (without tickets) from half-past ten till eleven o'clock' at which time divine service will commence.
THE REV. GILES DAUBENY, M.A.,
Is appointed to preach the Sermon
Persons who may be desirous to obtain tickets, which will be distributed gratis, may apply, either personally or by letter, to the Vicar or Churchwardens, or to the Committee, who will attend at the Infant School Room, on Monday the 3rd of November, and the three following days, from 12 till 2 o'clock.
There will be an EVENING SERVICE, at 7 o'clock, and a Sermon will be preached by the
REV. THOMAS NOLAN, M.A.
Minister of St. John's Episcopal Chapel, Bedford Row, London.
Mr. W. T. Best, from London, will preside at the new organ.
A Collection will be made at each Service towards the deficiency in the funds for defraying the cost of the Building.
H. G. BAILY, Vicar.
JAMES BRADFORD, } Churchwardens
ROBERT REYNOLDS }

Newspaper Article 1851

Vicarage while *'the residents of nearly all the principle inhabitants of the town were thrown open for the reception of friends'*.

It was not until 4th December 1852, that Christ Church legally became the Parish Church of Swindon, however, when the Bishop granted a Faculty legalizing the change of status and permitting Holy Rood to be pulled down with the exception of the chancel. The churchyard there was to be maintained *'as a sacred and consecrated place for ever'*.

Henry Baily was a staunch Evangelical and a strong preacher. He would always give his sermon in his favourite black gown and white cravat. These would usually last three-quarters of an hour. On one occasion, however, it is noted that his sermon lasted for one hour and twenty minutes *'without any sign of impatience from the congregation'!* Amongst the church silver and brassware still used today in services are the chalices, patens and alms dishes used by Henry Baily.[1]

Baily also looked outwards from the walls of his own church and became involved with the development of the parish and town it was built to serve. He, like James Grooby

Revd. Henry Baily

---

1   These include a flagon, hall-marked 1738, presented to Holy Rood in memory of John Neate (Vicar 1703-19), a pair of chalices with patens, hall-marked 1851, a credence and paten presented by James E.G. Bradford and his wife, Charlotte, in 1886, and three brass alms dishes inscribed 1885.

before him, supported the attempts to establish a Local Board for Old Town. At the time, the hygiene and moral health of the town were of concern to many people. An overindulgence in alcohol concerned many, and poor sanitation had already seen many taken ill, or even die (as mentioned above). Public Houses close to Christ Church, such as The Lord Raglan, The Oddfellows Arms, the Saracen's Head, the Carpenter's Arms, and the King of Prussia did not enjoy the best of reputations. Baily firmly believed that the health and sanitation in the parish could be greatly improved (as recommended in his Report to the General Board of Health). In 1864 two District Councils were set up, one for Old Swindon and one for New Swindon. Henry Baily later served on the 'Old Town Board' for many years on which he was often to 'cross swords' with William Morris, the Proprietor and Editor of the *Swindon Advertiser*, who was a Liberal and used his newspaper to forcibly reflect his views. Morris described the services at Christ Church during the 1850s in the Swindon Advertiser as follows:

William Morris, Editor of the Swindon Advertiser.

'Services at this new church are conducted on precisely the same lines as were the services in the old Parish Church were for generations: a surplice choir has never been introduced, processions are unknown. Altar lights have never been used, and the preacher preaches in the orthodox black gown.'

Despite the cool feeling between Baily and Morris, meetings were held at the Town Hall, built in the Market Square in 1853, to discuss various plans for the Parish. The adjacent Market House and Corn Exchange opened later, on 9th April 1866, and these were also often used for large social gatherings by the Church. Indeed, the Corn Exchange building (in its various guises) would become a social hub for the people of Swindon for the next century. Its sad demise is one that needs urgent addressing.

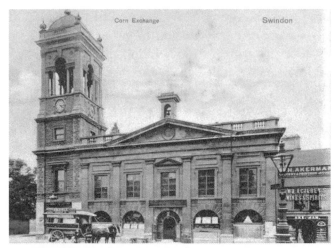

The Corn Exchange in Old Town was often used for Church meetings.

Perhaps to help offset his own personal expense in helping to raise enough funds for the building of the new church, Henry Baily advertised in various newspapers. He offered to prepare young men for university as lodgers within the vicarage, and advertised regularly in the newspapers from 1857 onwards. This was a common practice among clergy at the time, and a useful way to supplement their income.

Vandalism, it appears, is not just a scourge in modern times. There were two recorded incidents during the 1860s. One in which damage was done to the main door, during an unsuccessful break in attempt, and again in 1866 when three youths, Henry Frowd, Walter Page and Frank Page, were ordered to pay costs of seven shillings for breaking 22 windows at the church, vicarage and Churchwarden's cottage.

Charles Ellicott Bishop of Gloucester (portrait by Herbert Barraud).

The Revd. Baily appeared in court once again in 1870. Once again as a witness, this time in a libel case against the *Swindon Advertiser.* Mr Barnes, proprietor of Broom Farm, had taken great exception to the newspaper's report regarding the treatment of his tenants. Baily gave evidence, telling how both he and his wife had supplied parochial relief to the tenants in the form of meat and wine.

In 1879 William Baker Pitt was appointed as Curate. He remained for three years until he accepted the rectorship of Liddington, where he remained for 54 years until his death in 1936, aged 81 (The unique contribution of Pitt to the town is dealt with in the chapter on the sporting activities of Christ Church). The appointment of yet another Curate, and the firm views of Revd. Baily, seemed to cause some disquiet with both the *Swindon Advertiser* and with Charles Ellicot, the Bishop of Gloucester and Bristol. William Morris, editor of the *Swindon Advertiser* wrote*: 'The circumstances attending the leaving of curate after curate are too vividly remembered in the town to need recapitulation'*. Charles Ellicot, tiring of Henry Baily's outspoken views, regarded Christ Church as *'the one black spot in my diocese'*.

Henry Baily was also keen on Church teaching for children, and was a member of the first Swindon School Board; in which he immediately opposed its undenominational policy. A new parochial school was built in King William Street in 1871. In 1877 a legacy from a Mr. Anderson allowed the Parish to endow four almshouses to be built in Cricklade Street, next to the church, known as Anderson's Hostel. In 1880 the organ was rebuilt and in 1881, a fine brass Lectern was given to the church by Henry and Harriet Kinneir, in memory of their son. It is still in use to this day. Two further bells were also added to the peal in 1881. The chancel was refurbished in 1883 and an oak screen added to the west porch in 1888.

Henry Baily was also a farmer, both at Swindon and later at Lydiard, and kept at one time a famous breed of pigs. Baily frequently exhibited at local agricultural shows, buying and selling his livestock. He was a Tory of the old school and a great supporter of the party. Ambrose Lethbridge Goddard, as mentioned above, was Conservative Member of Parliament for the Cricklade and North Wiltshire Constituency for a total of twenty-seven years (Swindon did not have its own M.P. until 1918). This fact, however, did not prevent Baily from opposing the Squire (who had succeeded his father as Lord of the Manor in 1854) where he thought that the interests of the Lord of the Manor were in opposition to those of his parishioners. In 1872, a scheme was put forward to build a railway line through Old Town between a junction to the east of the Swindon Junction station on the main GWR line southwards to join the London & South Western Railway at Andover. The new railway was to be called the Swindon, Marlborough & Andover Railway. Ambrose L. Goddard became Deputy- Chairman of the newly-formed company. Goddard was soon approached by the Company's other directors, who tried to persuade him to sell some of his family's land at the Lawn so that the railway might pass Old Town to the east. The request was met with a stubborn refusal and Goddard supported an alternative plan, involving a tunnel beneath Old Swindon, and this was adopted, although the costs of this scheme would be excessive. A public meeting was held at Old Swindon Town Hall in August 1875, where fears were expressed that the tunneling would interfere with local water supplies, leaving the people of Old Town literally high and dry. Led by Revd. Henry Baily, those opposed to the tunnel formed a deputation to Mr. Goddard, hoping he would reconsider his decision not to sell off the land but to no avail. Work on the tunnel (at the south of what is now Queen's Park) went ahead but nature itself provided the final answer – heavy autumn rains caused continual roof falls and the tunnel workings were finally abandoned. The railway company were eventually forced to take another route to the west of Swindon Hill. In 1884, Henry Baily would again join

Christ Church 1885

forces with William Morris, Editor of the *Swindon Advertiser*, in opposing the Lord of the Manor after he closed the right of way across the old church road by The Planks. The local authorities sued the Squire and Mr. Goddard changed his plea to 'Guilty' when the case came up at the Salisbury Assizes.

Henry Baily (1815-1900)
Taken towards the end of his life.
(courtesy of Friends of Lydiard Tregoz).

In 1884 the original building debt on the church was finally paid off (more than 33 years after the foundation stone was laid). The following year, to the surprise of his congregation, Henry Baily accepted the nomination of Lord Bolingbroke to become Rector of Lydiard Tregoze - after thirty-eight years energetic and distinguished work as Vicar of Swindon. The 'Living' at Christ Church, at that time, was £302 p.a., at Lydiard it was £628, so perhaps the reason was financial. At his last service at Christ Church the attendance was so large that, for many hundreds of people who wished to attend, there was no room. A presentation followed at the Corn Exchange where, it is reported, he received a handsome clock, vases and a purse of £50. His old adversary, William Morris, wrote in the *Swindon Advertiser* in March 1885 an appreciative article about Baily's service to the community: '*He had loved and endeavoured to maintain those principles as he believed them to be clearly and prominently set forth in the Prayer Book of their reformed Church of England and that book he had loved to maintain in all its integrity*'.

Memorial to Ambrose L. Goddard.

Baily died on 8th May 1900, aged 84, and his body was brought back to be buried by the south-east corner of Christ Church. His widow, Elizabeth, aged 92, was buried with him in 1910. A memorial tablet was erected to Baily in the chancel of Christ Church adjacent to the pulpit, where it remains today as a reminder of the extraordinary vision and dedication of the first Vicar of Christ Church.

3

Discord and Scandal

1885 was a difficult year for Old Town and Christ Church. Not only did Henry Baily leave the parish but the Goddard family were in mourning for the premature death of Colonel Ambrose Ayshford at the age of 37 years, the eldest son of the Lord of the Manor, Ambrose Lethbridge Goddard. A Lieutenant-Colonel in the Grenadier Guards, he died on board of H.M.S. *Tyne* in May, whilst homeward bound from active service in Suakin on the Red Sea. He was buried in the Military Cemetery at Valetta, in Malta, and a memorial plaque placed in the church (which can still be seen today).

The Goddard Family

Back in Swindon there was much discord and argument regarding the attempts to introduce Anglo-Catholic ritual and teaching into the churches of New Swindon. At St. Paul's Church in Edgeware

Road (built in 1881) the *Swindon Advertiser* reported that *'the services are highly ritualistic. On special occasions the Altar is ablaze with candles, there are processions with banners, and the chanting of processional hymns, members of the congregation bow their heads and cross themselves, and those in office bend the knee as they pass the Altar'*. Attempts to introduce High Church practices were also been made at St. Mark's Church. By contrast, the services in Christ Church were still maintained in a strongly Evangelical tradition. The appointment of the successor to Henry Baily in 1885 was, therefore, of much

interest. This was Henry Armstrong Hall. He had become a deacon in 1876 and a priest the following year. He had served as Curate, at the Church of the Holy Trinity, Lee, Kent from 1876-78, Curate of St. George's, Isle of Man, 1878-80, and Vicar of Holy Trinity, Bristol, 1880-85. Hall was a man of great personality and eloquence, a break from the past, who boded great changes to come. Of striking manner and possessing a rich, deep voice Hall soon filled the Church to overflowing. It is reported that on one occasion *'the crowd extended from the doors to the road; one had to be there at 5.30 p.m. (service at 6.30 p.m.) for a seat'*.

In 1885, shortly after arriving in Swindon, H. Armstrong Hall instigated the sale of the old Vicarage house in The Planks for the sum of £1,880. It had fallen so seriously into decay and disrepair that the cost of refurbishing would have been excessive. In 1886, a Committee was formed to consider the building a new Vicarage house. A site was found in Bath Road and a new Vicarage built there (to the design of Mr. W.H. Read of Swindon); the cost of land and building being £3,400 – approximately £430,000 today. After taking the amount derived by selling the old vicarage, together with other grants, about £850 remained to be found. This new debt was to cause problems during the next few years.

The 'honeymoon' period for the new Vicar was not to last long.

He spent a disproportionate amount of time in London, delivering lectures to the YMCA. Hall also introduced altar lights and a surpliced choir, to lead services *'reverent and hearty though with no excessive ritual'*. Even these innovations aroused great opposition within the parish and were, probably, the reason why he left after only two years. Hall subsequently became Minister of Brunswick Chapelry, in St Marylebone, from 1887-88. He then took on various other duties before becoming Residential Canon of Ripon in 1908. Hall became Chaplain to King George V in 1912, Official Chaplain to the Armed Forces during the Great War; and was awarded the CBE in 1919. He died, aged 67, on 12th May 1921 at the Rectory, Methley in Leeds and was buried in Oswald Churchyard in Methley.

The arrival of Newton Ebenezer Howe as Vicar of Swindon in 1887 began a period of steep decline in the fortunes of the parish that was to continue until he left in 1901. The story of those traumatic years has never been fully told before . . .

Newton E. Howe was born in Lewisham, Kent in 1848, the seventh child of schoolmaster and author Thomas Howe. After being educated privately he was admitted to Magdalene College, Cambridge University, in 1867, at the age of 19 years, but left early without gaining his degree. In his 20s Howe moved in with brother's family in Heavitree, close to Exeter in Devon. Although without a formal degree he described himself as a *'student of philosophy'*, which seems to have impressed the church authorities enough to secure him his first appointment. In 1879, Howe was ordained as Deacon at St Albans and became Curate at St Saviour's Church, Walthamstow, in the same year. Three years later, under the patronage of one George Frederick Ottley, he became Rector of Luckington, near Malmesbury. Ordained a Priest in 1882, Howe remained as Rector there until 1887, during which time he married Susannah Wigzell, from Halifax in Yorkshire, and had a son, Ernest, born in 1884. During his time at Luckington, whilst presenting prizes at a local agricultural show, he chose to deliver an ill-advised and inappropriate speech about extending the franchise to women. His pontifications surprised the audience and perhaps demonstrated his unseemly behaviour in certain situations. At the age of 37 years, in May 1886, he was admitted to Merton College, Oxford as a commoner. Still listed as being at

Merton College, when Henry Armstrong Hall left Christ Church, Howe applied for the vacant living at Swindon.

After the short incumbency of Henry Hall at Christ Church, there was much interest and speculation in the town regarding his successor. On 11th June 1887, the *Swindon Advertiser* published a long leading article in which William Morris, commented on the state of affairs in the Church of England and the circumstances under which the new Vicar of Swindon had been appointed. He asked *'What doctrine would he preach? Was he an open Protestant or a disguised Romanist?'* However, other matters, not even considered at this time, were soon to occupy the minds of the congregation of Christ Church.

The Revd. Newton E. Howe made himself known to the people of Swindon by having the following notice put up on the door of Christ Church: *'The Vicar-Designate asks the prayers of the parishioners on behalf of himself and fellow helpers in the future work of the parish. Luckington Rectory, May 1887'*. However, the minds of his new parishioners were distracted for a while by the celebrations for the Golden Jubilee of Queen Victoria on 21st June. The streets and buildings of Swindon were festooned with decorations and banners and, at night, rows of burning gas jets illuminating the town. Howe arrived in Swindon in July and was inducted as Vicar of Swindon by the Ven. J.P. Norris, Archdeacon of Bristol, during the following month. The new Vicar's Churchwarden at this time was William Reynolds, Shoe & Harness Maker and Leather Merchant, whose premises were in the Market Square. Alfred Plummer was the People's Warden. The Reynolds family had been connected with Christ Church for many years and William's father, Robert, had been churchwarden when it was opened in 1851. However, they would soon find dealing with their new Vicar very difficult as he was often an absentee from the parish (he is listed as continuing to be a student at Merton College until December 1888). The majority of the services and other Parish affairs where often left to the curates, John Colmer Godwin and Jonathan Puckeridge. Thus, began a long period of decline in fortunes of the parish.

In April 1889, differences were already coming to light between Newton E. Howe and his flock. The organist, George Whitehead, was dismissed after 12 years-service. It seems that Whitehead may not have been paid for his work, as was the agreement. As a result, the two

High Street

churchwardens claimed that they could not work with the Vicar, due to his long absences from the Parish and his secretive nature regarding the administration of parish funds and charities. They both agreed, however, to stand again until the following year. By 1889 Howe had taken over the New Vicarage Fund from the Curate, the Revd. John Colmer Godwin, who had been looking after this since the departure of Armstrong Hall. A three-day 'Ice Carnival and Grand Fancy Fair' was held in June 1889 in the Corn Exchange to help in clearing the outstanding debt on the Vicarage. This consisted of stalls and tableaus, based around a winter theme, of various countries including Canada, Russia, Norway, Germany, Iceland and England. There was also entertainment and band concerts each day by the Orchestral Band of the 2nd Vol. Batt. The Duke of Edinburgh's (Wiltshire Regiment). A great undertaking with many taking part to make the occasion a success. This bazaar, however, would appear to have been the last time that the Vicar and his congregation would work together in an amicable manner.

By the end of the summer in 1889, the town was deluged with rumours and reports as to the alleged behaviour of Newton E. Howe, regarding his dealings as a Trustee for

Golden Jubilee celebrations of Queen Victoria 1887. Wood Street.

the various Church and National School charities. There were also allegations made that he had received payments from the Lord of the Manor for the New Vicarage Fund which had found their way into his own private funds. Few answers were forthcoming from Howe regarding these allegations. Many parishioners began to drift away from services at Christ Church including the two Churchwardens, William Reynolds and Alfred Plummer. The final act came in early

Extract from Church Bazaar programme 1889. (Myra Hartshorn)

November when Revd. Howe dissolved the Church Council because of *'the way some members interpreted their duties'*. This effectively divided the congregation into two parts, those who still supported the Vicar and those, the great majority, who agreed with the views of Reynolds and Plummer. Things became so bitter between the warring factions that two separate meetings were held in King William Street School in the last week of November. The first, called by the Vicar, entrance being by ticket alone, was in secret. A public meeting three days later, called by the Churchwardens, and open to all was attended by 120-130 persons. These included the majority of the regular worshippers at Christ Church. Gradually the Churchwardens and bulk of the congregation switched their allegiance and began attending Sunday services at St Mark's Church and St Paul's Church in New Town. Public feeling against Howe was so strong that even the building of a new church for Old Town, near North Street, was given active consideration! One of the persons attending the meeting was Charles F. Goddard, youngest son of the Lord of the Manor, Ambrose Lethbridge Goddard.

All these events, of course, were dutifully reported in the local press. In fact, *'Church Affairs in Swindon'* became a regular column in the newspapers. Howe continued to have frequent and uncertain absences from the Parish and could not be contacted. The services at the Church, his parish obligations and duties were often left for his latest curates, M.L. Eaton and R.L. Atkinson, to carry out. The administration by Howe of the Christmas Offertories in December brought about a new wave of debate in the Parish. A *'Paper War'* commenced in the readers' letters column of the *Swindon Advertiser* with accusations and recriminations being exchanged weekly, for a period of several months, with both Reynolds and Plummer and their supporters trading views with Howe and his followers. The Vicar's cause was not helped by accounts of litigation against him in the Swindon County Court also appearing in the newspaper. During September 1889 Howe was forced to appear in court over non-payment of a loan secured against church property. Despite his inability to keep up with the instalments on the debt, he suddenly, and miraculously, found £500 to lodge with the court and the case was dropped. In February 1890 details were carried of a case in which Howe was sued for non-payment of his newspaper account by the *North Wilts Herald*, from 8th August 1887 to 31st November 1889. This was settled out of court but added to the damage to Howe's reputation.

Over 100 people attended the annual Vestry Meeting of the Church in April 1890. Here there was a head-on collision with the Churchwardens. Howe complained that he had taken on a poor living by coming to Swindon (value about £300 per annum) and had been needlessly persecuted by his parishioners and inferred this was why the previous vicar (Hall) had left. It was said by his opponents that, by ceasing to attend Church services, he had effectively lost all spiritual guidance over the congregation. The meeting ended in deadlock and plans were made to gather again in May. On 8th May, at the reconvened meeting, the disagreements continued. Conflicting statements were issued by both parties regarding the accounts and Howe intimated that, in future, he was to administer the offertories himself alone. Mr. Robert Croome, was chosen as the Vicar's Warden for the next year whilst William J. Smith, a chemist in the High Street, was elected the People's Warden. William Smith was to play a major part in the events of the next ten years. The *Swindon Church Monthly* magazine for June 1890 carried a somewhat confusing analysis of the various accounts together with the story from the Vicar's point of view.

The opposition to Howe in Old Town now took their grievances to the Bishop of Gloucester and Bristol (the re-establishment of the latter as a separate Diocese did not take place until 1897). He declared himself, however, unable to interfere regarding the administration of charities. It was then decided to take their case to the Charity Commission and it was agreed that the matter would be discussed at a meeting in Swindon during August. Unfortunately, before this meeting could take place other rumours regarding the behaviour of the Vicar began to spread throughout the town. It was reported, on more than one occasion that Revd. Howe required a police escort home from the church to the vicarage.

Amongst those who supported Howe was a 23-year-old lady, Marion Ormond, a Sunday School Teacher and District Visitor, whose father, William Ormond, was a well-known and respected local solicitor, as well as being Treasurer for the Society for the Promotion of Christian Knowledge. Marion was a friend of Mrs. Susannah

Howe, the Vicar's wife, and was often invited to the Vicarage. Against the wishes of her parents she continued to see both the Vicar and Mrs. Howe. In the spring of 1890 Revd. Newton E. Howe (20 years her senior) started to show increasing affection towards the young girl, often visiting her family home at The Limes, in Devizes Road. Thus began a relationship that was to eventually bring about his downfall. Clandestine meetings between the couple were held from May onwards in the countryside around Swindon, at Walcot and along Marlborough Lane, off the Coate Road. Often they would meet under the Midland & South Western Junction Railway bridge adjacent to the Coate Road (now Evelyn Street) before walking down the lane into the woods together. The unavoidable occurred, they were seen by various passers-by and men working on the railway line. Despite the inevitable rumours, Howe could still be seen parading proudly about Old Town, presenting a cool and collected front. The *Western Daily Press* reported that Howe had been seen, '*walking and being alone with her in secluded places, putting his arms around her waist and kissing her.*' News soon reached William Smith, the People's Warden, who immediately contacted the Archdeacon and the Bishop of Gloucester and Bristol. On 21st June 1890 the latter served a notice of inhibition on Howe to prevent him officiating at any services until the matter was investigated.

The outcry the news caused in Swindon can be imagined. The position of a Church of England clergyman in the late Victorian era was a privileged one. He was considered to be ranked in class after the aristocracy having, generally, the benefits that money and a good education could bring. For a man in this position to be charged with improper conduct was considered a scandal. On the evening of 21st June 1890 a large crowd gathered in the Sands (Bath Road) and wended its way towards the Vicarage where they stayed until a late hour; hooting, whistling, shouting and throwing missiles at the house which was protected by a ring of twenty policemen. There was no sign of life at the Vicarage, however, as the Revd. Howe had been warned to vacate the premises until the situation had calmed down. Similar demonstrations followed on the next two evenings with many young children taking part. Gradually, however, these '*Extraordinary Scenes*' (as described in the *Swindon Advertiser*) calmed down as it became obvious to the crowd that Howe was absent from Swindon. On Sunday, 22nd June, the services at Christ Church were conducted, at the request of the Archdeacon of Bristol, by the Revd. Hon. M. Ponsonby (Vicar of St Mark's) and one of his curates. On the following Saturday, 28th June 1890, William Morris wrote a long leading article in his newspaper regarding the affair in which he gave his opinions on the problems at Christ Church since Howe had arrived and the inability of the Church authorities to deal with them.

A Court of Enquiry was called for 15th August at the Town Hall, Old Town, to see if there was enough evidence to carry the case to the Lord Bishop. Howe was charged *'with having occasioned grave scandal in the parish by having been guilty of improper familiarity with Miss Marion Ormond, of lewd and indecent behaviour, and of soliciting her chastity on more than one occasion.'* After a five-hour hearing in front of a packed courtroom it was agreed to take the matter to the next stage. Howe indignantly denied all the charges at the hearing. Referring to William Smith and his friends, on leaving the court, Howe was heard to say: *'he would take care they did not get rid of him!'*. Strangely enough the enquiry into the charities took place the day before the above case at Swindon, this time to an almost deserted courtroom. Howe could not be indicted because he had not attended this hearing, claiming he had been detained in London on clerical duties.

Correspondence continued in the columns of the *Swindon Advertiser* and *North Wilts Herald* over the next four months whilst waiting for the hearing at Bristol to take place. During all of this time Newton E. Howe continued to protest his innocence of the charges against him, supported by his wife, so that it came as a great shock to the congregation of Christ Church that at the Consistorial Court in the Chapter House of Bristol Cathedral on 12th December 1890, Howe changed his plea to guilty on all charges. The Bishop decreed that the Revd. Newton E. Howe was to be suspended from all duties for three years from 21st December and would be liable for the costs of the hearing. Howe pleaded with the court that the loss of his salary and the burden of the costs of the hearing would leave him no option but to declare himself bankrupt. Nonetheless, his pleading fell on unsympathetic ears.

Marion Ormond, whose part in the affair may not have been dealt with as sympathetically as perhaps it would today, left Swindon immediately and took a position of employment in a convalescent home near Newbury. It appears the public disgrace was too much for her to bear and she never returned to Swindon. After a period working as a nurse in Harley Street, London, she moved to the south coast, eventually retiring to the Old Hastings Hotel in Warninglid, Sussex. She remained a spinster. Her father, William Ormond, died in 1908, leaving a considerable fortune of £51,000 (more than £6 million today). Did the Revd. Howe have an envious eye on the Ormond fortune when he began his illicit affair with Marion? We will probably never know.

To those back in Swindon it still seemed justice had not been done as Howe remained Vicar of Swindon and, although the living had been sequestered for three years, he was to return. Therefore, few medium or long-term plans could be made to rescue Christ Church from the trough into which it had fallen. Nevertheless, church life continued, the plans for a new church were dropped and many of those who had deserted the congregation returned to the fold including William Reynolds. For the next three years the Church was put in the charge of two Curates, the Revd. Ernest J. Houghton, and then the Revd. Charles F. Goddard, the youngest son of Ambrose Lethbridge Goddard. He had been ordained a Deacon in 1889 and Priest in 1891, at Southwark. Curate of St Paul's, Swindon, 1890-91, he served at Christ Church from 1892-95 until leaving the Parish to become Vicar of Clearwell. To mark his ordination, members of the church presented Charles Goddard with a white silk stole and a Morocco-bound prayer book.

The Goddard family also showed further support for the Church when Captain Fitzroy Pleydell Goddard, the second son of Mr A. L. Goddard, became a churchwarden during this difficult period, despite many other conflicting commitments.

Letters were written and published in the *Swindon Advertiser*, exalting the virtues of the Revd. Houghton and Revd. Goddard, and lamenting the sorry state of the church under the Revd. Howe. One example, signed only L.M.T., stated *'we do not want a man who will only disgust an intelligent congregation and drive them from the church!'*

Howe was also summoned in March 1891 to Swindon Court for non-payment of the Poor Rate (a tax levied on householders within a parish, to help towards relief of the poor).

Parish life continued at Christ Church. At Christmas 1891, the fine Reredos (ornamental screens) behind the high altar was erected by Pleydell and Jessie Goddard, in memory of their brother, Ambrose Goddard. A Grand Military Bazaar & Mess Canteen was held in the Corn Exchange and Town Hall for three days in November 1892 to clear the balance that was still outstanding on the New Vicarage Fund of some £450. This consisted of displays by various famous British regiments, music by the Swindon Town Orchestral Band and various other stalls and entertainment.

The annual Easter Vestry meeting (held in April 1892; and chaired by the Revd. Charles Goddard) at least could report some good news for the beleaguered church. In the absence of Newton Howe, numbers attending services had increased, particularly among the poorer people of the parish. Collections were now averaging '*nearly six guineas a week, which was very good indeed.*' (A guinea was a gold coin - named after the Guinea region in West Africa, where much of the gold used to make the coins originated – it's value was 21 shillings. Although the actual coins themselves had fallen out of use, the term was still used. One guinea, in 1892, would be today's equivalent of approximately £130.)

Newton E. Howe mostly disappeared from the public eye in Swindon during the years 1891-94. After a short period living in Liscard, Wallasey (it appears without his wife) he spent several months in Douglas, on the Isle of Man, apparently engaged in clerical duties (despite an order from the Ecclesiastical Court preventing him from earning a living in this way). Here he became friends with a Mr Joseph Roskyll, his wife Eliza, and their daughter, Mary, who was then aged 39. Joseph Roskyll died shortly after (in 1892) and Mary's mother Eliza just two years later. These unfortunate circumstances, coupled with plenty of time on his hands, seems to have strengthened Howe's relationship and influence over Mary.

During these years, Howe would later claim, that he had made efforts to find another living within the Church so that he would not have to return to his post at Swindon. He was unable to do this, however, and took up his position as Vicar of Swindon once again at the end of 1894. A long-winded notice comprising several pages, confirming Howe's return to the office of Vicar, was posted on the church door and large congregations gathered for Howe's first service.

His financial position by this time was very precarious, not surprisingly after the loss of income for three years from the living at Swindon. William Smith was still one of the Churchwardens so that relations between the Church Council and the Vicar must have been extremely difficult. For two or three years everyday affairs in the Parish seemed to return to normal and the Church took part in the celebration for the Diamond Jubilee of Queen Victoria in 1897. However, perhaps with the recent scandal involving the Revd. Howe still fresh in their mind, one member of Christ Church's congregation did write to the *Swindon Advertiser* following the Diamond Jubilee celebrations at the County Ground, complaining that *'the cyclists' attire was simply filthy, especially after they dismounted'*, and how this *'rudely shocked the ladies and the girls, causing our already fearfully demoralised country some degree of further declension'*. Unfortunately, this was to be just the tip of the iceberg . . .

Newton Howe still spent much time away from Swindon and rumours began to be circulated in the town regarding his relationship with Miss Mary Roskyll (mentioned above). It appears that in 1894, after the death of her parents, Howe had become her guardian. She took property in Oxford and he was often seen with her here and elsewhere. They also spent holidays together. Miss Roskyll sometimes visited Swindon and stayed at the Vicarage, with the pair often seen promenading the streets of Swindon together. This state of affairs continued and it was inevitable that gossip would follow. The matter would soon come to the notice of the Church authorities. In October 1898 Mary Roskyll took up permanent residence at the Vicarage and remained there until February 1899. In early 1899 the Bishop sent Howe a letter telling him that, in view of all the bad publicity that was circulating he should cease his involvement with the lady. Howe was not to be persuaded and the situation continued as before during the remainder of 1899. Finally, a Parish meeting was convened in late October by William Smith *'to consider certain matters of vital importance to the Parish at large'*. It was chaired by Fitzroy Pleydell

Queen Victoria's Diamond Jubillee Arch in County Road 1897.

Goddard with about thirty parishioners attending. When asked about the meeting the Vicar said that '*he was unaware of it and had no idea what was the object - he took no notice of rumours*'. A letter of complaint regarding Howe's behaviour duly went to the Lord Bishop of Bristol, Dr. Forrest Browne, outlining how the Vicar's conduct had contravened the Clergy Discipline Act of 1892. The Bishop issued an order then inhibiting Howe from taking part in any religious act in the Diocese until the matter had been resolved. In mid-November the Revd. William Scott was appointed Curate-in-charge of the Parish.

Churchwarden William John Smith, who owned the chemist shop in the High Street, decided to take proceeding into his own hands and personally financed the case against Howe. The hearing was heard at the end of January 1900 at the Consistory Court, Guildhall, Bristol, charging Howe with adultery under the Clergy Discipline Act, stating that he had '*brought discredit upon his cloth and (that he) ought not to be allowed to remain vicar of the important parish of Swindon*'. Witnesses reported that Howe referred to Miss Roskyll as '*darling*' and that, during a visit to an aunt, Miss Roskyll had taken two cups of tea upstairs in the morning and promptly disappeared into Howe's room! On another occasion Bessie Crowest, the cook at the vicarage, observed Howe leaving Miss Roskyll's room in a state of undress. It was generally noted that, wherever the pair stayed, they requested rooms that were close together or with adjoining doors. It was reported that they frequently stayed up late together in the dining room, after Mrs Howe had retired to bed, and were often seen holding hands.

Revd. Howe was defended by the considerably talented and respected Lord Bernard Coleridge, a relation of the poet Samuel Coleridge, who would later become Lord Chief Justice of England. Just how the Reverend was able to afford the services of such an eminent barrister remains a mystery, however it was certainly effective. Lord Coleridge produced Mary Roskyll as a defending witness. She testified to the fact that she being a *'lady of independent means, who never took up any occupation, never married, and all her life was looked after by a servant.'* Mary insisted that the vicar's interest in her affairs had been solely at her own instigation and only with the consent of his wife Susannah. Lord Coleridge further argued that the proceedings had only been brought to court in the first place because of Howe's admitted adultery in the case of Marion Ormond a decade earlier. Lord Coleridge told the jury that he failed to understand how adultery could have taken place if Mrs Howe was living with them on the same premises. Coleridge explained that he believed the truth was, in fact, nothing more than financial necessity on the part on Howe, who could not afford to lose Mary Roskyll as a paying guest at the Vicarage, and had merely *'gone out of his way to show her attention and make things pleasant.'*

After two days, the case was adjourned until the last week in March. Finally, a verdict was declared on 26th April 1900. Despite some seemingly damning evidence, to the surprise of many it was 'Not Guilty' of the charges. The support of his wife, Susannah, throughout the hearing had proved decisive, coupled with the fact that the evidence produced was largely circumstantial. Cases of adultery

Lord Coleridge who defended Revd. Howe.

were notoriously hard to prove in Victorian courts. Costs were ordered against the Churchwarden of £800 – today's equivalent of almost £100,000! Clearly beyond the means of any single person, an appeal was immediately set up to cover the cost of the legal fees. 'The Prosecution Fund' was advertised in all the Wiltshire newspapers and members of the Christ Church congregation canvassed door-to-door in Old Town in a desperate attempt to raise funds. The strength of feeling against Revd. Howe can be gauged by the level of support for the cause. Major F. Goddard contributed and the Churchwardens themselves raised over £700. Eventual costs would run to £1,117. Over 1,700 circulars were distributed and over 500 house calls were made in an attempt to raise the funds. Mr G. Butterworth (the Churchwarden's solicitor) agreed to reduce his fees; and his partners even contributed to the fund! Eventually, after more than 10 years enough money was collected and the legal fees finally paid. An extraordinary endeavour on the part of the people of Old Town; and probably an occurrence without parallel in the history of the Church of England.

What was to happen now at Christ Church? The Revd. Ernest Houghton left his role as Curate to become Vicar at St Luke's in Gloucester, where he was to meet with further misfortune. Whilst out visiting his parishioners on his bicycle, he collided with a Brewer's Dray and was thrown onto the cobbled street, receiving serious injuries, from which he never fully recovered. Meanwhile Miss Roskyll continued to live at the Vicarage with Newton Howe and his wife. Matters carried on as before with the Vicar able to take services once again. But Howe's victory proved to be his last. Although Miss Rosykll was able to help him financially to some extent the cost of the loss of income during the trial proved Howe's downfall. He continued to live as if he had little in the way of money problems, however. Soon complaints began to surface from several local businessmen, stating that Howe was asking for credit and that cheques were being received that were not honoured when presented at the bank. This finally led to him being arrested on 25th September 1900 in Llandrindod Wells, whilst on holiday there with Miss Roskyll, and charged with obtaining money by false pretenses from H. George English, a grocer of Fleet Street. Howe was charged with obtaining credit by means of fraud.

In an era when normal daily and business life was based on trust in the system of settling accounts in a timely fashion, and in honouring cheques, these allegations were far more serious than, perhaps, we would consider them today. Howe, who at that time owed 14 shillings and 2 old pence to the grocer, presented him with a cheque for £10 14s 2d, and persuaded Mr English to give him the £10 as change. This was a not insignificant sum in 1900, today's equivalent of more than £1,200. When the cheque was returned from the bank marked 'unpaid', Mr English had immediately gone to the police. Howe was directly summoned to Swindon. Whilst on the way back on the train, it was noted by another passenger that he was reading a book on Ecclesiastical law and was heard to say: *'to get me out of my living they will have to get me a term of imprisonment with hard labour'*. Yet another notice of inhibition was affixed to the west door of Christ Church from the Bishop of Bristol to prevent Howe taking part in any services. The case came up at the Wiltshire Autumn Assize in Salisbury in the last week of October 1900, the Vicar pleaded 'not guilty' and after a five-hour hearing the jury were unable to agree on a verdict. The case was then adjourned until the Winter Assize at Devizes in January 1901. During the period of the adjournment further allegations emerged, including an outstanding debt of £19 to Edwin Morris, a coal merchant from Devizes Road. Finally at the Winter Assizes, on 14th January 1901, following another five-hour hearing, he was found 'Guilty'. It was reported that Howe was very pale when Judge Day pronounced sentence of twelve months with hard labour, to be served at Devizes Jail – a notorious prison at which the conditions for prisoners were uncompromising to say the least. Judge Day told the court that he *'could only regard it as benefit to the public at large to be rid of his services'*.

Howe left the dock a broken and humiliated man, the story received national and international press attention, being reported as far away as Australia. Ironically Howe was correct about his sentence – this finally allowed the authorities to dismiss him from his position as the Vicar of Swindon. Mr Justice Day (during his summing up in court) heavily criticized the Ecclesiastical Court for previously allowing Howe to return to his role at the church, following his first suspension. By an official order, dated 4th February 1901, the living of

Rev. Newton Ebenezer Howe.

SUSPENDED FOR IMPROPER BEHAVIOUR.

TO A SUNDAY SCHOOL SCHOLAR.

HIS DISHONOURED CHEQUES.

At Wilts Assizes on Monday, the 14th January, the Rev. Newton Ebenezer Howe, vicar of Swindon, was charged with obtaining by false pretences £10 from Henry George English, with intent to defraud, at Swindon, on July 28. The case was sent down from the last assizes in consequence of the jury then disagreeing. Prosecutor swore that defendant obtained from him £10 for a cheque on making representations that he had a large amount to come in from tithes; that he also had cheques to present from his bank; and that the cheque would be all right. In point of fact the living was at that time sequestrated, and the tithes were being paid to the registrar of the diocese. There was only a balance of

A FEW SHILLINGS AT HIS BANK,

and no cheques were paid in for some time afterwards. Several witnesses gave evidence as to cheques from Mr. Howe being dishonoured, and also as to extensive county court and bankruptcy proceedings. Defendant gave evidence denying fraudulent intention. In cross-examination he admitted having told untruths in letters as excuses for cheques being dishonoured. He was found guilty. Sentence was deferred.

The case was reported as far away as Australia.

Swindon was declared vacant by W. Hurle Clarke, Registrar. Howe was listed as a 'common prisoner'. He was confined to one of the 210 cells at the prison. Inmates were required to spend long periods isolated in their cells, which measured 10 feet high, 7ft. 5 inches wide, and 8ft. 5 inches long. Those of the women's 7ft. high, 5ft.wide, and 7ft. 5 inches long. During these long periods of confinement Howe could only communicate with his fellow prisoners through a small aperture in the cell door. He was expected to attend the prison chapel daily, during which time he received instruction from the Prison Chaplain – much to the chagrin of the discredited Vicar. Each morning he was required to grind corn on the Devizes Prison treadmill along with other prisoners. The task was an exhausting one and the inmates frequently returned wearily to their cells, complaining of sore feet and aching limbs.

Howe served his sentence without privileges or incident among what he considered to be *'a lower class of person'*. He was eventually released in January 1902.

The humiliation of her involvement in such a public scandal proved too much for Mary Roskyll, who wasted no time in informing the people of Swindon that she would be distancing herself from the convicted Revd. Howe. (This does not seem to have been the case however – see below). Mary moved to

*Contemporary illustration of prisoners on the Devizes
Prison Treadmill.*

Bognor Regis initially, eventually settling in Oxford in 1910.

The colourful Howe's subsequent career was not known at the time to the people of Swindon (his name disappears from *Crockford's Clerical Register* from 1901 onwards), nor at the time of the original publication of *The Old Lady on the Hill* in 2001. However, for this revised and updated edition, we are able, for the first time, to complete the story of the notorious Newton Ebenezer Howe.

Following his release from Devizes Jail, the disgraced Howe moved to number 96 Tulse Hill, in Norwood, London, where he seems to have found employment teaching in a small school. Perhaps to distance himself from his previous misdemeanors, Howe now referred to himself as 'William Howe' rather than 'Newton' or Ebenezer'. It seems unlikely that a school would employ a stranger, replying to a job advertisement in the newspaper, without first asking for a reference. It was common in the Edwardian era for prospective applicants to arrive at their interview with a handwritten *'To Whom It May Concern'* reference already prepared. Did Howe falsify a reference? Commonsense tells us that the school would, almost certainly, not have employed Howe if they had known the truth. However, a Vicar conveniently named William Howe had recently passed away in Crewe, after a short illness. The death was reported in the church press but was not otherwise widely known. Did Howe

Tulse Hill, Norwood in 1902.

'steal' the Revd. William Howe's name and identity for the purposes of gaining employment? It certainly seems likely. Once a satisfactory reference had been presented, a cursory check would have revealed the existence of a 'Revd. William Howe' and the document would have been taken on trust, as was the convention at the time. Howe's long suffering wife Susannah appeared with him at his interview for the appointment, however there is no record that she ever lived with him at Tulse Hill.

The appointment came with a small house attached to the school, but it was not long until Howe fell foul of his neighbours. It appears that he began constantly knocking on his neighbours' doors, claiming that he was collecting for charity. However, his appeals bordered on harassment and, when challenged, was unable to provide satisfactory details of the charities in question. The governors of the school were forced to, first, warn him and then finally dismiss him in 1906.

Howe then moved (somewhat ironically!) to 192 Church Road in Worthing, Sussex and, initially, found employment hard to secure. For a while he obtained some work as a tutor, however an incident in 1908 was to cost him this position. The former Vicar started a charity collection on behalf of a schoolmaster who, Howe claimed, was in ill health and financial difficulties. He managed to gain the trust of several ladies – partly through charm and partly through falsely

Lewes Prison.

representing himself as a member of the clergy – and obtained various sums of money, including 5 shillings from a Mrs Katherine Hunt, 2s 6d from Mrs Mary Holman and 10s from Mrs Mary Reval.

However, his subterfuge was unearthed when inquiries found the schoolmaster to be alive and well. Howe was again arrested. After a period on remand at Lewes Prison, he appeared before Justice Grantham at the Lewes Assizes on Monday November 9th 1908 – still dressed as a clergyman. On this occasion he admitted his guilt to the charge of obtaining money on false pretences, and to that of impersonating a member of the clergy; and was sentenced to 12 months in prison with hard labour. Had he not admitted his guilt, his sentence would undoubtedly have been much longer. Lewes Prison was a large, and uncompromising, Victorian prison which, during the early part of the 20th century, notoriously housed political troublemakers from Ireland, such as Éamon de Valera. Later in the century it would infamously cage Reggie Kray and Mick Jagger. Security was high and discipline tough. Hard labour for the prisoners involved rock breaking and the now middle-aged Howe found his prison term back-breaking and humiliating.

He was eventually released on 9th September 1909 and returned to Church Road in Hove. Prison had taken its toll on the former Vicar. He was now 61 years of age, grey and balding, his bravado and swagger gone. Unfortunately, Howe was now unable to afford the rent payment at these lodgings and, remembering Mary Roskyll's kind and generous nature, wrote to her in Headington, Oxford, pleading for help. Howe had contacted her before, knowing that she had substantial private means, and it is likely that she paid his rent arrears during his incarceration. Mary, with her forgiving and warm nature, and perhaps still besotted with Howe, took him in as a lodger in 1910. Mary lived alone (apart from a maid) at number 13 Stile Road, a pleasant, bay windowed Edwardian villa and now led a secluded life, supported by private means. Howe, although still legally married but estranged, seems to have relied on Mary's charity for the remainder of his life, living in her house as a lodger. He listed his occupation as 'tutor', although there is no record of him ever having worked again. Unable to now return to tutoring or to the church, he remained a penniless recluse until his death in 1927. Mary lived out the remainder of her life in Headington, before passing away in 1933 at the age of 81.

The beginning of the 20th century signaled the end of an era for the country and for life in Swindon. On 22nd January 1900 the Charter of Incorporation, signed by Queen Victoria, had been received in Swindon and the two towns joined together to officially become the Borough of Swindon on 9th November. The main protagonists in our story had already begun to exit 'stage left'. William Morris, Editor of the *Swindon Advertiser* since its inception in 1854, had died in Bournemouth in June 1891 at the age of 65. He is buried in the churchyard at Christ Church. Ambrose Lethbridge Goddard died in November 1898 to be succeeded by his son, Fitzroy Pleydell. Finally, on 22nd January 1901, the long reign of Queen Victoria herself came to end and Britain entered the Edwardian era.

4

Renewal & Growth 1901-1929

The new Borough of Swindon in 1901 had a population of 45,000 people of whom some 6000 lived in Old Town. When Canon Edmund Walter Southerton Estcourt was appointed as Vicar of Swindon (with a stipend of £300 p.a.) the people of the town and the congregation of Christ Church were anxious to put the years of neglect, discord, and recession behind them. The new Vicar was to enjoy much goodwill amongst his new parishioners. Estcourt proved to be a wise choice. Born in 1850, he was educated at Balliol College, Oxford, where he obtained his BA in 1874 and MA degree in 1878. Estcourt had become a deacon in 1876 and a priest in 1877. Curate and then Rector of Long Newnton, Gloucestershire from 1876-1901, and an Honorary Canon of Bristol Cathedral from 1898. He came to Swindon with many years of experience in running the affairs of a parish. Edmund Estcourt was a member of an old and land-owning

Cricklade Street in 1905. Number 36 (on the left in the middle of the photograph) housed the Parish Office for a short period of time.

Wiltshire family, originally called the De La Estcourts. He was a man of great energy, warm sympathy and considerable organizing skill. The *Swindon Advertiser* described him as *a 'moderate high churchman who will pander to no party or clique.'*

An early priority was to strike up a good relationship with the lay members of the Church. This accomplished Estcourt set about developing a vigorous corporate life in the parish. He believed in taking Christianity out to the people of Old Town. In 1902, following various fundraising events, including a garden fete and a concert at the Church

The former Parish Office in Cricklade Street, photographed in 1908.

Hall, the Little London Mission was opened in the street opposite the parish church, Church Road, on the corner of the area known as Little London. The area had been the home of a small migrant population from the capital from the early nineteenth century. It was (and still is today) a narrow steep lane which is thought to have seen use by stage coaches when Cricklade Street became impassable in bad weather. In 1902 it was still lined with thatched cottages (some remained here until the 1960s) and was the home for many of the poorer people of Old Town. The creation of the Mission Hall initially caused problems with residents, and a court case ensued, however the building was eventually established from two cottages gifted to the church by Mr James Hinton of The Brow, in Swindon. By 1903 £120 of the estimated £200 building costs, had been raised, so a further Garden Fete was held in the grounds of The Lawns mansion to raise the balance. A 60 feet by 35 feet marquee made an eye-catching centerpiece and a large giant chess game was played on a manicured area of the grass, in which volunteers were dressed as the chess pieces and moved accordingly by the players.

Garden Fete in aid of the Little London Mission.

The Mission was run almost entirely by lay members of Christ Church. One lay member who worked there later said that the Mission was provided for *'people who couldn't stand the sight of a clergyman!'* Major Buchan, a Church Army Captain, later joined the parish staff with the Little London Mission being his particular responsibility. The small hall was fully equipped as a church, complete with a harmonium, and soon boasted a thriving Sunday School and a large evening congregation. A weeknight club, 'The Dawn' was formed, which was held in a small hall in Devizes Road and attended by some of the older boys from the Mission. Amongst its activities were boxing sessions and a football team was formed. The Little London Mission continued to flourish until the Second World War when the building fell into disrepair. In 1949 the Mission was finally closed (see also Chapter 5).

After eleven arduous years, William Smith retired as Church-warden, with William Reynolds returned for a third time in this position. Another well-known local businessman, Edward Bays, a local ironmonger and engineer, also served as Churchwarden during this period. Bays would also become a Justice of the Peace for the Borough of Swindon, before eventually passing away in 1922 at the age of 74. A plaque in his honour was placed on the wall of the church.

In the typical terraced house at the beginning of the Century a bathroom was very much an extra amenity and the one W.C. would have been outside. In rural areas this was an earth closet at the end of the garden. Fireplaces and chimney stacks were standard, even in the two main bedrooms. Larger houses had a wash-house, with a brick copper boiler with its chimney stack adjoining the kitchen. Small houses had the 'copper' in the very tiny kitchen, which also had a pantry and a small shallow stone sink. Cooking was done on the range in the small living-room until gas cookers were wedged into the tiny kitchen.

The early years of the twentieth century also saw lengthy casualty lists published in the *Swindon Advertiser*, as the South African War raged (later known as The Boer War). The population of Swindon did not escape, with many more men dying of infections and cholera, whilst 'recovering' in the camps, than from actual injuries inflicted on the battlefield. One such unfortunate hero was Private J. Hitchman (No. 4986 2nd Wilts), a member of Christ Church's congregation, who succumbed to disease on 19th October 1900.

Canon Estcourt, however, found the new Vicarage in Bath Road too small for his family and his domestic staff. He, therefore, arranged that a large extra wing be added to the property. This was to prove a burden to his successors as Vicar of Swindon as they did not have as many servants! Already a large building, it would become an even more substantial house. With its large garden, surely one of the larger townhouses in Swindon.

Urgent fundraising was required in 1904 following damage to the steeple, and, in 1905, to aid improvements to the heating system within the building. In February 1904 a large piece of masonry, weighing one hundredweight, fell from the cove of the cornice beneath the spire, and crashed into the roof. Fortunately, it bounced off and landed harmlessly in the grass, rather than crashing through the roof of the main building. Despite howling gales, and with little regard for health and safety, a team of intrepid steeplejacks were urgently employed to scale the spire and repair the (extensive) damage.

In July 1905 a fete was organized in the Town Gardens towards the heating fund. Tea, refreshments, entertainments, and an outdoor concert were held. Note the original spelling of coconut!

Also, in July 1905, a new Font was presented to Christ Church

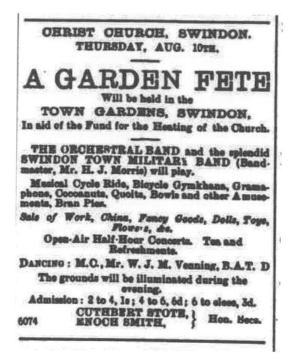

Garden Fete in aid of the Church Heating Fund.

by Edward Hesketh Goddard (brother of Fitzroy Pleydell Goddard) in memory of his wife Dulcie Gwendoline. On Ascension Day, 1906 Jessie and Pleydell Goddard also continued to show their family's love and care for the Church by erecting a new Pulpit in memory of their parents, Ambrose Lethbridge Goddard and Charlotte Goddard. The original pulpit and font were placed in the chancel of Holy Rood where they remain to this day. Major F. Pleydell Goddard also gave further land around Christ Church to extend the churchyard and a Burial Board was established in February 1902 to administer the burial ground.

The need for fundraising is highlighted by the deficit in Church Accounts which was scrutinized at a meeting in 1903. Key expenses were three annual Curates' salaries of £150 (one of which was paid by the Vicar from his own account), an annual caretaker's bill of £63, £26 on fuel and £2 for winding the clock! The Offertory Account (used to pay for clergy staff) showed an expenditure of £300 and an income of £273.

The Mothers' Union, formed in Old Alresford in the Winchester Diocese in 1876 by Mary Sumner, had spread throughout the country by the 1900s. By the beginning of the 20th century its worldwide

membership had swelled to 169,000 with branches throughout the British Empire. The Christ Church branch was established in 1906 with a membership of 87 (its membership had increased to 242 by 1914). A Mrs. Brodie being the Enrolling member. Despite already being 78 years of age at the time, founder Mary Sumner visited Christ Church to open the Christ Church branch.

Mary Sumner, founder of the Mothers' Union

In June 1906 the Bath and West Show came to the town, and the new Swindon Tram Service was ready to carry passengers from New Town to and from the Market Square in Old Town. Unfortunately, a major accident occurred when tramcar No 11 suffered a brake failure on Victoria Hill and crashed at the bottom of the hill killing 5 people. Prayers and a collection were held in Christ Church. Many elderly people were frightened from using the new tram service, following this incident, but the younger generation, having had the convenience of the service, soon resumed using it. However, the incident resulted in a levy on the rates for many years afterwards to pay the compensation required.

The churches in Swindon showed their social responsibility when the Swindon Unemployed Aid Fund was launched in 1909 (in the days before the Welfare State). Large contributions from Christ Church (£11), the Kinneir family, and many other members of the congregation were among a pleasing show of awareness from the more affluent organisations and individuals in the town.

Canon Estcourt, who also held the position of Rural Dean of Cricklade from 1903-10, left Christ Church in 1910 to become Rector of St John the Baptist Church in Shipton Moyne, in the Diocese of Gloucester. Estcourt remained there until his death in 1938 and is buried within the churchyard. He was succeeded as

Swindon Tram Disaster 1906.

Vicar of Swindon by Charles Augustine Mayall. Revd. Mayall was a graduate of Corpus Christi College, Cambridge, obtaining his BA in 1874 and MA degree in 1906. He had been ordained a deacon in 1897 and priest in 1898 at Ely. Previously, Mayall had been Curate of Cherry Hinton, Cambridge from 1897-99, and St. Paul's, Bedminster, Bristol from 1899-1907. During his time at St. Paul's, Charles Mayall was known as an extremely hard working and much loved curate and received the highest praise from his Vicar, Charles Griffith (himself a highly influential and respected parish priest of true Victorian values). He bestowed the highest of references upon his curate – that of granting his daughter Ida's hand in marriage. Ida was later to have a large influence on parish life during their time in Swindon. Charles Mayall left St. Paul's in Bedminster to become Vicar of Holy Trinity Church, Hinckley, in Leicestershire, in 1907, then succeeding Canon Estcourt at Christ Church in 1910.

Mayall soon built up a close relationship with his congregation gaining their respect and affection. He continued Canon Estcourt's work to develop the corporate life of the

Charles Mayall, Vicar of Christ Church 1910-1929.

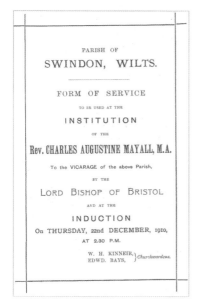

PARISH OF

SWINDON, WILTS.

FORM OF SERVICE

TO BE USED AT THE

INSTITUTION

OF THE

Rev. CHARLES AUGUSTINE MAYALL, M.A.

To the VICARAGE of the above Parish,

BY THE

LORD BISHOP OF BRISTOL

AND AT THE

INDUCTION

On THURSDAY, 22nd DECEMBER, 1910,

AT 2.30 P.M.

W. H. KINNEIR, } *Churchwardens.*
EDWD. BAYS,

Order of Service for the institution of Charles Mayall as Vicar. 1910.

Parish. An early undertaking was to build a new Church Hall in Devizes Road. From 1910 the original small hall on the site was being used as a Sunday School whilst, during the week, it was occupied by the Dawn Club (see above). The growth in the number of people wishing to attend the services at Christ Church, especially Evensong, proved too large to accommodate in the Parish Church so it had also become necessary to also take this into account. On 6th June 1913 the foundation stone of the new Church Hall was laid by Fitzroy Pleydell Goddard, the Lord of the Manor. When completed, at a cost of £3,000, (almost £350,000 today) the Hall was used for overflow services for the people who could not be accommodated in Christ Church. Later, the organ in Liddington Church was purchased and installed in the Church Hall and a new Hall Choir recruited. The chairs used there were obtained from the Picture House Cinema in Regent Circus, cleaned, sand-papered and polished by men from the Church of England Men's Society.

National events impinged on the congregation of Christ Church during these years. A period of mourning at the death of Edward VII in May 1910 was observed together with the celebrations for the coronation of King George V in June 1911. The people of the Parish Church also joined in the grief at the sinking of the liner S.S. *Titanic* in April 1912 and helped towards the fund set up for the families of those who had died in the disaster. Mr Benjamin Howard, from Cheltenham Street in Swindon, was among the 1,500 people who perished. Swindon, and society itself, was markedly different in the pre-war years than they appear today. There was a small middle and upper class and a large working class, many of whom lived in a state of poverty which would be completely unacceptable today. Most homes

Church Hall Foundation Stone 1913.

Ceremony for the laying of the Church Hall Foundation Stone, Devizes Road, 1913.

Interior of Christ Church 1907.

were heated by coal, electricity was still the preserve of the wealthy. Motor vehicles were not a common sight on the streets of Swindon, and tended to be the preserve of either prosperous businessmen or wealthy private citizens. The horse still dominated, and the tram was the sole form of motorised transport available to ordinary townsfolk.

It seemed as if war in Europe was inevitable in 1914, as two opposing power blocks began arming - the Triple Entente, consisting of France, Russia and Britain on one side, and, the Triple Alliance comprising Italy, Austria-Hungary and Germany on the other. Tensions escalated until the assassination of Archduke Franz Ferdinand of Austria tipped

Exterior of Christ Church c.1914, showing insert of Revd. Charles Mayall.

the countries into war. On 4th August 1914 Britain declared war on Germany. This was to signal the beginning of the Great War that was to change the world for ever. The only light relief provided in the town during the dark days of 1914 seems to have been Swindon's 1 – 0 defeat of Manchester United in the F.A. Cup, as 18,000 people crammed into the County Ground on a cold January afternoon.

In 1914 Swindon was still essentially two separate towns linked by Victoria Road and Drove Road. The latter being – as its name suggests – a road along which cattle and other domesticated beasts were driven. At 7.49pm on 4th August, despite the distance between the two parts of the town, Old Town was alerted by ten blasts on the GWR Works hooter – war had been declared and reservists were to report for duty. Soon afterwards, hundreds of men left the M.S.W.J.R .station in Old Town, waved off by a dense crowd that had assembled there. All told, 45 troop trains left Swindon in those early days of the war. Within a few days many more troops arrived in the town and billets had to be found for them. Many members of the congregation

Christ Church in the snow (1908).

1911 Patriotic postcard depicting Christ Church (far from accurately!).

at Christ Church welcomed soldiers into their homes. Marquees (dubbed 'The Soldier's Rest') were erected adjacent to the Church Hall in Devizes Road to serve as recreation rooms for the troops. Facilities for reading and writing were provided, and concerts arranged under the management of the Revd. Robert W. Philipson, Curate at Christ Church. These proved so popular that 3,000 soldiers attended in just one weekend. With costs increasing beyond the income from subscriptions, the committee decided it would have to charge 3d. a head per visit.

Charles Mayall placed the Vicarage in Bath Road at the disposal of the local Red Cross Society at the commencement of the war for use as a hospital or a convalescent home. In October 1914, however, it was felt that larger premises would be required in view of the large army camp which was being established at Draycott, near Chiseldon. The Red Cross Society then rented the large Baths of the GWR Medical Fund in Faringdon Street, paid by the War Office, for use as a hospital. The ladies of Christ Church and Swindon were kept busy making the medical items and garments so badly needed by the Red Cross, bandages, draw-sheets, socks, night-shirts, day-shirts, vests, pyjamas, bed-jackets, pillows, mittens, and scarves. Mary Slade, the first Headmistress of King William Street school, led the efforts to get Red Cross parcels to the troops on the Western Front.

By September 1914, casualty lists, and then the list of prisoners of war, began to include names familiar in the Parish. On 5th September Swindon's first casualty was reported when William George Sheldon was blown up by a mine aboard his ship, *HMS Pathfinder*. Then came the news of the death of Captain Gerald Ponsonby, son of the former vicar of St Mark's Church. On 23rd October 1914 it was reported that Captain T.E. Estcourt of the Scots Greys, son of Canon Estcourt, had become a prisoner of war. Two of Swindon Town's popular footballers, George Bathe and Jim Chalmers, were also killed, meaning the team were forced to start the season with a fully amateur team. They lost 5 – 2 to Portsmouth FC. All football was cancelled soon afterwards. Swindon Town would lose several players during the course of the Great War, perhaps more than any other English football team.

Public sympathy in Swindon was roused, as elsewhere, by the plight of the many Belgian refugees who had fled to Britain after the invasion of their country by the German army. A Committee was set up in Swindon, with responsibility for the welfare of the Belgian refugees in the town. Charles Mayall placed the Vicarage in Bath Road at the disposal of the Committee for use as a Hostel and it soon became the headquarters for the work. A section of the building was used as a store-house and was soon filled to capacity with parcels of clothing and other necessities. The hostel later moved to 53, Bath Road, and then to 88, Bath Road. Houses were also taken in Devizes Road, Goddard Avenue, Ashford Road, South Street, Victoria Road, Hythe Road, Westlecot Road, Kingshill Road and King William Street in Old Town as 'Belgian houses'. In many cases the houses were let free of rent, and furniture was loaned for the refugees to use.

The reality of the struggle finally came home to the British people in 1915 and any ideas of a quick victory were dispelled, especially when the hopes of decisive success in the summer were found to be deceptive. On 2nd January 1916, the day was marked as a day of Public Intercession when Charles Mayall, Vicar of Christ Church, joined the Mayor (Mr. W. E. Morse), the Town Council and many other distinguished local officials, and walked in procession from the Town Hall to the Parish Church; there a unified service was held with the Vicar being assisted by the Mayor's Chaplain and representatives of the clergy of the Primitive Methodist and Free Churches.

If the horrific news from the front was not tragic enough, in 1915 another incident sent shockwaves through the congregation. A young man called Sidney Dixon from Devizes Road was killed on the eve of his wedding at Christ Church. Having recently been given the news that he had lost his job at Draycott Camp in Chiseldon, Dixon was last seen wandering along the M.S.W.J. Railway line at Broome Crossing in Swindon. At last possible moment he stepped in front of the 9.10 train from Swindon to Marlborough and was killed instantly. A verdict of *'suicide while temporarily insane'* was brought in at the inquest. The episode caused much sorrow among the members of the church. A handful of guests, who had not received the bad news, arrived at the church the following day; still expecting the wedding to take place.

In the winter of 1915-16, lighting restrictions imposed earlier in the year, due to fear of air raids by German Zeppelin airships, were stringently enforced on the public to ensure all lights were obscured from an hour and a half after sunset to nearly sunrise. This resulted in Christ Church, with all other churches, having to fix an earlier time for the evening service, which were often finished in semi-darkness. In November the bells of the Parish Church ceased to be rung for the

WARNING.

Defence of the Realm

Discussion in Public of Naval and Military matters may convey information to the enemy.

BE ON YOUR GUARD.

J. Walker, Printer, Northallerton.

Defence of the Realm Act.

Men not considered fit enough to return to the front line were put to work in the town.

evening service, *'lest their notes should be a guide to some prowling foe in the air.'* Under the Defence of the Realm Act, restrictions were placed on drinking, shop opening hours and seditious talk. It was declared that the GWR hooter would sound six times in the event of a Zeppelin raid. Daylight saving time was introduced shortly afterwards. Troops injured in the fighting were returned home to Swindon. Those considered fit enough to work (but not fit enough to return to the Front) were put to work in the town.

In 1916 following the Battle of the Somme, in which more 600,000 Allied soldiers lost their lives, the cost of the War came home fully to the people of Swindon, and the congregation of Christ Church mourned the loss of so many young men known to them. Long lists of casualties were a harrowingly regular sight in the *Evening Advertiser* and *North Wilts Herald*. These included the death of 2nd. Lieut. William H.W. Moore of the 6th Battalion of the Wiltshire Regiment in France on 25th September 1915 in France - he was their second son and only 18 years old. Later his parents Dr. S.J. Moore and Mrs. Moore erected a tablet in his memory in the North Transept of Christ Church. Back home the War Savings Campaign for the war effort was in full flow and special sermons were preached at Christ Church by the Vicar to assist the appeal. The stalemate continued in France throughout 1917, and into 1918. Following the German offensive, in the spring of 1918, many feared that the terrible slaughter would never end. However, this proved to be the German's final effort and on Monday, 11th November 1918 the Armistice was signed. The bells of Christ Church rang out in praise and celebration in the afternoon and a special Thanksgiving service held in the evening, attended by the Mayor (Alderman C.A. Plaister) and the Mayoress in a church filled to overflowing. The war, however, had taken a terrible toll on the town. More than 5,000 men – or about one in five of the male population of Swindon – fought in the Great War. The official death toll was 920, although inconsistencies in record keeping meant the true figure might be as high as 1,300.

After the Armistice celebrations the town settled down to its ordinary life again waiting patiently for the actual Peace treaty to be signed. Charles Mayall attended a dinner at the Large Swimming Baths in Milton Road in January 1919 to entertain former prisoners of war who had returned from Germany. Finally, on Saturday, 28th June 1919, the Peace treaty was signed with Germany. A service of thanksgiving was held the following day and again on 6 July, 'Peace Sunday'. The Mayor and other officials attended service at the Parish Church. The procession included a large number of discharged and disabled soldiers. A united memorial service was held on 20th July in the GWR Works which was attended by Charles Mayall as Vicar of Swindon. Between 10,000 and 12,000 people assembled to take part in this service which was reported to be *'both beautiful and touching.'* The War Memorial in Christ Church, bearing the names of men from

The Unveiling of Swindon War Memorial 1920.

the Parish who had died in the War, was unveiled by Field Marshall Lord Methuen in 1919 – about a thousand men in all from Swindon were killed or died whilst on active service in the conflict. Revd. Charles Mayall also attended the unveiling of the Swindon War Memorial on 30th October 1920. The *Swindon Advertiser* reported that, '*All the approaches to the Town Hall were densely packed with people. Especially touching was the scene when the relatives of the fallen came forward to deposit their floral tributes at the base of the memorial*'.

Due to the pressures exerted by the War, little had been done to the Church during 1914-18. A porch, however, had been added over the south-west door, given in memory of Henry and Harriet Kinneir, in 1916. In 1922, Major Fitzroy Pleydell Goddard erected a stained-glass window in the North Transept in memory of his sister, Jessie. By 1924 the peal of bells had become unsafe and out of tune and they were replaced and two extra bells added (see Chapter 14). St. Mary's, a new church for the members of Christ Church who lived at the western end of the Parish was built on land '*half way down the Mall*' and presented by Fitzroy Pleydell Goddard and dedicated on 6th October 1926 (see Chapter 11).

In 1919 John Bodycombe from Swansea left his employment in banking to take up the curacy of Christ Church. He later became Vicar of St Oswald's in Bristol in 1925, before passing away while on holiday in 1939.

Charles Mayall became an Honorary Canon of Bristol Cathedral in 1923. William Dean, who had been Parish Clerk for forty years and for ten years previously Verger, died in early 1924. He was one of only a few who remembered worshipping in the old church of Holy Rood prior to 1851. A further link with the early years of the Church was also lost when Henry Bizley died in 1923; he had been a member of the choir for 69 years since 1854. During these years an annual service was held in Holy Rood during the summer months. Another era ended with the death of Major Fitzroy Pleydell Goddard in August 1927 at the age of 74 years.

Christ Church in 1924.

The last Lord of the Manor of Swindon and a prominent Freemason, he had been a churchwarden of Christ Church from 1918-26. Even as late as the 1920s the Goddards insisted that their staff attend church on Sundays and Major Goddard would want to know where they were if he did not see them there! His funeral was a grand affair; he was not buried in the family vault at Holy Rood but in Christ Church burial ground. His wife, Eugenia Kathleen Goddard, continued to live at the Lawn until 1931 when she left to live at Fernham House, near Faringdon.

The *'Swindon Advertiser & Wiltshire, Berkshire and Gloucestershire Chronicle'* ceased to be a weekly newspaper in 1925 and became the *'Evening Advertiser'*, having been acquired by the Swindon Press Ltd in 1920.

By 1924, 14,369 people were employed in the Railway Works and it was during this decade that the peak employment figures were reached there, much of the later decline being attributed to improved technical efficiency.

The General Strike in May 1926 caused much disruption and excitement in the town. The burning of effigies in the street of neighbours who worked through the strike became a common sight in Swindon.

In 1928 a new boiler was fitted at Christ Church and the Parish buildings were badly damaged by a gale in November 1928 that led to a considerable outlay on repairs. In March 1929 memorial tablets were erected for two former Churchwardens, William Reynolds and Edward Timms, and were dedicated by the Bishop of Malmesbury.

There was much great regret in the Parish when Canon Mayall resigned as Vicar of Swindon in 1929. During his eighteen years at Christ Church the population of the Parish had increased to over 10,000

Fitzroy Pleydell Goddard. The last Lord of the Manor of Swindon, at home at The Lawn. 1920s.

with a corresponding increase in active church membership. Church attendances increased generally in the years following the Great War as the population searched for meaning and for solace. The number of children in the Sunday Schools, about 250 in 1910, had grown to

The Lawn. Home of the Goddard family and adjacent to the old parish church, Holy Rood. 1920s.

93

between 700 - 800. There were over 100 Confirmation candidates each year and the Easter communicants had increased from 300 to 1,200. The Mothers' Meeting had 250 members whilst the Men's Club (the Brotherhood) had 100. The latter was formed in 1909 and met in the old Church of England School in Newport Street. It is reported that thirteen coaches were needed for the annual Mothers' Union outing!

In May 1929, Canon Mayall was instituted as Vicar of Almondsbury, near Bristol. A large contingent of people from Christ Church made the journey to take part in his institution service. He remained here until his retirement from the priesthood.

The town and its people had changed hugely since the turn of the century. Swindon had survived the Great War and the 'Spanish Flu' pandemic, soon the Great Depression of the 1930s would begin to be felt across the town. As if to mark the end of an era, as Canon Mayall left Swindon for the last time, the final tram service ran in the town. It was time to say goodbye to the tram and herald in the era of the motor car.

Revd. Mayall with an unidentified group 1920s.

5

Consolidation And Change 1929-1953

After the progress under the leadership of Canon Mayall, the affairs of the Parish were to pursue a more mundane course with consolidation of the gains made being the priority. The new Vicar was John Gilbert; educated at Exeter College, Oxford, he had obtained his BA degree there in 1913, returning there later to have his MA awarded in 1923 at Wycliffe Hall. Ordained a deacon in 1913 and priest in 1914, he became Curate of St. Clement's in Oxford, from 1913-15, and subsequently served as a temporary Chaplain to the Forces from 1915-20. Curate of Jesmond, Newcastle, from 1921-23, he became Vicar of St. Nathaniel's, Bristol, from 1923-29. A man of a rather retiring disposition and of a scholarly nature, he took over at Christ Church in 1929.

Dr R.P. Beatty, Churchwarden from 1926-30, seen at home with his daughter.

At the time John Gilbert became Vicar of Swindon, the Churchwardens were Dr. R.P. Beatty and Mr. E.C. Beard. Dr. Beatty was replaced by Mr. A.E. Dean in 1930 and, with Mr. Beard, he was to serve in this post for over ten years. A new organist, Mr. W.A. Vivian May, was appointed in October 1929 to replace Mr. W.H. Painter, who resigned after nearly forty years' service; he had been originally appointed at Easter 1890. In December 1929 Charles Adkins became Curate. A native of Newhaven in Sussex, he had been blind since the age of 10. A fact that was widely reported in the papers with some fascination!

Captain Walter H. Wheeler.

In 1931, a new stained-glass window, designed by Mr. M. Travers, was placed in the North Transept to commemorate Fitzroy Pleydell Goddard (see also chapter 16).

August 1931 also saw Christ Church host a full military funeral with honours. The occasion, a rare one, attracted a large crowd with many also lining the streets to the church. Popular and well known local newsagent Walter Henry Wheeler had passed away following a steady decline in his health. Although aged only 44, Wheeler had never fully recovered from his harrowing experiences in the Great War. After attaining the rank of Captain in 1915 with the Royal Artillery his right hand was shattered in a shell explosion one year later. After the remains of his hand were amputated he was invalided home. Despite this horrific injury he continued to serve in the territorials and to run the family newsagents in Victoria Road. Full military honours were accorded to Captain Wheeler as his coffin, draped with the Union Jack, his medals and sword, was paraded through the town atop a gun carriage. Revd. Gilbert performed the service at which *The Last Post* was played and a 12-gun salute was fired by the 220th Wiltshire Royal Artillery.

Funeral of Captain Wheeler 1931.

The early 1930s were overshadowed by the world-wide economic depression which caused much unemployment and hardship in Britain. At its peak over 3,000,000 men were out-of-work nationally. This included many in Swindon. In 1933 the Mayor of Swindon's 'Committee For the Help of the Unemployed' asked the Vicar of

Christ Church if the Parish could help feed the many hungry townsfolk, so a 'Soup Kitchen' was set up at the Church Hall in Devizes Road. Here, the ladies of Christ Church and St. Mary's, led by Mrs. Clarke and Mrs. Green, took up the entire task of organization, preparation and distribution, of the food. Some 4,257 portions were prepared and approximately 615 gallons of soup distributed by 30 ladies from the Church.

George Churchward 1857-1933.

On 19th December 1933, the town of Swindon suffered the loss of the great railway engineer, Mr. George J. Churchward, former Chief Mechanical Engineer of the Great Western Railway, who was killed crossing the main London to Bristol line, near his house at Newburn House. Despite being 76 years of age and with failing eyesight, he retained an interest in the GWR's affairs and was inspecting a defective sleeper on the

George Churchward memorial plaque.

tracks, when he was struck by the Paddington to Fishguard express. The first Mayor and Freeman of the Borough of Swindon, he was buried in Christ Church churchyard, as he had wished. His funeral was attended by a large crowd of mourners. Mr. Ernest Bishop who had been 'Master of the Tower' at the Parish Church for some 35 years died in 1935 (see also Chapter 14). Mrs Rose Ethel Bishop, his wife, was also active in church life and had been a District Visitor since the early 1920s. She had been awarded the OBE for organization of Canteens for Troops from 1914-18 (she died in 1950).

National events again had their impact in the Parish during the 1930s. The Silver Jubilee of King George V and Queen Mary in May 1935 was widely celebrated with bunting, flags and flowers decking the streets of Old Town and beacons being lit on the hilltops around the

Christ Church, floodlit for the first time 1937.

country. King George V's death in January 1936 brought nationwide mourning. The Abdication, on a grey and damp day in the following November, of the uncrowned King Edward VIII was greeted with much regret and sorrow within the Parish. It was, however, with much rejoicing that the Coronation of the new King George VI and Queen Elizabeth was celebrated in Swindon in May 1937. Once again the streets were decorated and, for the first time, Christ Church and its spire was floodlit.

In 1935, Revd. Gilbert oversaw the marriage ceremony between Henry Deacon, from Dartmouth, and Gladys Ann Dixon, from Swindon, at Christ Church. This splendid wedding photograph gives us a unique insight into the fashions of the time,

Henry Deacon and Gladys Ann Dixon Wedding at Christ Church 1935.

KING EDWARD ANNOUNCES HIS ABDICATION

DUKE OF YORK SUCCEEDS AS GEORGE VI.

CORONATION REMAINS FIXED FOR MAY 12.

THE announcement of King Edward's abdication was made on Thursday afternoon by the Speaker in the House of Commons, following a week of intense national anxiety.

King Edward is to be succeeded by his brother, the Duke of York, who will take the title of George the Sixth, and not that of Albert the First. The date of the Coronation will remain that fixed for King Edward's Coronation—May 12.

Princess Elizabeth, the Duke of York's elder daughter, will become Heiress-Presumptive to the Throne. With a Queen Consort again on the Throne, Queen Mary may now take the title of Mary the Queen-Mother.

King Edward's Abdication 1936.

a theme which would again be highlighted at the '100 Years of Weddings' celebrations in 2011.

Various alterations and improvements were carried out in the 1930s to the Church building. Due in very great measure to the enthusiasm of Mr. E.C. Beard, the old curtains in the chancel were replaced by oak panelling in 1933 and the old vestry to the south of the chancel (at the time just a lumber-room) was transformed into a Side Chapel in 1934-35. The architect of this lovely addition to the Church (now known as the Lady Chapel) was Sir Harold Brakspear. Sir Harold had been knighted in 1931 for his work on Lacock Abbey, Bath Abbey and Windsor Castle. His attachment to the design was a considerable coup for the Parish. Sadly, he proved to be his final project. He died in November 1934, aged 64, following a short illness. In 1936 a deaf-aid installation was made available in the Church. Finally, roof lighting was installed inside the Church in August 1939 in memory of Arthur, Martha and Alice Deacon. A brass plaque marking this can still be seen by

PARISH CHURCH - SWINDON

PROGRAMME OF

Tableaux
Canaan to Canaan

To be given in the

CHURCH HALL, Devizes Road

Choir under the direction of - Mr. VIVIAN MAY
Contralto Soloist - - - Miss M. GIBBONS
Tenor Soloist - - - Mr. J. BEASANT
Violin - - - Mr. SETH PERKINS

ON

Tuesday, Wednesday & Thursday
November 3rd, 4th & 5th, 1936

TO COMMENCE AT 8 p.m.

PROGRAMME - - - THREEPENCE
Silver Collection at each service

PRINTED BY THE ADVERTISER PRINTING WORKS, SWINDON.

Programme from an event at the Church Hall, 1936.

the south west door inside the church.

John Gilbert was appointed an Honorary Canon of Bristol Cathedral in 1937. During the 1930s, Parish organizations continued to flourish. The Mothers' Union and Meeting had 280 members on its register in 1938. Annual outings to such places as Winchester, Windsor, Symonds Yat and Warwick were very popular and successful. Similarly, the Men's Club in Newport Street also prospered as did the youth uniformed organizations; the Girl Guides (with two Companies), Rangers, Brownies, Rovers, Wolf Cubs and Scouts. The 12th Swindon (Christ Church) Scout Group had been formed about 1930; Eddie Perkins was the Scoutmaster in these early years with Donald Vince, George Prisnall and a Mr. Barker as his assistants.

In March 1939 a collection at Christ Church raised £10 (approximately £650 today) towards *'Foodship for Spain'*. The Bristol Diocese, including Christ Church, had formed the Bristol & West Region Fund which raised more than £5,000 (£325,000 today) towards the assistance of refugees from the Spanish Civil War. Before

Foodship for Spain 1939.

long, however, the people of Christ Church would find themselves involved far more deeply in yet another war.

By the late 1930s, it became apparent that the years of peace would soon be over. The aggressive policies being pursued by Adolf Hitler and the Nazis in Europe made it obvious that a new war would follow before long. As early as 1937, the Air Raid Precautions Act compelled local authorities to recruit and train volunteers as Air Raid Wardens and for other services. Members of the Parish 'joined up' as Wardens in case of conflict breaking out. When hostilities commenced on 3rd

September 1939, it was thought that air raids would immediately take place on Britain, so all cinemas were closed along with all other places of entertainment. Churches, however, remained open and services continued more or less as normal, subject to the strict 'blackout' restrictions (by the winter of 1939-40 the Sunday Evensong at Christ Church was brought forward to 3 p.m.). The *Evening Advertiser* carried advertisements offering '*rolls of brown gummed tape, 500 feet long, two inches wide, for tuppence.*' Ration books were issued together with identity cards and gas masks. Townsfolk were called to collect these items in alphabetical order at a school or church hall. Notices headed O.H.M.S. (On His Majesty's Service) came through the letterboxes almost daily and needed to be read and acted upon. They gave details of blackout regulations and what the warnings meant. Whistles, handbells or rattles would warn of gas attack. Swindonians were encouraged to '*dig for victory*', '*lend a hand*' or '*keep mum*'. But above all, remember that '*careless talk costs lives*' – Mr Hitler might just be listening! Members of the congregation and clergy were obliged to arrive at Church carrying their gasmasks with them. New faces soon appeared in Church; soldiers billeted in the town together with

Ministry of Information posters were displayed around Old Town.

evacuee children from London (many were lodged in the Parish, in Drove Road, Goddard Avenue, The Mall and Belmont Crescent). The Church Hall in Devizes Road was commandeered by the Army and the door was soon surrounded by heaps of sandbags. Organizations had to find other places for their meetings, including Christ Church and the Vicarage.

In October Leonard Golledge left, after three years as Curate, to become Vicar of St Paul's in Chippenham.

The invasion of France and the Low Countries by the Germans in May 1940 brought the war home to the people of Swindon. After the evacuation of Dunkirk, hundreds of survivors, begrimed and fatigued after their ordeal, arrived in Swindon. The people of Christ Church played their part in providing accommodation and relief for the soldiers. Men also joined the newly formed Local Defence Volunteers (renamed the Home Guard in July). The Church was packed for services as the fear of imminent invasion brought the community together. However, there was still time in March 1940 for Christ Church to grace the pages of Scoiety magazine *The Tatler*, for the society wedding of Mr Douglas Story, of Grove House, Swindon, and Elsa Milton (whose first husband had died in the Great War). It was to be one of the last times that the bells rang out in joy across Old Town.

On 13th June 1940, the order was given that church bells were not to be rung for services in the foreseeable future – they were only to be used in the event of an invasion. Happily, this never happened, but the war would drag on for a further five years. Swindon was extremely lucky that, despite the presence of the GWR Works in the town, relatively few air raids were carried out on Swindon although those that did resulted in 48 deaths and 105 injured (38 seriously). After escaping lightly in 1940 and 1941, Swindon suffered a catastrophic raid on 17th August 1942. Two separate incidents caused 19 deaths in Ferndale Road and another 10 in Kembrey Street. Among the dead that night were a mother and her tiny child who was *'still clasped to her breast'*. It took several days to remove some of the bodies in Ferndale Road. Prayers were said in Christ Church as the story spread throughout the town, despite efforts to censor the worst of the news.

Old Town escaped until 29th August 1942 when a single bomber, flying around 38,000 feet, dropped a bomb that hit the carriageway of Drove Road, about seventy yards south of Groundwell Road. Eight people were killed outright or fatally injured. The force of the explosion rattled the stained-glass windows in the church. One of the victims, Mrs. Freda M. Taylor aged 46, of 83 Drove Road, was the organist at St. Mary's and was later buried in Christ Church graveyard.

Also, in August 1942, the Revd. Charles Frederick Goddard (son of Lt-Colonel Ambrose William Goddard) died at the age of 78. He left an estate valued at £35,511 12s 4d – today's equivalent of £1.64 million. Within his will was a provision of £100 for a

View towards Christ Church with anti-invasion obstacles in Church Street 1941.

brass tablet to be erected in his honour inside Christ Church. Another member of the Goddard family, Ambrose Michael Andrew Goddard, the eldest son of Lt.-Colonel Ambrose William Goddard, died on active service in July 1944 and his family later erected a stained-glass

The Weathercock, complete with bullet holes!.

window in the Lady Chapel in his memory. The fabric of the church did not escape entirely intact either. The weathercock, which sat atop the spire, (until later replaced by a cross) carries several bullet holes allegedly made by soldiers during the war who used it for target practice!

Viewed today, the attitude of the congregation to the war and to the enemy makes interesting reading. Attendances at services dropped, especially during the winter months. Revd. Gilbert found this entirely understandable but did express his concern when numbers did not pick again with the warmer weather. In his regular column in the Parish Magazine he spoke of:

'the disquieting tendency that for many people the winter marks, not a revival in Christian activity but rather the withdrawal from the Church's work until the spring. The most subtle influence, however, has been customs caused by the war. The early period of national danger naturally forced all other considerations aside. The first paramount duty was to save the future of England and civilisation. The question now, however, is to what extent this has become habit.'

It seems the question of Christian worship and attitudes in Germany was often discussed within the church. The congregation received much comfort from a story leaked from Germany about a German pastor who had recently given a series of talks on 'The Principles of the Christian Faith' to a packed church. More than 4,000 people had wanted to attend and a bigger building had to be found. Revd. Gilbert mused that *'that experience is not unique; if the same thing is happening in other parts of the Reich, then there is still a base upon which a purged and cleansed Germany can be built.'*

American troops began to arrive in Swindon from 1942 onwards, as the numbers in the south of England were built up for the 'D' Day landings in June 1944. They were based at Chiseldon Camp and in Drove Road Senior School and the Lawn mansion, former home of the Goddard family. At Christmas 1942, Major Dworin of the U.S. Red Cross gave bags of sweets to the children at Christ Church; these had been given by men of the U.S. Army who had given up their monthly ration of sweets. Many American servicemen attended services at the Parish Church and the *Parish Magazine* for May 1944 told the story of a note written to Canon Gilbert which was found in Christ Church with an Easter offering; *'From an American Soldier who has never heard you – but whose faith in God was restored on April 1st 1944, while these beautiful chimes rang out the hope and joy of the whole world. Please pray for my wife and children in America'.*

The end of the Second World War was celebrated on V.E. Day, 8th May 1945. In Swindon on this day, and the next, many street parties were held and the celebrations continued well into the night. At the Parish Church and St. Mary's prayers were said and services held giving thanks for the victory. Christ Church and the Town Hall clock were illuminated for the first time since before the War. In August 1945, the V.J. celebrations were rather more muted and orderly than those of V.E. Day but, again, the Church and its people gave thanks for their deliverance and prayed for all those who had lost their lives in the conflict.

The Mayor of Swindon, Alderman Charles MacPherson attending the VE Day service at Christ Church, May 1945. To his left is Town Clerk, Mr David Murray John.

During the war years, although services had continued throughout, little development of Parish life was achieved. Existing organizations continued to be supported with membership of the Mothers' Union and Meeting being maintained at over 250 on the register every year. To meet the needs of the growing community of the north side of the Parish, a Sunday School was organized in Drove Road School from January 1942, with the agreement of the Vicar of St. Paul's Church, in whose parish the school was situated. The early post war years were difficult ones and the conflict had caused a sea change in the attitudes and expectations of people in Britain. The ravages of the War years had also created further problems; the chancel of the old parish church of Holy Rood had become a serious problem to the Church officers. It had been badly treated during the conflict by visiting troops, and any attempts to keep it in a reasonable condition were frustrated by vandalism. The only alternative to allowing it to fall into ruin was to transfer the chancel and churchyard to the local authority; to be preserved as a building of historic interest. The necessary Faculty was obtained in 1949.

Sadly, the Lawn house of the Goddards had also deteriorated badly by this time and after being acquired – together with its grounds - by the Borough of Swindon in 1946, it was demolished in 1952. The Little London Mission had also fallen into disrepair during the Second World War and, in 1949, was closed, the thirty or so children then attending the Sunday School being transferred to the one held in King William Street School. In 1953, the building was sold to a local building film, Pope Bros, and was used as a store for many years. Until approximately 2018 one clue to the building's original use was still visible to the eagle eyed – a small cross on the roof. However, this cross has now disappeared and planning permission has been granted to convert the old mission into apartments.

There was one addition to the furniture of the Parish Church during these early post war years – an anonymous member of the congregation gave a painting of 'The Crucifixion' to the Church in 1948 in memory of the fiftieth anniversary of the marriage of her parents. The painting, which was originally hung in the Lady Chapel, is painted on slate and probably dates from the 17th Century. However, once its true value was discovered, it was promptly taken down and put in storage for safe keeping!

A loss to the Parish in 1946 was Mr. A.E. Dean, who had attended Christ Church for over 35 years including 17 years as Churchwarden.

There was much amusement – and some annoyance – in August 1948 when Canon John Gilbert and a photographer were the only people present at the wedding of Mr John Brooke and Miss Ida Alderman at Christ Church. The Vicar was less than amused (having given up his Bank Holiday to marry the couple) when they failed to turn up for their own wedding, despite the banns having been read for the three previous weeks. Apparently, the couple had married a month earlier in Plymouth and '*quite forget*' to let anyone know!

1951 saw The Archers broadcast for the first time on the BBC Light Programme and Winston Churchill returned as Prime Minister just before his 77th birthday. It was also the Centenary year of Christ

Church. The Parochial Church Council undertook several major tasks as a Centenary thanksgiving. These were the most extensive since the Church was opened in 1851; the rebuilding, enlarging and modernization of the organ (see also chapter 9); major repairs to the roof and wiring; maintenance work and the removal of seventeen dangerous elm trees along the north edge of the churchyard. The Centenary itself was celebrated in November by special services attended by the Lord Bishop of Gloucester and the Lord Bishop of Bristol, organ recitals, a Centenary Supper and Social, held in the Church Hall, and a performance of Handel's *Messiah* by the Bath Road Methodist Church Choir. The bells of Christ Church were recorded by the BBC West Region in 1951 and, later, a recording of

Scene from a production of 'Through A Stained Glass Window', February 1950, produced by Church Warden Jack Turner.

Scene from a production of 'Through A Stained Glass Window', February 1950, produced by Church Warden Jack Turner.

Christ Church from the west 1950.

Christ Church from the north west c. 1950s.

the bells was made by HMV on a 10-inch vinyl record. A '*Centenary Souvenir*' booklet was also written and published in 1951.

Royal events still made a large impact on Parish life. Following a service of remembrance at Christ Church, to mark the death of King George VI in 1952, a period of national mourning took place. The following summer (following a 15-month period of mourning,

108

something which seems impossible to imagine in the 21st century) the coronation of his daughter Elizabeth took place. Coronation Day, 2nd June 1953, commenced with Holy Communion at Christ Church, at which about 100 people were present. The Church Hall opened at 9.30 a.m. and a large queue formed, which eventually reached the Devizes Road traffic lights. The Old Headlandians' Orchestra (Conductor: Ben Battson) played '*patriotic selections*' from 9.45 a.m. to 10.00 a.m., when the Mayor of Swindon (Ald. H.W. Gardner) and the Mayoress opened the day's celebrations. Television coverage began at 10.15 a.m. It must be remembered that very few had televisions at this time, so it was arranged to show the coronation on 14 sets borrowed by the Parochial Church Council (twelve from G. Skinner of Modern-Radio, Commercial Road, and two by W.J. Moran Electrical, Victoria Road). Entrance, by programme, was 1 shilling each, lunch boxes being available at 1s 9d. Viewing terminated well after 4.30 p.m. Work then commenced on cleaning the hall and the preparation for high tea and a Carnival Evening. Well over 200 people returned to enjoy the evening, commencing at 6.30 p.m. Tickets for the Carnival Evening and high tea were 1s 6d. High tea was reported as being "*a most appetizing meal*" and those attending were again entertained by the Old Headlandians' Orchestra. The Evening Carnival continued with games and dancing with a break at 9.00 p.m. to hear the speech by Queen Elizabeth. Queens Park in Drove Road had been officially opened three days previously to celebrate the coronation. Elsewhere in Old Town, street parties were held for the children. Rationing, extra taxation, cold winters and fuel shortages could be forgotten temporarily for one magnificent summer's day. News even reached home that Edmund Hillary and Tenzing Norgay became the first men to conquer Mount Everest. Shortly afterwards Jim Laker took 19 wickets in a match as England beat Australia to win back the Ashes.

The glorious events of that summer were tinged with regret, however, when Canon John Gilbert announced his retirement at the end of August 1953, after holding the position of Vicar for some 24 years (at that time he had been the longest serving incumbent, other than the first vicar Henry Baily). John Gilbert died in January 1962.

The uplifting events of 1953 were a prelude to a new Vicar and a new era for the church, and although rationing had not yet finished, there was a new feeling of optimism and a hope that times were – at last – changing.

6

Halcyon Years 1953-76

Whilst waiting for the installation of the next Vicar of Swindon, following the retirement of John Gilbert, a former Curate of Christ Church, the Revd. J. Holmer Green (then in his 80s), was temporarily placed in charge of the Parish.

The arrival of a familiar face, in the form of the Revd. Frank Thomas as the new Vicar of Christ Church, at the end of November 1953 brought a new injection of energy into Parish life. Francis William Thomas was educated at the London College of Divinity and St. Joseph's College, Durham, where he obtained his BA degree in 1931. He was ordained a deacon in 1931, and then as a priest in 1932, at Malmesbury for work in the Bristol diocese. Frank Thomas first came to Swindon in 1931 and was Curate at Christ Church from 1931-36. He then became Curate-in-Charge of Christ Church in Hengrove from 1936-40 before becoming Vicar of Hengrove from 1940-47. After receiving his MA in 1947, he

Canon Thomas, Vicar of Christ Church 1953-64.

became Vicar of Bishopston, in the Diocese of Bristol, from 1947-53. Frank Thomas was well remembered by the older members of the congregation of Christ Church for his sterling work as a curate in the 1930s. Those who could recall Frank Thomas from his first stint at Christ Church regarded him as a softly spoken man, who exuded warmth when he spoke. Full of new ideas and vitality, with a deep concern for each individual person, his work in the Parish will long be remembered. Frank Thomas left his mark on almost every aspect of church life during his years as Vicar.

In the 1950s, everyday life for those in the parish generally continued as they had in previous years. There was not the hectic pace, commercial pressures and continual change of today. Many of the shortages of the early post war years were still in place and money was short. Rationing of confectionery and sugar did not end until 1953 and of meat until July 1954. Harsh winters, fuel shortages and workers' strikes did nothing to alleviate the situation. The distractions offered today by television, smartphones and the ability to travel with ease were not present. Foreign holidays were only for a lucky few. Men were the chief wage earner and most married women did not work after their children were born. By the mid-1950s there was a feeling in the air though that life was slowly starting to improve.

At this time the church in England still provided a focus for family and community life. Under Frank Thomas's leadership, the organizations at Christ Church and St. Mary's blossomed and membership increased rapidly for some during these years. The Church of England Men's Society reformed in January 1954 (it had originally been formed in 1899), at Frank Thomas's suggestion, with sixteen members, and grew to nearly 200 members in the next few years (the largest branch of CEMS anywhere in the World). The Christ Church Dramatic Society formed in 1963 and remained active for many years.

In May 1954 the Hillingdon Bellringers' Guild arrived at

Christ Church, as part of their annual outing, ringing bells at five different churches in five counties, all on the same day! There seemed, however, to be some competition between the churches, with the Vicar of St Andrew's in East Hagbourne, Berkshire, declaring his church bells as *'the best in England'*!

Those who smoked, and that was a huge

CEMS logo.

percentage of the population in 1954, over 80% of men and half of all women, received a shock when, for the first time, a scientific study proved the link between cancer and smoking. By 2020 the rate had dropped to less than 14%.

Programme for the 1955 Garden Party.

Church services also developed in 1954 and the number of people attending these increased rapidly. In February, the new service of Family Communion was started. Some fifty attended the first service and then the congregation rose steadily to about 300 every Sunday. The New Year's Eve service in 1955 was broadcast on the BBC Home Service. Attendance at the nine Sunday Schools in different parts of the Parish reached approximately 600. In 1961-62, the number of Communions for the year at Christ Church alone totalled 32,400, and at St.Mary's 2,300 people. At Easter 1962, 1,200 people took their Communion at Christ Church.

The population of the Parish doubled in the 1950s. This resulted in a second Curate being added to the staff in 1954 and a third in 1957. The Revd. John Poarch, Curate from 1956-59, later became a missionary in the Seychelles from 1961-63, featuring in Donald Taylor's book *'The Anglican Church in the History of the Seychelles'*. During the 1950s several curates came from overseas, including as far afield as New Zealand. In 1955, Mr. W.A. Vivian May resigned as Organist and Choir Master at Christ Church after twenty-six years' service; he was replaced by Gordon Crabbe. Gordon had started to play the organ for St. Mary's Church, Commonweal Road, at the age of fifteen. He was to raise the musical standards to a new height during his many years during the post.

Various changes took place in the church building in the 1950s. In October 1953, the central heating system was converted to oil firing and new carpets laid in 1954. A new Processional Cross was given by the church of St. Michael and All Angels, Bishopston (Frank Thomas's old parish), in May 1954, and is still used today. A new Mothers' Union banner was dedicated on Mothering Sunday in March 1957 (membership had been maintained at around 200). Prime Minister Harold Macmillan told the country *'most people have never had it so good'* and prayers were said in church for the victims of the Munich Air Disaster, in which many of Manchester United's players lost their lives.

Unfortunately, much expense was incurred by the church in 1959-60; the North Aisle roof was re-slated and the top 12 feet of the spire had to be removed, the vane and weathercock taken down, and the spire rebuilt. A new cross, designed by Oswald Brakspear (son of Sir Harold Brakspear, the architect of the Lady Chapel) of bronze treated with gold leaf, was placed on the top of the spire to replace the weathercock and vane. The spire was finished by March 1960. When the old weathercock was taken down it was found to have several bullet holes in it (as mentioned in the previous chapter). These are thought to have been made during the Second World War by bullets, from rifles fired by American soldiers during unauthorized target practice! However, in a later edition of the *Parish Magazine* for December 1984, Frank Foord, a member of Christ Church for many years, claimed that he had seen a German aircraft firing tracer bullets at the Church *'one wet and misty day in 1943'*, hence the bullet holes. Either account could be true.

The old Empire Theatre was demolished in 1959 and replaced with Empire House. However, as part of the Diamond Jubilee of the Borough of Swindon in 1960, the council also carried out some restoration on the old chancel of Holy Rood in the Lawns. After the work had been completed, a pilgrimage was made to the old church for an evening service in June 1962, this being the first time for some twenty years. In 1963, a cupboard in the North Transept of Christ Church was dedicated to the memory of the Revd. Charles Frederick Goddard, the youngest son of Ambrose and Charlotte Goddard. He had died in May 1942 and had been buried in the Goddard vault at Holy Rood.

In 1955, the Bishop of Bristol asked Christ Church to take part in the launch of a new church to serve the new Walcot housing estate. Christ Church was responsible for raising £6,000, one quarter of the total cost, over a period of ten years. This was achieved well within this period. Representatives of the new estate of Walcot sat on the Christ Church Parish Council in 1956 and services were held in a hut in Raleigh Avenue from November 1956. In January 1958, a church hall was finished, and the services transferred there. The new church, St. Andrew's, in Raleigh Avenue (designed by R.J. Beswick and Son) was built and dedicated by the Bishop of Bristol on 3rd May 1958. For the next eight years St. Andrew's became the second daughter church of Christ Church. On 1st January 1967, however, it became a member of the East Swindon Group of Churches, which included Anglicans and Methodists in the Walcot, Park, Nythe and Covingham estates (St Andrew's closed in the 1990s but has since been rebuilt and reopened).

St Andrews Raleigh Ave.

By the early 1960s, the Sunday programme was incredible with services at Christ Church at 7.00 a.m.; 8.00 a.m.; 9.30 a.m.; 11.00 a.m. and 6.30 p.m. In addition, there were the services at St. Mary's and at St. Andrew's. In 1955, Frank Thomas initiated a stewardship campaign for Home and Overseas Missions, by which one tenth of Sunday collections were given away annually. He was a strong believer in the development of a family spirit within the congregation of Christ Church and, in 1959, arranged for birthday cards to be delivered each week in the name of the Parish. His work in visiting the sick and bereaved was also outstanding and he instituted the Memory Table in Christ Church in 1956 and the Memorial Rose Garden behind the Church.

For his work in the Diocese, Frank Thomas was made a Surrogate (a deputy for a Bishop or Chancellor) from 1953 onwards, and became Honorary Canon of Bristol Cathedral from 1955-64. He also the first Anglican chaplain of the newly built Princess Margaret Hospital in Swindon. Prime Minister Harold Macmillan made his famous *'Wind of Change'* speech in 1960, and it seemed that changes were taking place in Swindon too,

Christ Church in the snow, during the bad winter of 1963.

which would have an effect on the Church. The Christ Church Men's Club in Newport Street was closed in December 1960, the premises being sold to Swindon Corporation for demolishing as part of a road widening scheme. Its membership, on closure, had dwindled to about twenty-five.

Christmas 1962 was followed by blizzards with deep drifts, cutting off supplies to homes which still depended on doorstep deliveries of milk, bread and solid fuel. Frozen pipes, followed by the inevitable bursts, delayed many schools re-opening after the Christmas holiday. In many remote places on the Downs south of Swindon there was snow to be seen until March.

Young people were well catered for with regular Saturday night dancing at McIlroy's ballroom and the Locarno in Old Town. Pop groups began appearing in the town, the Beatles famously playing at McIlroy's in July 1962. Rock 'n' Roll, followed by the 'beat boom' had created a new interest in music among the young, and an ending to the era of deference towards the older generation.

1963 was an eventful and traumatic year for the country and for those at Christ Church. Already shellshocked by the events of the

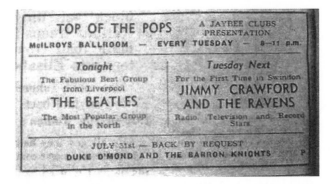

year, Canon Frank Thomas' resignation at the end of 1963 came as a great shock to many in the Parish. Following from the harsh winter, the 'Beeching Cuts' to Britain's railways, the Profumo scandal, the Great Train Robbery and the assassination of John F. Kennedy, the news of the loss of Frank Thomas to the parish brought great sorrow to the congregation. His health was causing his family concern and he wrote a letter to his Parishioners in the *Parish Magazine* for February 1964, in which he stated that he was *'leaving ... for the ultimate good of the Parish, for this is one of the key places of the Diocese and must be served by a Priest who is better able to bear the burden of responsibility than I whose health is far from what it used to be'*. Frank Thomas left Swindon to work in a new area on the outskirts of Preston, Lancashire, at the invitation of the Bishop of Blackburn, and there to help in the building of a new church. Later, he would become Curate of Ashton-under-Ribble (in charge of St. Margaret's, Ingol) from 1964-67 and was appointed Vicar of Stoke-sub-Hamdon, Diocese Bath & West,

Christ Church in 1965.

116

from 1967. He died in July 1975.

The Revd. John Wilson Jackson was appointed Vicar in July 1964 (in the intervening months from Canon Thomas's departure, the Archdeacon of Swindon, Cyril W.J. Bowles had been in-charge of the Parish). John Jackson, born in 1914, had been educated at St. Joseph's College, Durham, obtaining his BA degree in 1938, and Wycliffe Hall, Oxford. He was ordained a deacon in 1940 and a priest in 1941, at Birmingham. Curate of Holy Trinity, Bordesley, 1940-41, St. John, Sparkhill, 1941-44 and St. Matthew's, Walsall, 1944-46, and Rector of All Saints, City and Diocese of Birmingham, 1946-

Revd. John Jackson, Vicar of Christ Church 1964-68.

50. From 1950-52, he was Perpetual Curate of St. Augustine's, Bromley Common, then became Vicar of Sparkhill and Chaplain of the Women's Hospital, Birmingham, from 1952-64. John Wilson became a Surrogate from 1957-64 and an Honorary Canon of Birmingham Cathedral from 1961. A very experienced priest, Canon Jackson took over Christ Church, and although he resigned after

Aerial view of Christ Church 1965.

117

Good Shepherd Service at Christ Church mid 1960s.

only 3 ½ years, left his mark on the Parish.

There was great excitement in the town during the early months of Canon Jackson's tenure when, in October 1964, the nationwide manhunt for escaped Dartmoor convict Gerald Johnson focused on Swindon. After a huge police operation, he was eventually traced to an address in Old Town and arrested.

A new venture during these years was the television recording and broadcasting of the BBC's *'Songs of Praise'* from Christ Church on 22nd May 1966. During the year in which England won the World Cup at Wembley and of the Aberfan mining disaster in Wales, a tour of the Holy Land was held in July/August 1966 and a Parish Mission in September 1966, by the staff and students of St. John's College, Durham, proved successful. The vestry was extended at Christ Church, in memory of Mrs. Beatrice Long, and dedicated by the Venerable C.W.J. Bowles, in October 1966. As mentioned above, St. Andrew's Church, Walcot, left the Parish of Christ Church at the end of 1966. Canon Jackson is best remembered in Swindon for his part in founding the Swindon Samaritans in the, now demolished, Congregational Church Hall in Sanford Street in 1967. Canon Jackson, the Revd C.S. Ross of the Trinity Presbyterian Church at the bottom of Victoria

Congregation in Christ Church. mid 1960s.

Road, and Baptist minister Revd. G.E. Boocock were joined by the branch's first 70 volunteers at the inaugural meeting on August 20th, 1967. It was agreed upon to launch the service on 1st November. This proved to be Canon Jackson's last action as Vicar of Christ Church. He left Swindon at the end of 1967 to become Vicar and Rural Dean of Walsall, a position he held until 1981. A Prebendary of Lichfield Cathedral from 1972-81, Canon Jackson retired in 1981.

Again, awaiting the arrival of a new Vicar, Archdeacon Cyril Bowles took charge of the Parish in early 1968. On 3rd June 1968, the Revd. Derek George Palmer was inducted as the new Vicar of Swindon. Born in 1928, Derek Palmer had been educated at Selwyn College, Cambridge, and Wells Theological College, receiving his BA in 1950 and MA in 1954. Ordained a deacon in 1952 and priest in 1953, he became Curate of Stapleton, Bristol, 1952-54, and then Bishopston, 1954-58. Following a period as Curate-in-Charge, Hartcliffe, Bristol, from 1958-62, he became Vicar

Revd. Derek Palmer, Vicar of Christ Church 1968-1977.

of Hartcliffe from 1962-68, when he was also editor of the West of England Church Newspaper *Contact*. A man of impressive presence and personality, Derek Palmer brought to Christ Church a new vigour and purpose. One of his first aims was to bring together Christians of different denominations within Old Town. There was already a long history of close co-operation between Bath Road Methodist, Immanuel Congregational Church in Upham Road and Christ Church with St. Mary's that had existed for many years. In the middle of 1968, the Swindon Council of Churches decided to decentralize a large portion of its work and this coincided with the arrival of Derek Palmer and new Ministers, Arthur Bott at Bath Road Methodist Church and Norman Charlton at Immanuel. By a happy coincidence all three had enjoyed very close co-operation in previous positions before taking up posts in Swindon.

In the autumn of 1968, the three clergymen started joint staff meetings on a regular basis, and not just to discuss particular services and events but to begin to plan the whole life of a new Ecumenical Parish including all three Churches. An Ecumenical Parish Council was set up in early 1969 soon after the first joint service in January and the Ecumenical Parish of Swindon Old Town was formed officially on 19th March 1969. It has the distinction of being the oldest Ecumenical Parish in the country (celebrating its 50th anniversary in 2019). The symbol for the new Parish showing the Churches pointing into the Cross and, at the same time, pointing out from the Cross into the world, was designed by Mr. Peter Hunt, a Methodist art teacher, the following year.

Derek Palmer also saw a need for a new hall for Church and community

Celebrating the formation of the Ecumenical Parish. Derek Palmer, Arthur Bott and Norman Charlton.

use near to Christ Church and launched an appeal for money to build a hall next to the Church. To be known as the Leisure Centre, work commenced in January 1969 and the building was officially opened in September of the same year. Much voluntary labour was offered in the construction by members of the congregation including Edgar Baish, Peter Jones, Ben Battson and Reg Williams, who became the first Warden. The speed of the project perhaps mirrored the new 'anything is possible' optimism of the era, highlighted by Neil Armstrong's walk on the moon during that summer, and the celebrations of Prince Charles' investiture at Caernarvon Castle. A short history of Christ Church was also published in 1969, by Rosemary Stephens and Denis Bird.

Early in 1968 the Swindon Floral Art Society approached Derek Palmer to ask permission to decorate the Church for a Flower Festival. From this conversation, came the first idea for a Swindon Floral Festival, to be called 'A Town speaking in Flowers'.

. The first Festival, run by Christ Church, the Floral Art Society

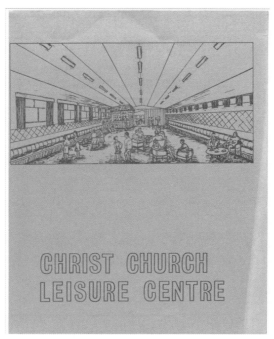

Programme celebrating the 1969 opening of the
Leisure Centre.

and the Swindon Borough Council, took place in mid-September 1969 and was a four-day event based mostly on Old Town and around the Church. It attracted 20,000 visitors and won wide acclaim both from within Swindon and elsewhere. A second Floral Festival was held in September 1972, when the original sponsors were joined by the Chamber of Commerce. A number of new events were added to make it more of a carnival event including a Saturday Procession of Floral Floats, a Round Table event on the Polo Ground and the Lions Club National Dance Festival outside the newly opened Wyvern Theatre. For the third Festival, held in September 1975, the Thamesdown Council of Churches took over from Christ Church as one of the sponsors. Christ Church continued to house the main exhibition, with no less than sixteen other Churches throughout the town also took part. Unfortunately, the Festival in September 1979 proved to be the final event in this series to be held in Swindon.

Programme for the Swindon Floral Festival 1969.

Vicarage Garden Party 1968.

Children from Sunday School outside the Church Hall in Devizes Road, 1968.

In 1969 preparations were well under way for the construction of the M4 motorway that would cut through the countryside south of the town bringing London within one hour's drive of Swindon. A large temporary caravan site opened near the site to accommodate the workers who were to construct the road.

At the end of the decade the town was gripped with football fever as Swindon Town F.C. beat Arsenal 3 – 1 at Wembley and won the League Cup also gaining a place in the 2nd Division of the Football League in the same season. A crowd of nearly 100,000 gathered at Wembley Stadium in London, and it seemed as if the town of Swindon was empty!

The 1970s opened with world events once again having an effect on Parish life. One of the curates, the Revd. John Stephens, left for former Biafra in West Africa to help in the aftermath of the bitter civil war in Nigeria. Curates came and went including John Hewitson, from Australia, who, at a Mothering Sunday service at Lawn Infants' School, upset the headmistress there by inviting the children to pick daffodils in the school gardens to give to their mothers! A retired clergyman, the Revd. Canon Lewis L. Thomas, also served as an honorary assistant Priest at Christ Church from 1964 until his death in

Ecumenical Service at Holy Rood Whitsun 1971.

1972. A small library was established in memory of Canon Thomas, using books left by him and Canon Christelow in the west corner of the North Aisle, and dedicated on Whit Sunday, June 1973.

After several years of preparation, decimal coinage was introduced in February 1971. Several very small businesses run by elderly people chose this time to retire and close down rather than change to new cash tills, completely new coinage and a new way of trading.

At this time the grocery chains were still in the main streets, names like Home & Colonial, Maypole, Peark's Stores, International and Liptons. David Greigs had moved to new premises in Regent Circus, but they still served customers from behind counters, with many goods cut to size and weight. The large stores, British Home Stores, Littlewoods, Woolworths and newly opened Bon Marche (now Debenhams) all had food halls and were soon joined by the new style supermarkets Fine Fare, Tesco and Sainsburys. Most of the 'old style' shops themselves became 'self-service stores' with check-outs. Even some of the remaining corner shops provided wire baskets and called themselves 'mini-markets'.

The M4 motorway opened in 1971, with junctions 15 to the east and 16 to the west of Swindon. The countryside nearby then began to settle down as the road builders moved away westward. The centre of Swindon became a huge building site, the skyline pierced by cranes.

The newly opened M4 Motorway 1972.

The Magic Roundabout.

Princes Street was demolished block by block, the Magistrates Court was built while the few small houses near the Town Hall that still stood finally gave way to the building of the Princes Street footbridge and the Wyvern Theatre (which was officially opened by Her Majesty the Queen on a wet day in 1971). For many years to come a shopping trip into the town centre would need the careful negotiation of routes around building sites. Careful driving would also soon be needed, as plans for the Magic Roundabout were announced – striking fear into visitors to Swindon for the next 50 years!

In Christ Church, the organ was rededicated in October 1970 after a five-month, £6000 refit (see chapter 8). The chancel of the old church of Holy Rood had also been restored as a Chapel of Unity for the Ecumenical Parish by the Borough of Swindon in the winter of 1970-71. Bartlett Bros. were commissioned to make a new stone altar for the Chapel and a stone cross and candlesticks were donated by Mr. Murray John, Town Clerk of Swindon, in memory of his wife. The restored Chapel was dedicated at an Ecumenical service on Whit Sunday, May 1971. Another memorable event for the church was the live broadcast on BBC Radio 2 of the People's Service on 21st November 1971. Considerations for the comfort of the congregation were needed in 1972 and 1973 following the Miners' Strike and subsequent power crisis. The ever-present threat of fuel shortages and power cuts meant the threat of a freezing cold, or an extremely dark, church! This continued for several years.

The needs of the modern world resulted in a car park for the Church being proposed in 1972. Permission was granted and the car park was opened in July 1973. Graves had to be moved to necessitate this but, as they were over 100 years old, no-one in fact objected. It was a difficult and sensitive time, however, and some members of the church needed a lot of convincing that it was the correct thing to do. Many of these stones can still be seen against the carpark wall. A coffee bar was also added in the Leisure Centre in 1973 in memory of Ben Battson.

Derek Palmer was made an Honorary Canon of Bristol Cathedral in 1974 and the Palmer family during these years continued to live in the old Vicarage in Bath Road. This large building contained the Parish office as well as a good four-bed house for a curate (Eddie and Hilda Newton and John and Rosemary Stephens at one time or another). In the 'Green Hut' attached to the Vicarage, known as the Vicarage Room, Ruth Port still ran her own Sunday School (she had been a Sunday School teacher since the 1920s). Margaret Williams, at that time Headmistress of Lainesmead Infants' School in Old Walcot, became the first woman Lay Reader of the Bristol Diocese when she was licensed in June 1974 at Chippenham. John Jarvis, who has been a server at Christ Church since 1952, Youth Fellowship leader and well-known for his service with the 18th Swindon Scouts, was another prominent member of the congregation at this time and, until old age prevented him, attended regularly. Ken Miles (who was Headmaster of King William Street School from 1968-72 before becoming head of Moredon Junior School) became leader of the Quest youth group during the 1970s, serving in that role for many years.

Christ Church in 1975.

The new South Porch was built in 1975. The small window, on the left showing the Coat-of-Arms of the Great Western Railway, was designed by a Bristol firm of stained-glass artists, in memory of Nancy Davis. Interior glass doors were designed and manufactured in County Durham. The chancel step was also enlarged by Duncan McCosh in 1975. A television presentation of *Songs of Praise* was recorded by the BBC in October 1975 at a packed Christ Church. Those lucky enough to be in attendance had to wait until January 1976 for the programme to be broadcast on BBC 1 during the Week of Prayer for Christian Unity. Whilst many were lucky enough to own a colour television at this time, many did not. Radio Rentals in the town reported an increase in those arranging 'easy terms' in order to acquire a colour set in time for the broadcast! Large numbers of people in Swindon settled down in front of their television sets

Floral Festival at Holy Rood, display by the pupils of Lawn Junior School, 1975.

128

Christ Church Youth Club mid 1970s.

that evening for The Prince and the Pauper, Holiday '76 with Cliff Michelmore, Songs of Praise from Christ Church, and Poldark!

Another step forward was the first united Confirmation service for the Ecumenical Parish, which was held in December 1975.

During 1976, the hottest summer on record in Britain, Canon Derek Palmer resigned as Vicar of Christ Church to become Archdeacon of Rochester and residentiary Canon of Rochester Cathedral. He later became Secretary for the General Synod Board for Missions & Unity from 1983-87, Team Rector, Dronfield, Derby from 1987-90 and Dronfield with Holmsfield from 1990-95. Derek Palmer served as Chaplain to Queen Elizabeth II from 1990. His final appointment was as Honorary Canon of Derby Cathedral from 1992-95, at which point he retired to live in Banbury. He passed away, shortly after the original publication of 'The Old Lady on the Hill', in March 2002 at the age of 74. Working tirelessly until the end, he died while attending a meeting of county ecumenical officers.

7

Changing Times 1976-2001

The new incumbent as Vicar of Swindon was the Revd. Owen Conrad Barraclough, aged 45, who was inducted in February 1977. Owen, born in 1932, had been educated at Pembroke College, Cambridge, and received his BA in 1955 and MA in 1959. After training at Westcott House, Cambridge, in 1956, he had become a deacon in 1957 and was ordained a priest in 1958 at Malmesbury. Curate of Chippenham, St. Andrew with Tytherton Lucas, Bristol, from 1957-62, he was Vicar of Harringay, St. Paul, in the Diocese of London, from 1962-70. Owen then worked in the Diocese of Coventry and was involved in race and community relations, being the Bishop's Chaplain for Community Relations from 1970-77. He was Priest-in-charge of Baginton from 1972-77. A peal of 5057 Grandsire Caters rung in 3 hours 7 minutes to welcome the new Vicar on 26th February 1977.

Revd. Owen Barraclough, Vicar of Christ Church 1977-1998.

One of his early duties was to lead prayers and blessings from the church for BBC Radio 2's *'Sunday Half Hour'*, broadcast in April 1978.

In the Parish, the old 'temporary' church of St. Mary's held its last service in July 1977 and meetings were held in the Vicarage Room in Bath Road whilst a new church was built. This opened in 1978 (see chapter 11). Britain emerged from the 'winter of discontent' into a spring that brought with it a General Election that would deliver a Conservative Government under Margaret Thatcher, the country's first £1 million footballer and mortgage rates of 17%. What transpired to be the last of the Swindon wide Floral Festivals was held in September 1979, while life in the Parish continued in a mostly quiet fashion. The buildings continued to cause maintenance problems with some £12,000 being spent in 1980 for work on the roof on the south side of the Nave, the west face of the South Transept and North Aisle, South Aisle, and south side of the Chancel. A new men's club, the Men's Society of the Ecumenical Parish of Old Town, was formed in January 1981 and called AMICUS (= Friendly, Amicable, Pleasing). Mainly due to the formation of this new club, the Christ Church branch of the Church of England Men's Society was eventually disbanded at the end of 1985. Unfortunately, AMICUS itself only lasted a few years longer, closing down with effect from December 1988.

Some reordering of the Crossing and the Transept was undertaken in 1984 and 1985, in memory of Frederick Hazell, former churchwarden who passed away in 1984 (aged 68) and of his wife Ruth who had passed away 11 years earlier. A plaque was placed on the wall of the north transept as a memorial.

The changing world, with its many other opportunities for relaxation, education and travel, was to alter many of the long-established traditions and outlook of the general population. Over many years, the Church had been their centre for community affairs and brotherhood. This was no longer the case. An imperative need to adapt, and to become involved in helping the general community in Swindon, was recognised by both the previous and new Vicar of Christ Church. A 'Day Care Centre' had been opened in the Church Hall in Devizes Room in February 1974, a pioneering venture between Parish, Social Services and the Health Service. This was followed by the 'Green Hut' project, set up by curate, the Revd. Alistair Stevenson, in 1985 in the garden of the old Vicarage in Bath Road, as a *'club for the unwaged'* which offered a place for those who could not find employment. Here, they would receive a warm welcome, some occupation and somewhere that a cheap meal and tea would be available. Later, in 1987, the project moved to the Scout hut at St.

Barnabas Church in Gorse Hill.

Until the 1980s missionary work in the Parish tended to be dealt with by one representative. Over the years, links had been made with the Seychelles (where the former curate, Revd. John Poarch, had been from 1961-63) and Kenya in the 1970s (with Link Missionaries, Tony and Myra Idle). A Missionary Support Group was then set up to increase the awareness of the congregation in the work of the worldwide Church through establishing links with specific societies, CMS (Church Missionary Society) and the United Society for the Propagation of the Gospel, the Leprosy Mission, Tearfund and the Bible Society.

At this time Christ Church had two very personal links with CMS through former curates Revd. Michael West in Tel Aviv and the Revd. John Stephens in Nigeria. Christ Church also had a link with Tearfund as Ian Wallace (son of Malcolm and Megan Wallace) went to work for them in Juba, Southern Sudan and, later, in Guinea Bissau. Link Dioceses were also established in 1984 with Namirembe, Kampala, and Muskono, Uganda. In January 1984. Owen Barraclough, attended the enthronement of the Archbishop of Uganda in Kampala to represent the Deanery of Cricklade and Parish of Old Town. He travelled again to Uganda to visit Bishop Livingstone Mpalanyi-Nkoyoyo for his enthronement as the new Archbishop of Uganda in 1995. A Landrover was also supplied to Uganda in 1985-86. In 1989, the Ecumenical Parish's project '*Pool Your Resources*' raised £10,000 for water pumps to supply an irrigation system and a solar powered pump for St. Matthew's Childrens' Fund School in Ethiopia. A donation of Bibles to the Uganda Bible Society was also made in 1996. In 1999, £1,000 was given to the European Childrens' Trust and £1,000 to the Besaniya Childrens' Home in Uganda. In 1985, Lynda Kerley, a member of Christ Church, went out to Papua, New Guinea to work for Wycliffe Bible Translators and the Parochial Church Council agreed to be one of the main sponsors for her self-funding. Lynda also worked in Melanesia, Philippines, from 1987-92, and later at the Pan African Christian College, Nairobi, from 1994-97. Lynda returned to the UK and married Chris Greaves in 1998. The Group also supported Rebecca Dunn in Sri Lanka from 1991-93. Since the mid-1990s, the CMS link has been the Revd. Marlene

Wilkinson, who travelled to teach English language at Sungkonghoe University in Seoul, South Korea.

Meanwhile in Swindon Parish life continued. The fabric of the Christ Church building continued to cause problems due to age and weathering, a faculty was applied for in 1983 to remove all the stone crosses from atop the dormer windows on the steeple, for safety reasons. The steeple itself also required repointing. Cracks on the North Transept wall also caused concern and calibrated *'tell-tales'* were fixed to the walls. A new stone cross was placed on top of the North Transept to replace one that had fallen down during the severe gales of 1990.

New West Doors to the Church were dedicated in September 1984 and the interior porch was removed. The wooden pews were removed from the North and South Transepts and, in 1985, a platform built out from front of pulpit and lectern area. A new Nave altar, made by John Densam, was provided in 1988 in memory of John Wirdnam, former Churchwarden, who sadly died at the early age of 43 years. Later, in 1990, John Bremner made new choir lights from the wood of the old pews in memory of his daughter. A new window for the Lady Chapel, by the artist John Hayward, depicting the Annunciation was also added in 1987, to replace a window that had unfortunately been vandalized. Kneelers on the Lady Chapel step were made by John, Aila and Janet English between 1989 and 1991. Further kneelers for the Lady Chapel were made and added by branch members under the guidance of Winnie Sedgwick, then the Mothers' Union Enrolling Member. Following a succession of wet summers the churchyard had developed into a maintenance

Kneelers in the Lady Chapel, provided by the Mothers' Union.

headache, and keeping the grass at an acceptable and suitable height proved difficult – one of the curates, the Revd. Tony Lynett, even employed goats at one stage to help keep the grass cut! A section of the old churchyard near to the gateway became a conservation area for wild flowers. The churchyard won the Bishop's Award in the Wiltshire Wildlife Trust's Church Survey Competition in 1997. July

The Vicarage in Bath Road, prior to its sale.

The changing face of the Vicarage, during its conversion into apartments, 2000.

The Vicarage, showing substantial alterations following conversion.

1984 saw the first 'Great Cycle Ride'(now called the 'Ride & Stride', see also the following chapter), on behalf of the Wiltshire Historic Churches Trust, an event that continued to be held annually, usually during September.

The closure of the Swindon Railway Works came in 1986. Rumours of closure had circulated for many years and, although the date had been an established fact for over a year, it was a devastating blow for the town. The familiar sound of the hooter fell silent over the town. It was to be another year before the works were completely deserted but the site remained derelict until the end of the decade, a graveyard of what had been the industrial heart of the town and the largest factory complex in Europe. Garrards who manufactured record turntables, also ceased manufacturing in 1982 and Wills Tobacco Factory closed in 1987 with the loss of many jobs. The buildings were demolished, including the landmark chimney at the side of the main railway line. Tesco purchased the site and began building an all-purpose superstore.

The face of employment in the town changed too, with the arrival of high tech and administrative companies, replacing the traditional 'blue collar' employers. From the late 1970s onwards, the arrival of Hambro Life, Burmah Oil, Intel, Nationwide and others heralded a new beginning for the town.

Owen Barraclough became the first Anglican Chaplain of Princess Margaret Hospital, Swindon, from 1977-89 and an Honorary Canon of Bristol Cathedral in 1987. One notable feature of Owen's years as Vicar was the annual foreign pilgrimage visiting Jerusalem in 1985 and 1988, Taizé in 1986 and 1987, Assisi, Rome and Florence in 1989, Greece in 1990, Portugal in 1991, Jordan in 1992, Turkey in 1993 and 1994, Cyprus in 1995, Crete in 1996 and Sri Lanka in 1998. He also represented the town on the 1996 trip to Salzgitter, as part of Swindon's twinning programme.

For *'A weekend of Renewal'* a production of *'The Torn Curtain'*, by the musician and writer, Roger Jones, took place in October 1989, followed by a performance of his musical *'Mary Magdalene'* at the Oasis Leisure Centre in April 1990. The three Churches of the Ecumenical Parish of Swindon Old Town were involved in this production and later came together to present his musicals *'Saints Alive'* in 1994 and *'From Pharaoh to Freedom'* in 1997. The Ecumenical Music Group was also set up in March 1987 and has since given many concerts locally and in North Wiltshire. Away from music, further Ecumenical Parish projects were undertaken including '*Shakers*' in 1991, the objective being to provide a place in Old Town where young people can meet, relax, enjoy a bite to eat or have a drink without having to break the law. '*Shakers*' opened in temporary premises at the Pilgrim Centre in May 1992 and later, in January 1994, in the rear room at the Church Hall in Devizes Road. In 1994, the Parish Project 'Help Our Homeless' raised £10,200 for the homeless in Swindon.

The old Vicarage was now proving to be too large and expensive to maintain, so in 1988 it was sold to White Horse Holdings, a property development company. The Vicarage moved to 26 Cricklade Street, a large modern house just to the north of Christ Church, at the beginning of 1989. However, the old building remained empty and forlorn for several years until rescued in 1999 when it was attractively converted into residential flats. In Christ Church, new lighting was provided. When this was completed in November 1993, it once more allowed the spire and Church to be floodlit. Planning permission was received in 1991 for the reorganization of the Almshouses in Cricklade Street from four houses to four flats, these were officially opened by Lady Benson in April 1992 (see chapter 11). This venture received the top award for Design and Architecture in the Borough of Thamesdown in May 1993. A new flagpole was also presented in 1994 to the Church in memory of Francis and Doris Pronger. Further repair work was also carried out on the church organ in 1998.

The Men's Breakfast was started in 1994 by the, then, Curate Robert Sanday. It has continued ever since on the first Saturday of each month. Usually a full English breakfast, cooked by men and eaten with relish by men and women. During Lent, only toast and croissants are served. The club usually have an interesting speaker as well. The Men's breakfast team also perform useful duties such as putting up and taking down the Christmas tree in Christ church.

Work with children and young people also took a high priority during the decade. In 1992 the Sunday School and Young Pilgrims became Scramblers, Climbers, Explorers and Pathfinders to cover ages from 3 to 14 plus. A group called '*STICKY*' (Secondary Teenage Independent Christian Kids' Youth Group) was also set up in 1996.

*Janet English (with pencil and clipboard running Guess the Weight of the Cake),
Aila English, Aileen Britt, Barbara Trowbridge, Sylvia Kitching, obscured figure in
background, Dorothy French, Elsie Willies, Mary Hampson, Peggy Morse, and
Joan Jones.*

The stalls at the Summer Fete proved a big hit in 1995. With the Vicarage having been sold, the Fete took place in the grounds of the church. All the stallholders chose a country as a theme and dressed themselves and their stalls accordingly. The Mothers' Union, pictured opposite (left to right):

Gordon Crabbe retired as organist at Christ Church at the end of December 1995. During his tenure as organist and choirmaster the Christ Church choir had been asked to sing in Salisbury, Gloucester, Bristol Cathedrals and in Magdalen College, Oxford. From 1976 - 86 over eighty services had been sung in the various cathedrals. The 70th Anniversary of the dedication of the ring of ten bells was held in April 1994 and broadcast on BBC Radio 4. In 1996, the Christ Church clock was regilded, the dial repainted, and automatic winding added to the function. Bill Daniel, for years, had the task of winding it up twice a week, a job then taken over by Eric Sutton. The clock originated from Holy Rood on the Lawns and is dated 1843. It used to chime on the hour until this function was removed in the early

1920s. Also, during the 1990s Belinda Scarlett (who had produced an altar frontal for Winchester Cathedral and the nave of Westminster Abbey) designed and made from hand-dyed silk, a Covenant Cope for Christ Church. In 1995, the Revd. Janet House, joined Christ Church as a curate, becoming the first lady minister to join the staff.

The 1990s saw much development in Swindon. Sainsbury's launched their second large out-of-town store at Bridgemead, Honda opened their massive factory in South Marston. New housing developments to the west and north seemed to expand almost daily. In March 1997, the Great Western Outlet Village was opened with bands and a carnival. The Outlet Village is entirely contained within the old Railway Works with many of the original features preserved. These were pleasing to the workers who had been employed there and to whom it meant so much. In 2000 '*Steam*', the Heritage Centre Railway Museum, also opened nearby. In contrast, the main shopping street in Swindon lost its oldest department store, McIlroys. At the beginning of the 20th century the store had built its handsome clock tower which for 60 years was the dominating feature of the main street. The building was completely demolished in 1998 and new shop units were built, with a small modern version of the original clock tower bearing the new datestone of 1999.

St Briavel's Castle, in the Forest of Dean.

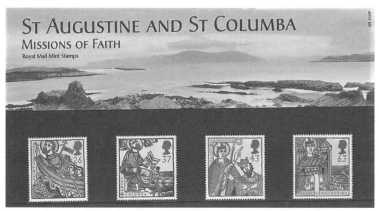

Special stamps issued to mark the 1400th anniversary of St.
Augustine in Britain.

In February 1995 Daphne Hardwick organised a Christ Church Families Weekend at the stunning St Briavel's Castle Youth Hostel in the Forest of Dean. Ten families enjoyed experiencing new skills and events, learning some of the region's history, while temporarily bring transported back to a simpler time. King William Street School celebrated its 125th anniversary (see chapter 13) with a Thanksgiving Service in May 1996. An open-air service was held at Barbury Castle in June 1997 to support of the planned ecumenical pilgrimage to mark the 1400th anniversary of St. Augustine in Britain and death of St. Columba of Iona in 597 A.D. Special commemorative stamps were also produced by the Royal Mail to mark the anniversary. The growing connection of Christ Church with the world-wide Christian community was continued by the visit to Swindon in September 1997 by the Lutheran Church of Salzgitter, Germany (Swindon's twin-town), during which their

Princess Diana during her visit to
Swindon in 1985.

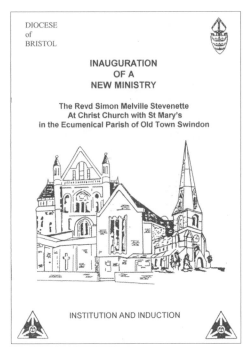

Pastor, Wolfhart Freisleben, preached a sermon in Christ Church. Showing the need that still exists in the modern world for spiritual guidance, the death of Diana, Princess of Wales, brought a huge response in August 1997 with the Church being filled to overflowing for her memorial service. Diana was regarded with much affection in the town, having visited Swindon on numerous occasions.

Owen Barraclough retired from his position as Vicar of Christ Church at the end of 1997. Although he has continued to be involved in church life in the west country even today (marking his astonishing 60th anniversary of service to the church in 2018). On his departure he was presented with a large cross which was erected on the west wall of Christ Church near the West door. The early months of 1998 proved difficult with Janet House having to manage Church affairs and take services; with the help of Peter Dawes (Hon. Assistant), Margaret Williams and John Seacombe, the Lay Readers. Ministers from the two other churches in the Ecumenical Parish also assisted. The Interregnum finally came to an end when the Revd. Simon Stevenette was appointed the new Vicar of Swindon in September 1998 – he was inducted at Christ Church on 6 October 1998.

*First service by Revd. Simon Stevenette as Vicar of Christ Church,
at Holy Rood, October 1998.*

Simon Stevenette, then 36 years old, came to Swindon after several years' experience as Team Vicar of Keynsham in Bristol. Educated at Hull University, where he met his wife, Nicola, Simon obtained his BA in 1984. After a year spent as a Nursing Auxiliary and working as a Pastoral Lay Assistant, he spent three years at Wycliffe Hall Theological College in Oxford. During this time he had a formative year's placement as a member of the Chaplaincy team at Campsfield Youth Comprehensive schools, St. Augustine, Oxford, and Faringdon School. He became a deacon in 1987 and ordained a priest in 1988. Simon served his curacy at St. John's, Carterton, in the Oxford Diocese, from 1987-90. He had married Nicola in 1986 and they moved to the Bath and Wells Diocese where he became firstly a curate from 1990-91, and then Team Vicar in the Keynsham Team Ministry covering five churches, including the three villages of Burnett, Chewton Keynsham and Queen Charlton. As Chaplain to the Keynsham Hospital, Bristol, from 1992-98, he also became involved with the local community there, becoming Chaplain of Bristol Rovers Football Club (he soon transferred his attention to Swindon Town FC as their Chaplain!). At Keynsham he was also Chairman of the Churches Together Schools team. With four young children, boys then aged from 12 weeks to 7 years, Simon and Nicola brought a new, youthful presence and vigour to the Church.

Three members of the Ecumenical Parish, Alice French and Henry Elliott from Christ Church and Muriel Baker from Immanuel Church, received Maundy Money from HM the Queen at Bristol Cathedral on 1st April 1999. Revd. Simon Stevenette waved the party off from Christ Church at 7.30am with a chorus of the National Anthem. After an interview and briefing at the Lord Lieutenant's Office in Bristol on etiquette, they made their way to the cathedral. Her Majesty the Queen entered, flanked by the Tower Warders (Beefeaters), and presented the party with their Maundy Money from a heavy silver salver. The Queen shook Henry's hand and gave him two purses, one red and one white. The red purse contained £5.50 (£3 for clothing, £1.50 for provisions and an extra £1). Inside the white purse were specially minted 1,2,3 and 4 pence coins, 73 in total – one for each year of the Queen's age at that time. Henry had the coins mounted into a special frame. In researching this book Henry recalled *'it was a glorious day which has lived in my memory for the last 21 years.'*

Henry was the last of 10 children and has outlived all the others. Originally from Essex, he worked for the Ford Motor company, before relocating to Swindon in 1958 to work for Pressed Steel. Henry subsequently became a driver for a local dairy, then a long-distance lorry driver for WH Smith. He has two children, a son and a daughter, both of whom live in Swindon.

The Church was filled when *'Roly the Clown'* (the Revd. Roly Bain) attended the Ecumenical Service at Christ Church in June. Additionally, in June 1999, there was also a service and celebration of the 25th anniversary of Margaret Williams licensing as a Lay Reader. Parish members joined the human chain for the Jubilee 2000 Coalition at Westminster in the summer of 1999.

Whilst the Vicarage at 26 Cricklade Street was redecorated the Parish Office moved to the Common Room at St. Mary's Church, where Ruth Haddrell continued her work as Parish Clerk, a position she had held since 1978. In 1997 she had been joined as Parish Administrator by Alisa Palmer. Several donors in the Parish allowed the Parish Office to be transferred to a cottage, a few doors from Christ Church, at 36 Cricklade Street from the end of September 2000.

The coming of the new Millennium was celebrated in style at Christ Church. Fears of the Millennium Bug paralyzing Britain's computer systems proved to be without foundation. New Year's Eve, 31st December 1999, began with an Ecumenical Service at the Church. A

A light above Old Town

BLAZING out above the town, the beacon at Christchurch was one of a chain lit throughout the country to mark the turn of the year, the century and the millennium.

Pictured standing with it are members of three generations of one family, the recently retired the Rev John Stevenette (right) lit the beacon at 8pm.

With him is his son, the vicar of Christchurch, the Rev Simon Stevenette.

Standing with them are three of Simon's four young sons, Thomas, Robert and Edward.

–JILL RYAN BROWNE

Welcoming in the year 2000.

2ft square Millennium cake was made and decorated by John Webb (it took a month to make and used 11 kg of fruit, 12 packets of marzipan and 9 kg of icing sugar!). and was cut in very generous slices and a glass of mulled wine was also provided. Christ Church had been chosen as a site for a beacon, one of a chain of a thousand torches throughout the country, to mark the new Millennium. This was then lit by the recently retired Revd. John Stevenette, Simon's father, and Simon's eldest son, Thomas. A party followed in the Leisure Centre and, after joining together in prayer, the bell ringers rang in the New Year. The celebrations continued on New Year's Day with a Millennium Ramble from Barbury Castle up to Smeathes Ridge, a total of about eight miles. An old tradition was revived on Rogation Sunday when an eleven mile 'beating the bounds' walk was held, an event continued in 2001.

Christ Church and the other Churches of the Ecumenical Parish joined the Millennium Pentecost celebrations on 11th June 2000, when many joined Christians from all over Swindon at the County Ground football stadium in '*Full Steam Ahead 2000*'. This event was attended by some 4,000 people. Two new priests were ordained for the

Christ Church staff at Bristol Cathedral in July 2000, Guy Donegan-Cross and Judy Ashby, a college lecturer, who became an Honorary Curate. Christ Church with St. Mary's held an Open Day on 22nd July 2000, a new venture, that gave the people of Swindon a chance to see the work and aims of the Church in the modern world. This event was very well supported and was attended by the Mayor and Mayoress of Swindon, Councillor Arthur Archer and Mrs. Archer, the Rt. Revd. Michael Doe, Bishop of Swindon, and the Swindon Town Crier, Mr Frederic Ferris. Another old tradition was revived when a service of Compline (night prayers) was held in the chancel of Holy Rood on the Lawns at the end of August. Apart from the early

Wooden Cross, looking eatwards down the Nave, Easter 2000.

morning service on Easter Day, few services had been held in the ruins of the old church in recent years due to bad weather and more

SWINDON HAS MANY GREAT ATTRACTIONS

It's easy to name places sightseers will travel for

IT SEEMS that no week's letters pages are complete without at least one person running Swindon down in some way.

The latest offering (EA December 5) comes from Trevor Wilson, of Walcot, who challenges readers to come up with five tourist attractions.

Well, here are six obvious tourist attractions for a start: STEAM Museum; the McArthurGlen Outlet Centre; the National Monuments Record Centre; the Oasis Leisure Centre (after which a well-known pop band was named); Coate Water Country Park; and Lydiard mansion and park - venue for the Wiltshire Festival.

The first two of these have recently won top regional awards, and are the envy of towns and cities for very many miles around.

I happen to work in London, and recently had occasion to visit a museum in one of the more fashionable areas of north London.

The curator I was dealing with asked me where I lived.

I told her Swindon, whereupon her eyes lit up. "You're very lucky then. What a beautiful area." We take breaks to stay there at the Marriott Hotel.

I wondered if she might have been exaggerating. A few weeks ago however, by remarkable coincidence, I bumped into her

with her husband and child in a Bishopstone pub car park - back here for another visit.

I agree entirely that a solution urgently needs to be found to the problem of restoring the Mechanics Institute.

We also need a concert hall, and to finalise a new route for the Wilts & Berks Canal.

And if we can only clinch some workshop space we can get going with restoring the old Swindon tram!

But, all in all, I really don't think we are nearly as bad as some make out.

Perhaps Mr Wilson might care to try out one or two other places of similar size for comparison - for example Barnsley, Basingstoke or Oldham, Milton Keynes?

The grass is not always greener on the other side.

NEIL BUTTERS
Tithe Barn Crescent,
Old Town,
Swindon

■ Inspiring sight ... Christ Church in Old Town

destructive vandalism which, unfortunately, destroyed or damaged many of the memorials and improvements (which had been carried out in 1970-71). It was hoped by everyone at the church, however, that the Swindon Borough Council would be able to undertake the much needed remedial work in the chancel in time for the proposed opening of

Holy Rood, in time for 'UK Heritage Weekend', due to take place during September 2001. This event was held in conjunction with an exhibition at Swindon Museum and the 150th anniversary of Christ Church, also due in 2001.

Another new venture at Christ Church was the first holding of the '*Alpha Course*' for Christians which took place from September to December 2000. The year 2001 began with a large Stewardship Campaign taking place to help people of all ages in the Church to grow spiritually, to worship together, and to play their part in showing their faith in Old Town and further afield. As the church approached its 150th anniversary, it had undoubtedly become one of the most welcoming and recognised places in Swindon.

In March 2001, after more than thirty years together, the 'Ecumenical Parish of Swindon Old Town' became known as the 'Swindon Old Town Partnership of Churches' – it had been decided that very few could spell the word '*ecumenical*' properly, with fewer still able pronounce it, and many more outside of the Church with little idea what the word actually meant!

8

The Skyline's the Limit!

Revd. Simon Stevenette's father, the Revd. John Stevenette, joined the Christ Church staff team after his retirement in November 1999. On 20th December 2001 he celebrated the 40th anniversary of his Ordination at Chichester Cathedral with a celebration service at Christ Church, attended by friends from all the six parishes he had served. John presided at Holy Communion with Simon preaching. They would do the same a decade later when John celebrated his 50th anniversary, sadly without his wife Angela who had died on 3rd July 2009 of Mesothelioma. This malignant and incurable cancer, caused by exposure to asbestos dust, has been dubbed 'the Swindon Disease' due to its prevalence among ex-railway workers in the town, with hundreds having succumbed since the closure of the Railway works.

Following the conclusion of the 150th anniversary celebrations at Christ Church, thoughts turned to the fabric of the building itself. Now in its third century as the parish church of Old Town, the ravages of time and weather were beginning to show.

A new organisation, *The Friends of Christ Church*, was created, with its main *raison d'être* being the upkeep and enhancement of the Church building. The inaugural general meeting of this group was held on 1st April 2001. Unfortunately, extensive work would be urgently required to the main fabric of the building. Most urgent, and foremost in everyone's minds, was the pressing need for

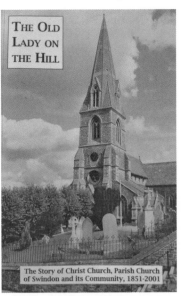

The Old Lady on the Hill was published in 2001.

146

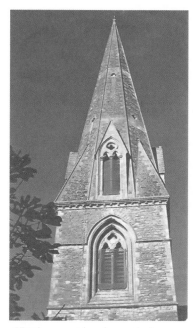

Netting was placed over the louvres.

repairs to the spire of the building. Small pieces of stonework had fallen from the spire and, should the heavy louvres fall out altogether, due to the eroded stonework, the risk to life was all too obvious. The church, although still sitting proudly above the town, required substantial repair and the need was immediate. To facilitate this, the Skyline Appeal was launched and the Friends given the responsibility of administering the fund. The cost would be considerable and, the effort needed to raise the funds, even greater. Margaret Williams became the first chairperson of the Friends. A feasibility study by the architect Terry Hopegood, from Wyvern Architects, had already highlighted the urgent need for repairs to the roof of the building. While carrying out his initial assessment, Mr Hopegood, became concerned about some parts of the spire. With a pair of binoculars he was able to see some erosion of the stonework, which would go some way to explaining the water penetration the church had experienced in the belfry. Green netting was placed over the heavy louvres (which help to control the sound of the bells). Despite this temporary 'fix', Terry Hopegood suspected that there might be further damage to the building and decided to seek expert help. Hopegood knew there was every danger of masonry falling from the roof.

In November 2000 expert climber Chris Milford (from the specialist climbing firm Wallwalkers) was employed to take on the vertigo inducing task of scaling the steep roof and spire. Chris braved the howling wind and cold to dangle from a rope more than 100ft up the tower of the church spire. Chris was able to help Terry Hopegood secure a closer look at the vulnerable parts of Christ Church through a video camera, without the architect ever having to leave the ground. Footage was relayed, from the video camera, to a television monitor on the ground, enabling Terry Hopegood to study and analyse the feed. WallWalkers were ideal for the task, with their expertise in accessing tall buildings in difficult-to-reach places, without the need for expensive and cumbersome scaffolding.

Parish administrator Ailsa Palmer said: *'We want to make sure the church is here for many more generations to enjoy'*.

Things moved quickly following the return of the feasibility study in June 2001. The constitution of the Friends of Christ Church was adopted in September and the terms of reference for the fundraising appeal were revealed in October, in time for the 150th anniversary in November. The 150th Anniversary Appeal (soon named the 'Skyline' appeal) was initially launched by the Friends on the 150th anniversary of the church, on 7th November 2001 against a backdrop of worrying recent world events. On 11th September, Islamic al-Qaeda terrorists had hijacked four aircraft, crashing them into targets in the USA. Two planes were flown into the twin towers of the World Trade Center in New York, a third into the Pentagon and a fourth crashed in open countryside after passengers tackled the hijackers. Almost 3,000 people were killed (67 of them British) and thousands more injured. Further terrorist atrocities would follow in Britain, including the London bombings in July 2005. Prime Minister Tony Blair offered US President George Bush British support for a campaign against international terrorism. The RAF joined in strikes against targets in Afghanistan and British troops were deployed as part of a NATO force.

The Skyline appeal would be directly responsible for the necessary repairs to the church, the re-ordering of the interior, and the building of a new Church Community Centre. A vision for the current and future use of Christ Church, for the whole of local community, was put forward by Revd. Simon Stevenette. This was followed by a talk to the congregation by the architect John Beauchamp, who highlighted the under-utilization of the building. This point, however, carried a caveat, John Beauchamp warned, that the appeal should not devote all its energies on the fabric of the building, at the expense of outreach into the Old Town community.

A new charity shop was launched at the former Fads store in Devizes Road; and raised £2,000 within the first week. Ivy Wilkins, a Christ Church stalwart managed the store alongside Immanuel Church's Muriel Baker. Ivy, Muriel, and their team of around 100 volunteers from Christ Church, Immanuel Church and Bath Road Methodist Church were all determined to raise as much as they could to help the Skyline appeal. Revd. Simon Stevenette also ran the London Marathon in April 2002, raising £8,000 towards the Skyline Appeal.

The Friends of Christ Church organised a 100 mile walk along the Ridgeway, on the weekend of the Queen's Jubilee in May 2002. The ambitious trek from Overton Hill, near Avebury, to Ivinghoe Beacon, in Buckinghamshire, would hopefully raise a further £5,000, to add the £40,000 already raised by that point. Francis Maples, who helped to plan the walk, felt certain that the Queen wouldn't mind the walk clashing with some of her Jubilee celebrations. After all, it was pointed out that Her Majesty had recently received, and thanked the church for, her copy of *The Old Lady On The Hill*!

The intrepid walkers were sent on their way by a blessing from Revd. Simon Stevenette and the Mayor of Swindon. To keep their spirits up on the long trek a special song was even composed by Caroline Pitt and the walkers to mark the occasion of the Ridgeway walk. Entitled '*The Ridgeway Song*', it was sung to the tune of '*John Brown's Body*':

Ridgeway Walk 2002.

Ridgeway Walk.

'We walked along the Ridgeway all the way to Ivinghoe
Some of us walked rather fast and others rather slow the luggage
in the minibus was driven by John Michaux
In aid of the Skyline Appeal.
(repeat the last line of the verse to the tune of Glory, glory,
alleluia)

We started off at Overton beneath the blazing sunthe Mayor
and the Vicar came to see the walk begun
We all had bright red faces by the time the day was done
In aid of the Skyline Appeal

Francis was our leader in a shirt as green could be
some had trouble with their feet and others with a knee
we all got very partial to a glass of ice cold tea
In aid of the Skyline Appeal

We all stopped off at Watlington to rem'mber Francis' Dad we
had a lovely service which made some of us quite sad
for super sandwiches and cakes we were all rather glad

The Skyline's the Limit!

With thanks to St Leonard's Church
But when we got to Ivinghoe we all were wet and cold
good waterproofs and jumpers were worth their weight in gold
and everyone who joins in has a story to be toldbut we ain't
going to walk no more!

John Michaux ferried the walkers' backpacks by minibus between overnight stops, and after five memorable, weary (and sometimes wet!) days, over £5,000 was raised for the appeal.

On 24th May 2002, thanks to an idea by Sarah Jefferies, a fundraising concert 'Music to Inspire' was organised. The event included the 'Ten in A Bar singers', Helen Pysanczyn, and the Swindon Young musicians Big Band. The evening raised £1,150 towards the appeal. Following the success of this event, an evening of classical and modern music with Bristol Cathedral choir was organised for Saturday November 16th.

The old church of Holy Rood also became involved in the fundraising efforts during 2002, the Queen's Golden Jubilee year, when it was chosen as the summer venue for an exhibition of floral arts by Students from Swindon College. Led by Lizzie Mathieson, the event also helped to raise money for the Skyline appeal.

A showcase of talent was held by the Swindon Artists' Forum and the Swindon Artists' Society to raise money for the appeal. To help the fundraising appeal 50 pictures went on display in Christ Church's leisure centre. The exhibition, which was the brainchild of local artist Diana Crafer, who had approached Francis Maples, chairman of the Friends of Christ Church, to see how the groups could help.

Diana said: *'The exhibition will feature pieces from many different local artists and there may be one or two pictures of Christ Church. It is very worthy cause; Christ Church is one of the town's most beautiful buildings.'*

Swindon's Mayor Peter Stoddart opened the event. The Mayor also named the Skyline Appeal as one of the chosen causes for the Swindon Charity Gala at the Wyvern Theatre in 2003. The show featured songs from the West End, performed by, among others, the Kentwood Youth Choir, Tanwood, and the Janet Thompson Concert Choir. In July of the same year, the Goddard Association of Europe referred to the appeal in their newsletter, referencing all the famous members of the Goddard family that had taken their place in Christ Church, or in Holy Rood before it.

Time was also found in 2002 and early 2003 for the cover to the font to be restored by Bernard Oxborrow. The original chain and pulley system for the font cover had long since disappeared, however the cover was discovered languishing in a dark and damp corner of the old boiler house. The iron cover had rusted badly, the paint had peeled away, and the oak base was rotten. In conjunction with advice from both the Swindon and British Museums, Bernard Oxborrow eventually completed the painstaking restoration (More detail about the font can be found in chapter 16).

The font at Christ Church.

The positive start to the fundraising campaign led to renewed optimism regarding the scope and vision of the appeal. Christ Church and St Mary's Parochial Church Council (PCC) welcomed architect John Beauchamp who explained a vision for the possibilities of the church's interior. A bold concept, that would involve a much more flexible re-ordering of the inside of the building, enabling the church to become a real hub and centre for the community of Old Town. Several meetings were held, in which Daniel Pitt spoke of Brian Bridgeman's vision that Christ Church would become a modern centre for Old Town, reaching out to the whole community.

Early fundraising efforts were positive. Nevertheless, in order to raise the huge sums required, it was clear substantial grants would be needed too. 2003 did see an early setback to the fundraising effort when, despite the best efforts of Peter Ford, an application to the Heritage Lottery Fund was unsuccessful. This was a significant blow to the appeal. The plans for renovation and improvement were ambitious and, in order for the work to start, a large sum of money would be needed. Small, local fundraising events – while successful –

tend to have a financial ceiling and larger injections of cash would be needed to ensure the momentum of the appeal kept rolling.

There were further setbacks too. Jean Hillman was tragically killed in a traffic accident, and both Brian Bridgeman and Michael Brougham passed away. Revd. Stevenette was diagnosed with Hodgkin's Lymphoma in July 2003 and began a year of treatment, including six months of intensive chemotherapy; severely limiting his ministry duties and beloved participation in sport. However, with typical determination and positivity, he set himself the target of being fit enough to participate in the 2004 Swindon Half Marathon, and to cycle again, *'I'd be in floods of tears - looking out of the window at the hospital, I could see Coate Water, I could see the spire of Christ Church. I thought to myself, one day I'll cycle again. It was the sense of being in one way so unbelievably weak and fragile but that the bike was almost a visualisation that one day I would cycle again.'*

His faith was undimmed, even though the treatment was gruelling. At one point he was unable even to push one pedal of a bike. Simon, and his wife Nicola's youngest son Hugo was born on Sunday 2nd May 2004. Later that morning, at the all age worship, Curate Revd. Ed Quibell posted an announcement on the screen in Church 'It's a boy!' – thus rather neatly completing Simon and Nicola's personal 5-aside football team! Unfortunately, in July Simon suffered a serious relapse. This necessitated a state-of-the-art Stem Cell Transplant at the Great Western Hospital, followed by radiotherapy in Oxford. He would be off work for nine months, eventually returning just after Easter, April 2005.

Revd. Simon Stevenette received many messages of support, but always found time to comfort fellow patients, as they had comforted him, even helping to set up a support group. He told the Swindon Advertiser that, *'this medical glitch is like an enforced sabbatical with infinite possibilities and much to learn. I was frightened and fearful the morning before my biopsy, the first anaesthetic I had ever had. My tears flowed freely as I returned to Swindon with a hand-held wooden cross, given to me by my dad, pressed into my hand. This cross has been a great source of strength subsequently.'*

The country, too, was in a subdued mood. The invasion of Iraq had taken place. Many from Swindon travelled to London to join the

2 million people demonstrating against the war, and Russian President Vladimir Putin openly mocked Britain's failure to locate weapons of mass destruction in Iraq.

Meanwhile, the enormous challenge facing the Skyline appeal continued. After much hard work and commitment to the project, Cilla Slipper, Angela Ruck and Mike Slipper (the Chair) all needed to step down from the Skyline Appeal subcommittee. Understandably the new chair, Francis Maples, was somewhat downbeat about the appeal. Nonetheless, new blood was drafted in, in the form of Nicola Grosvenor, Jim Sinclair, David Cox and Peter Jones. Pam Bridgeman became new treasurer.

On a more positive note the Christ Church Dramatic Society celebrated its 40th anniversary in 2003. The Society had been originally formed in April 1963 by members of the Christ Church Youth Fellowship, and the first play performed was The Gay Bachelor. Since 1963 the Society have staged 74 three act plays, almost two a year, the highlight being an appearance on HTV.

By July 2003 the Skyline appeal had raised over £150,000 – still well short of the £1.5 million target. The extensive plans for Christ Church included substantial renovation and re-ordering of the interior of the church, as well as cleaning the stonework, complying with modern legal requirements (such as disabled toilet facilities and emergency lighting). However, by the end of 2003, the monumental efforts of everyone involved meant that over £200,000 had been raised; and repairs to the spire could begin. A legacy gift of £61,000 from the estate of Jean Hillman, together with £50,000 from the PCC, meant the initial target had been reached.

The town of Swindon seemed to be moving in a positive direction too. The early years of new millennium saw the Railway Museum (known as 'STEAM') open its doors to great public acclaim. New patients were admitted to the Great Western Hospital and shoppers thronged to the new Orbital Shopping Centre in North Swindon. A new Town Centre Library would follow in 2008.

Further progress was made in 2004 and 2005 with additional income raised towards the Skyline Appeal. 'Seasonal Voices', with the Janice Thompson singers and a Burns Night being just two of events organised. A CD of Christ Church choir was recorded. Entitled '*Skyline*

Sounds' it raised over £4500 (The CD was sold out by December 2006). Funds of £222,000 were transferred to the PCC, so that work could at last commence on the spire. Good news also came just after Easter 2005 with the return to work of Revd. Simon Stevenette, following his long battle with illness. He announced himself with the quote, *'the old Simon has gone, this is a new resurrected Simon!'*.

Scaffolding contractors arrived in April 2005 to undertake assembly of the scaffolding around the spire. In 2004 Julia Kablak took over as Honorary Treasurer to manage the Friends' continuing contribution to the fundraising for the Skyline Appeal and the various projects to preserve and maintain the beautiful building and fabric of the Christ Church and its churchyard. The scaffolding, weighing 40 tonnes in total, was expected to take six weeks. Once completed, work on the spire was anticipated to take seven months. David Vowles, of the Parochial Church Council, explained the situation:

The spire, shrouded in scaffolding,
2005.

'The scaffolding is complex work. It has to cover all 151 feet of the spire. but it also has to wrap around the spire and over the church roof. So getting all of that correct will be complicated.'

Once erection of the 23 floors of scaffolding was completed, specialist contractors Ellis and Co, of Shepton Mallet, in Somerset, could begin the task of repairing the stonework, which had suffered from more than 150 years of exposure to pollution and the elements.

Revd. Simon Stevenette told *the 'Swindon Advertiser': 'The building has helped many over the years. Now it's time for the many to help the building, not to create a museum, but to secure and expand the base of our support to the people of Swindon.'*

Daniel Pitt atop the spire. 2005.

Fundraising Chair Daniel Pitt braved a climb to the top of the spire in June 2005 to witness for himself how phase one of the ongoing programme of works was progressing. Specialist mortar re-pointing and stone replacement carried on for several months, as the flaky and worn stonework was carefully repaired.

Finally, in January 2006, after nine months of hard work, the renovation of Christ Church's tower was completed. Delighted with the results, the PCC felt sure that the finished project would secure the integrity of the tower for at least another 100 years. The replacement of the clock face on 24th January marked the finishing touch to the repairs to the spire and church exterior. The completed and regilded clock face had a story of its own to tell. Following the renovation, the clock arrived back at the church in a horse box! It seems that the clock had set off on its journey from the clockmakers in a more traditional form of transport; but got slightly damaged en route. The clock had to be returned to the clockmakers, who decided on a horse box as the only form of transport large enough for the clock face! Margaret Williams happened to be on site, when the clock face arrived back at the church, and managed to grab her video camera in time to film the workmen hanging precariously on ropes as they guided the clock face into position. A DVD of the whole operation – complete with Haydn's Clock Symphony as background music - is kept in the bell tower.

To celebrate the completion of the project a service of thanksgiving was held on 26th February, attended by the Bishop of Swindon, Right Revd. Lee Rayfield. An exhibition detailing the work was planned for display in the church.

'*We will be showing examples of old stonework, as well as discussing future plans for the church,*' explained Daniel Pitt, '*The louvres were repaired, we have repointed all the stonework and the ball flowers have had to be replaced.*'

During this intense period of fundraising the church did not 'take its eye off the ball'. Other projects were still at the heart of life within the worshipping community. In April 2006 both a Barn

Workmen hanging over the clockface, 2006.

Dance and a cheese and wine party were held on behalf of the Kagitumba School Appeal, in Rwanda. The cheese and wine party, organised by Angela Ruck, raised £750 alone. A talent show was also held in January 2007, helping take the total raised for Kagitumba to over £22,000. David Godfrey donated two projectors to be sold on behalf of the appeal and books were sent to Rwanda and Kenya. Unfortunately, many of them took years to arrive! Meanwhile Britain resembled Africa – at least in temperatures – as one of the hottest summers on record saw the average temperature (including at night-time) rise to 19.7 degrees centigrade for most of July!

The Friends 100 Club began in 2007 and was run by Maggie Bird and Colin Simmons. Members paid £1 per month. Half of the proceeds from ticket sales were distributed in prizes; and the other half paid for taxis to take congregation members to services. The most popular service proved to be the 4 pm choral evensongs, followed by tea. The Friends 100 Club ran for five years.

Since the beginning of the new century there has been a huge growth in people undertaking vocations to Ordination and in joining the Licensed Lay Ministry. In addition to Curates coming from elsewhere, 14 people have discovered their Vocation, serving both in Old Town, across the Swindon Deanery and further afield. This was the largest amount at that time in the Bristol Diocese, for which thanks was given to God.

As a result of Revd. Simon Stevenette's mother Angela seeing an advertisement in *The Church Times,* the Revd. Ray Low, a retired Episcopalian Priest from the United States crossed the Atlantic to work voluntarily at Christ Church for three months. Ray arrived and settled in, eventually staying for a whole year. He returned in subsequent years for a further 18 months serving in the Bristol Diocese. Revd. Ray Low was a huge support and inspiration to many at Christ Church who still remember him fondly. Revd. Simon Stevenette and his family visited Ray and his wife Joan in Boston, Massachusetts, followed by a month long clergy exchange in Westborough Massachusetts in 2010, learning about the work of God around the world.

With a monumental effort still required to complete the urgent repairs to the building, the committee did not rest on their laurels. Next came proposals to re-order the interior of the church and the ambitious plans to replace the 40-year-old Leisure Centre with a new, purpose built, Community Centre. A re-ordering committee was set up in 2007, with John Michaux as chair, and Andrew Mottram in an advisory capacity. Andrew Mottram, who was diocesan Heritage Buildings & Community Development Officer, brought a wealth of experience to the project. During his tenure he visited almost 300 churches, bringing his own values to the role of advisor. He would eventually retire from a job well done in 2018:

'Churches must become social hubs – in order to survive they need people!' said Andrew, *'I'm a committed pew remover...but not if they're replaced with lines of chairs which never get moved! Having buildings that are fit for purpose is a key part of being Kingdom People and it's been great to help PCCs and congregations catch the vision – seeing their church buildings as a great resource rather than a burden or problem!"*

Andrew had his own Mission Statement for church buildings: *'If they are effectively to serve their communities as well as being places of worship, church buildings should be: a place of meeting for the community, a place for listening, learning and telling stories, a place for creative and artistic endeavour, and a threshold between heaven and earth'.*

Andrew visited Christ Church in December 2007. He identified further work required on the main section of the church's roof. In addition visits were also carried out to other churches, such as Abingdon, where re-ordering of the church's interior had already taken place.

Andrew Mottram wasn't the only visitor to Christ Church in December 2007, as the Friends Committee organised the first Christmas Market. The fundraising event proved an instant success and has expanded every year to include stalls, raffles, refreshments, entertainment, and, of course, Father Christmas!

In the meantime, in order to help with the building of the new Community Centre, the decision was made to sell the Devizes Road Church Hall to the Salvation Army. The sale, originally agreed in January 2006, released £310,000 – a significant boost to the fundraising efforts.

Preparatory work on the re-ordering of the interior carried on apace. In 2008 an Asset Management Plan and a Conservation Statement were commissioned. The fundraising and project management efforts were crystalized, however, in June 2009 when an examination and statement from the architect confirmed that repairs to the roof of Christ Church were urgent and could wait no longer. Unfortunately, the outlook did not improve when an application to the Heritage Lottery Fund of £226,000 was rejected in September. Another approach was clearly needed.

While efforts continued swiftly to secure the future of Christ Church, Old Town's other most recognisable listed building, The

Locarno in the High Street, suffered its second arson attack, leaving the structure as a charred shell. Swindon residents feared for its future.

In October 2009 the Parish Council endorsed the policy of securing an external fundraising consultant to head the campaign. Following a series of selection interviews, the unanimous choice was Gill Moody from Craigmyle Fundraising Consultants, based in St Albans. The company specialised in helping churches, cathedrals and hospitals and could boast more than 60 years' experience in helping organisations secure funding. However, it was ultimately decided not to go ahead with external help, and the other avenues of fundraising would need to be explored. In light of the failed Heritage Lottery Fund application it seemed prudent to defer the roof restoration in favour of a 'patch and maintain' policy. A surveyor's report also revealed the potentially high cost of repairs needed to the old Leisure Centre. Further bad news was to come in December 2009, just as the Office of National Statistics announced that the country was officially in recession.

The church was blighted by the scourge of vandalism during Christmas 2009. Almost 100 graves were vandalised in the churchyard. In a sickening act, headstones were smashed and pulled out of the ground, plaques on graves were bent, and ornaments left on graves were smashed during the incident. It was believed that the destruction took place on Christmas Eve and possibly over the following three

Christ Church Churchyard 2009, prior to the vandalism.

nights. It was certainly the worst act of vandalism in the church's history, and, luckily, the church has not suffered a similar occurrence since. The addition of more secure fencing around the churchyard in 2015 has no doubt helped.

The faith of those involved in the importance of the church's place in the community, and the ambitious renovation project, never wavered however. Bold moves and more positive news arrived in 2011. Firstly, it was decided to sell the former Curate's house in Upham Road, in the hope of raising a substantial amount towards kickstarting the Skyline appeal again. This was achieved in April 2012 when the property was

sold, swelling the coffers by more than £200,000. This, in turn, enabled new architect Antony Feltham-King, from St Ann's Gate Architects in Salisbury, to develop an innovative plan and source a modular wooden structure from a specialist firm called Timberworks. A video outlining the proposals was released and can still be viewed on youtube: https://www.youtube.com/watch?v=V2p5jpOw1WA

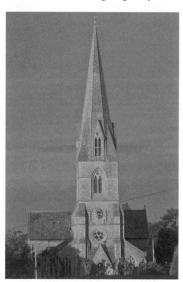

Christ Church 2011.

The sale of the Parish Office followed soon after, raising a further £128,000. The old office had been situated at 36 Cricklade Street, close to the church, and its sale helped release crucial funds. Soon the Parish administrators would have a purpose built office, housed within the planned new Community Centre. Revd. Simon Stevenette also contacted Swindon Council and was made aware of a possible '106' Development Grant, which could help swell the funds substantially. The church, at last, seemed within touching distance of achieving its goals.

2011 also saw a double celebration and anniversary for Christ Church. Revd. Simon Stevenette was pictured with two of the thousands of couples who have been married in the church during the previous one hundred years. Mary and David Priday, and Steven

Wedding Celebrations, 2011.

and Tracy Goldsworthy helped to mark the occasion. Weddings were selected as the theme for the forthcoming 160th milestone anniversary gala dinner and wedding dress fashion show is to be held at the STEAM railway museum on November 4th 2011.

The event was reported in the Swindon Advertiser:

> *'The Revd Simon Stevenette, the vicar of Christ Church with St Mary's, said: "160 years is a landmark and we are celebrating that and using it to springboard our development and renewal into the future. All money will go towards a £160,000 appeal to fund a development and renewal project to make the church more welcoming and accessible for future generations.*
>
> *Christ Church is at the heart of the community and we host various community events, as well as worship, and weddings, and baptisms and funerals. Weddings were picked as a theme because weddings are about one celebration, but almost everyone in Swindon will know somebody who has either been married; or has been to a wedding in Christ Church."*
>
> *Hundreds of couples have said 'I do' and pledged their eternal love at the altar of Christ Church, in Old Town, over its 160-year history.*
>
> *The bumper birthday bash will also kickstart the initiative to*

further develop the church as a community facility. They intend to replace the old heating system, level the floor to improve access and install more comfortable and flexible seating. They also want a new community centre to replace the ageing hall, which has been used by a host of local groups over the past 40 years. So far more than £437,000 has been secured, but a further £160,000 is needed.'

Revd. Stevenette, 2011.

The special celebration evening was headlined with a unique and nostalgic fashion show, by Wood Street based bridal store Trousseaux, who staged a fashion extravaganza of wedding gowns and clothing worn through the ages. This was complemented by hair designed by award winning Swindon hair stylist Steven Goldsworthy (one of the many Swindonians to have been married at Christ Church), and with music from the Nathan Jones' All Star Jazz Bands.

On the following Monday the anniversary was marked with a special celebration service at Christ Church, to mark the laying of the foundation stone in 1851. Retired Vicar, Revd. Canon Owen Barraclough, returned for the event as guest preacher. In fact, it seemed to be the season for anniversaries, as 2012 saw celebrations for the Queen's Diamond Jubilee take place at Christ Church. Many older members of the church remembered the Queen's coronation in 1953 and recalled street parties, spending hours on the coronation route to catch a glimpse of the young Queen; or travelling miles to visit a family member with a television set!

Lee Abbey Christian Community Centre in Devon hosted a group of 40 parishioners from Christ Church in September 2012. The event, called 'Entertaining Angels' gave those attending a chance to discuss 'He Hospitable God and he Hospitable Church'. The weekend, which was written enthusiastically about in the Parish Magazine by Maria Morcumb, posed the important question: *'Are we hosts or guests in church – or, indeed, can we be both?'*

*Revd, Stevenette and Gareth Hutchinson celebrate
the Beer Festival.*

Christ Church Beer Festival.

In 2013, the year that same sex marriages were legalised in England, a new and novel fundraising initiative took place in the church. The Old Town Beer Festival took place in Christ Church for the first time. Originally springing from an idea by Gareth Hutchinson, church warden at Christ Church, (now an ordained vicar in Leicester) and plenty of persuasion, the festival – which at first may not have seemed a natural fit for a church – proved to be an instant success. Thanks to lots of hard work from Mike Palmer, Stephen Grosvenor, Ailsa Palmer, Daniel Pitt, Nick Smith, Chris Smith and others, the festival

Revd. Stevenette with his family, as he receives his Canonship, 2013.

has grown every year into a valuable social occasion and fundraiser for Christ Church. The event has often been opened by local sports representatives, celebrities and local MP Robert Buckland.

The Parish Magazine, now called the Partnership Magazine in recognition of the work of the three churches, was given a refreshed, modern look during the decade too. Diana Swann and Margaret Williams continued their tireless efforts in bringing news and views from the Old Town Partnership of Churches to the people of Old Town and beyond.

In October 2013 Revd. Simon Stevenette was installed as an Honorary Canon of Bristol Cathedral. Coincidentally, he received his Canonship on the 15th anniversary of his licensing as the Vicar of Christ Church in 1998.

The newly titled Revd. Canon Simon Stevenette explained, *'This honorary title entitles me to have a stall in the cathedral and to wear a special red scarf. It was a remarkable day with over 100 family and friends, with about 50 coming over from Swindon on a coach and about 50 coming over from Keynsham, my previous parish.'*

Simon was joined by his family, wife Nicola, and sons Thomas, 22, Robert, 20, William, 15, and Hugo, nine. Eighteen-year-old Edward was unable to make the occasion as he has enrolled at Warwick University.

The next stage of Christ Church's Development and Renewal plan came on 30th November 2013 with the first booking in the new

Community Centre @ Christ Church. Following the exhaustive period of grant applications and fundraising work began with the demolition of the old Leisure Centre in March 2013. The new centre is truly a building for the 21st century, utilising as it does insulation efficient and sustainable materials wherever possible. Christ Church also recognised its responsibilities to the environment, achieving carbon negative energy efficiency for the building. This was accomplished by the innovative use of 20 KW photo voltaic solar panels and zoned underfloor heating, driven by a ground source heat pump. Flexibly designed, the new centre encompassed the parish office, a large hall, a garden room, store, well-equipped kitchen, toilets, and two meeting

The Shinde family helping to dismantle the old Leisure Centre, 2013

The Community Centre during construction.

rooms. The hall and garden room were divided by a movable screen which could be removed to create a larger single space for weddings, children's parties or big functions. The opening of the new innovatively designed Community Centre coincided with the unveiling by the Royal Mint of the new 12-sided £1 coin, designed to prevent fraud, and the country's wettest winter for over a century.

Television personality Nick Hewer (of *The Apprentice* and *Countdown* fame) officially opened the new Community Centre on 18th January 2014. Not only was the opening a major opportunity to introduce the versatile facilities to the wider Swindon public, it was also a perfect opportunity to thank all those who had provided valuable advice,

TV personality Nick Hewer, who officially opened the new Community Centre.

information and support to ensure that the project was completed. The opening was marked with the unveiling of an important new artwork by local artist Laurie Plant celebrating the central role that Christ Church plays in the life of Old Town and Swindon.

The new Community Centre Development Manager Chris Smith, together with children from King William Street School, and Revd. Daphne Hardwick, buried a time capsule in the foundations of the new Community Centre. An open day followed and the day finished with a family friendly quiz evening. To mark the 1 year anniversary in 2015 a toilet twinning quiz event was run raising over £100 for Tearfund and Cord charities.

It was identified, at the time, that a large number of older and socially isolated people lived in Old Town. In September 2016 a regular Tuesday afternoon tea was created. The teas run every week between 2-4pm with up to 25 older people, and carers, in attendance, many of whom have dementia. Attendees are invited for a cup of tea, slice of cake, chat and a planned activity such as bingo, exercise, or talk. The activity is run by the community centre volunteers.

Thanks to the success of the afternoon teas, it was also highlighted that a significant number of lonely and isolated people lived in the community. The Church therefore decided to create 'Alone at

Christmas' which first took place on Christmas Day 2016. 40 people attended, with a further 25 volunteers, for a three-course Christmas lunch followed by Christmas singing and the Queen's speech. Importantly, this meant that all those attending (including some of the volunteers) did not spend Christmas Day alone. 'Alone at Christmas' has now grown significantly, increasing to 80 attendees and 40+ volunteers in 2019. The event would not be possible without the help of all the volunteers, including professional chef Steve Mitchell who regularly gives up his time for free.

Attached to the Community Centre is the new Garden of Reflection, designed by local landscape designer Rachel Titcombe. This tranquil garden, with its neat paving, bushes and benches, provides a peaceful, calm and sheltered setting in which to pass a moment or two. Bordered by old gravestones and an attractive stone wall, it is hard to imagine the site was once a rubbish tip! Pride of place in the newly created Garden of Reflection goes to the impressive monument to William Morris, the founder of *Swindon Advertiser* in 1854, and the man who regularly locked horns with the Revd. Baily during the early days of Christ Church. The monument was moved from its original position, from what is now the entrance to the new Community Centre. Overlooking

The Garden of Reflection.

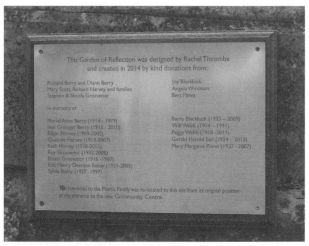

Garden of Reflection plaque.

the church and the town, the monument was repositioned with surviving members of the Morris family. It is also worth recording his large and interesting family (also recorded on the monument) many of whom played a significant role in the life of Swindon:

William Morris	Died 15th June 1891	Age 69 Author and Journalist
Martha	Died 14th Dec 1886	Age 63 Wife of William
Jessie	Died 6th Jan 1854	Age 7 Daughter
Frederick	Died 9th Jun 1865	Age 15 Son
Sydney	Died 21st Mar 1866	Age 7mths Son
Septimus	Died 11th Jul 1899	Age 25 Son
William Edwin	Died 22nd Apr 1902	Age 54 Son, Swindon Advertiser Editor
Walter George	Died 6th Feb 1905	Age 52 Son, Died in Cheyenne, Oklahoma
Edwin James	Died 29th Nov 1909	Age 49 Son
Valentine	Died 22nd Feb 1919	Age 63 Son
Kate Elizabeth	Died 29th Dec 1919	Age 57 Daughter
Jessie Emily	Died 27th Dec 1920	Age 63 Daughter
Frank Alfred	Died 18th Sep 1927	Age 60 Son, Swindon Advertiser Editor
Samuel Perry	Died 9th Apr 1928	Age 74 Son, Swindon Advertiser Editor

In a remarkable life, William Morris outlived his wife and three of his children. He was also the great grandfather of zoologist and author Desmond Morris.

Sadly, retired Choir Master and organist Gordon Crabbe passed away in June 2014. A special concert to raise money for Leukaemia and Lymphoma research was held in his honour. The achievements of Gordon are discussed in chapter 9.

Some good news arrived at Christmas 2014 with the announcement that, 40 years after becoming the Diocese of Bristol's first ever female lay minister, Margaret Williams was awarded an MBE in the Queen's New Year Honours List for 2015.

Margaret, then 83, was a retired headteacher of both Lainesmead and Oliver Tomkins primary schools in the town, and has given more than 40 years of service to the diocese.

Originally from Swansea, Margaret had married in 1955 and moved to Swindon, where she began an association with Christ Church,

Gordon Crabbe who passed away in 2014.

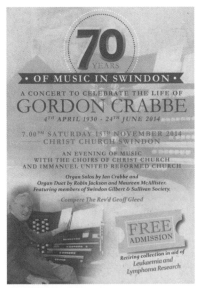

becoming a lay minister in 1974 after encouragement from Canon Derek Palmer.

'I was surprised because I'm sure lots of people have done good things and I don't consider myself to have done great things, I'm just an ordinary person', Margaret said, *'Perhaps having been a first female lay minister in this area 40 years ago, I have got stamina!'*

Margaret's story featured in the Swindon Advertiser, with a glowing tribute from Revd. Stevenette who

Celebrations for Margaret William's MBE, 2014.

highlighted her ability as a lay minister, especially at children's services, because of her love of storytelling which features in Margaret's book about her life *Bridging the Gap*, published in 2007. A special quarter peal of bells in Margaret's honour was sounded at Christ Church at 9.30am on New Year's Eve.

The work of Christ Church's parish administrator Ailsa Palmer was also recognised in 2016, when she received a Pride of Swindon Award for her 23 years of service to the church and the Old Town community.

2016 was a difficult one for the country, and for the Revd. Canon Simon Stevenette too. Firstly Prime Minister David Cameron announced that a referendum would be held in June to determine the country's continuing membership of the European Union. A period of fractious argument and division followed; before the result saw the people of Britain vote to leave the EU. Before the ink had dried on the agreement, Revd. Canon Simon Stevenette was taken ill again. After having survived one serious illness a decade earlier, Simon was admitted to the Great Western Hospital in Swindon with a mystery illness. Diagnosed as sepsis, the infection was a serious one, requiring a worrying stay in hospital. At the time of his admission Simon had been taking part in the 'Football Fans in Training' course; and was wearing his Swindon Town FC shirt. As official Chaplain to the football club he was delighted to receive a visit in hospital from Swindon Town Head Coach Luke Williams and First-Team Coach Ross Embleton. Thankfully, after a tough battle, Simon recovered and exactly one year later was able to compete in the Swindon Half Marathon. He even managed to clock in an impressive time of 1 hr 47m – 12 minutes ahead of Community Centre Development Manager Chris Smith!

Over 100 people from Christ Church and St Mary's attended a Parish Weekend at Lydiard Conference Centre in October 2016. The weekend, involving talks and discussions around re-imagining faith, hope and church in the 21st century, was led by Bishop Right Revd. Lee Rayfield and, once again, provided another example of Christ Church's commitment to finding new ways to worship and to reach out into the community.

The Historic Wiltshire Churches Trust, which provide grants for church repairs, contributed £3,000 to Christ Church in 2016 for the repair of the Lady Chapel roof. Both before and since that date, members of the Christ Church community have been significant participants in the Annual 'Ride and Stride' organised by the Historic Wiltshire Churches Trust. Taking place between 10am and 6pm on the third Saturday in September, participants are invited to choose their own routes between selected Wiltshire churches, which then open to receive them and often provide refreshments. The event traditionally commences at Christ Church with a prayer. Sponsorship contributions are then divided equally between the participant's parish and the Trust. Nearly £10,000 has been contributed by participants from Christ Church since 2000. Over the many years of the event Christ Church organisers have been Margaret Williams, Enid Sheldrake, Caroline Pitt and Arline Stovell, with as many as 15 taking part each year. In the early 1990s Janet French excelled, visiting 44 churches in one day! 2007 saw Caroline Pitt win the prize for best organiser, with the Silver Jubilee year of 2008 also proving to be a highly successful one for the event. Christ Church with St Mary's were also among the runners- up in 2010 and 2011 for The Brooke Cup (the competition for the best parish), presented by Peter Brooke the chairman of the Trust. In 2015 the event was launched at Lydiard by the Archbishop of Canterbury the Most Revd. Justin Welby.

For many years youngsters in the parish won prizes for raising the most sponsorship money during the event – especially Kate Pitt in the five years between 2000 and 2004 inclusively. In 2005 Paul Grosvenor and Eddie Gibney from Immanuel took both prizes for

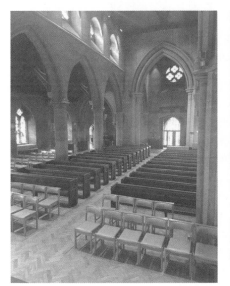

Renewal Works 2017.

the most funds raised and most churches visited in the Under 15s category. It was felt they more than deserved their prize as it was a very wet trip indeed! Other under-15 prize winners on the podium have been Robert Stevenette, Rachael White, Carl Godfrey, David Simmons, William Penfold, Alan Eyles and Emily Gibbs. Carl Godfrey won the under 15 prize in 2006 for visiting 38 Churches in one day and the following year was featured in the *Swindon Advertiser* accompanying his father on a tandem. Prizes were awarded, at a

2018 Pride of Swindon Award Winners.

magnificent ceremony in the splendid setting of Devizes Town Hall, by the Lord Lieutenant of Wiltshire and the Archdeacons of Salisbury and Malmesbury. The event celebrated walkers and cyclists from 6 to 96 years of age and restored faith in England's heritage. Sadly, because of falling income the prize ceremony no longer takes place.

In February 2017 a significant bequest from Pamela Gilbert, daughter of Revd. John Gilbert the vicar of Christ Church from 1929 – 1953, was made towards the internal re-ordering work needed within Christ Church. The work, and the costs involved, would again be substantial. However, thanks to the bequest, reclaimable VAT (under the Listed Places of Worship Scheme), and fundraising by the Friends of Christ Church, it would now be possible to fund the new tumbled oak block floor, LED lighting, audio-visual equipment and new radiators and underfloor heating system. The re-ordering was completed by April 2017, requiring a huge amount of work by all those involved, and the closure of the church for an eight-week period – for the first time in the church's history. The church's original Baltic oak pews were removed, taken away and restored. The central nave pews were returned to the church and the remaining side aisle pews were sold. 20,000 oak blocks were carefully laid, featuring an intricate compass emblem at the centre of the crossing to remind the congregation of their mission to constantly look for ways to engage

Christ Church during roof renovation.

Christ Church in winter.

with the local community. Christ Church reopened for Easter 2017, with a special service in which the Right Revd. Bishop of Bristol Mike Hill performed a special dedication to the renewed and reopened church.

Following the re-opening celebrations, recognition came in 2018 for the hard work and dedication shown by the Volunteer Project Managers on the Christ Church Building Committee, Stephen Grosvenor, Daniel Pitt and Mike Palmer. The team had worked tirelessly for the previous decade on, not only, the Community Centre project but also the conversion of the rubbish tip into the beautiful oasis of calm, now called the Garden of Reflection, and the re-ordering of the interior of Christ Church. Nominated by the Revd. Canon Stevenette for a Pride of Swindon Award, the team received their award in March, from Mayor Maureen Penny, during a glittering evening at the STEAM Museum in Swindon.

There was to be no resting on their laurels, however, there was still more work needed to complete the 21st century renewal programme of the church's fabric. The final phase involved the re-roofing of the church. Planning for the project began in 2018. A major and challenging task, not just from a financial viewpoint, but logistically and physically too. The Grade II listed building would require special permission to make any alterations to the steep roof. Robert Skinner and his team of intrepid roofers would need to replace 20,000 roof tiles, with best quality Cwt-Yi-Bugali Welsh roof slates, more than 50 metres of limestone ridge tiles, and 1,000 square metres of insulation. The story behind the replacement of the roof became, not a story of construction and administration, but a human drama, as contractor Robert Skinner suffered a major health crisis, just one week after signing his contract to begin the work. Without prompt medical care, surgery, and a period of convalescence, there was a real risk that the work might not have been completed. However, thanks to the brilliance of Robert's surgeon, a team effort by his friends, and a brave reappearance on the scaffolding by Robert, after surgery, the work was eventually finished. The results of the work are plain to see and pleasing to the eye. High praise from the architect Antony Feltham-King followed; and it is hoped that the new roof will last well into the 22nd century. After a delay, caused by Robert Skinner's illness, a service of celebration was held in July 2019, attended by the Mayor of Swindon, Robert Buckland MP, and Robert Skinner the roofing contractor. The work would not have been possible without the generosity, in the form of legacies, of Pamela Gilbert, Peter Ford, John Sondermann, John & Aila English, John Plaister, and Ken Trenery.

Swindon, and most of southern Britain emerged shivering from the winter of 2017/18 in which the 'beast from the east' battered the countryside. Heavy snow had affected much of the UK and dozens of vehicles became stranded on the country's roads. The weather improved dramatically in the spring as the country celebrated the wedding of Prince Harry and Meghan Markle at St George's Chapel, Windsor. The country wondered if the popular Prince would, perhaps, one day be King. Meanwhile a commemoration of a different kind was being proposed at Christ Church. 2018 marked the 100th anniversary of the armistice that ended the Great War. A 'Festival of Commemoration' was planned to take place in November to mark the occasion. Janet French and Stephen Grosvenor devised, created and co-ordinated the organisation of the festival. The event was planned to be a celebration of Swindon's role in the Great War, told in words, music, and pictures (using the new multi-media screen). Firstly, the Friends of Christ Church financed the renovation of the ornate War Memorial on the wall of the church. Faded lettering on the memorial required delicate repainting. The outside of the church was bathed in red light and the bellringers marked the occasion with a full peal, rung half muffled (see chapter 14). Even the sounding of the GWR Railway Works' hooter was played (from an original recording). The hooter had originally been used to signal the outbreak of war.

The festival itself, held on 10th November, combined with the Royal British Legion as a timely fundraiser for the organisation. Musical accompaniment was provided by the Aldbourne Brass Band,

2018 Festival of Commemoration.

war time songs were sung, and a local drama group supplied some simple props. Events of the Great War unfolded in sequence, and many personal stories of sacrifice and heroism involving local people were told, including that of the Belgian refugees who were housed in Swindon. The stories of some of those heroic individuals are dotted throughout this book. In addition, a visit to cast one's eyes over the names on the various war memorials in the church is a highly recommended and moving experience.

Revd. Daphne Hardwick.

These memorials also include the standard of the Burma Star Association, which was given to the church for safekeeping earlier in the decade. The last surviving veteran of the Burma campaign, Stanley Binns, decided to entrust the standard to Christ Church and a moving ceremony took place.

The offices of the Swindon Advertiser in Victoria Road were sold to a property developer in 2018, marking an end to the newspaper's long tenure at the site, after almost 150 years. Plans were proposed for a 13-storey block of flats in its place. Luckily planning consent was not granted, if it had been, Christ Church would have no longer been the highest point in the town.

In marked contrast however, Revd. Canon Simon Stevenette celebrated his 20th anniversary in the ministry at Christ Church. Simon, together his wife Nicola and four boys (soon to be five), had arrived in Swindon in 1998. During his time at Christ Church he had overcome the personal difficulty of not one, but two, life threatening illnesses to throw himself into the challenge of overseeing the transition from the 20th to the 21st Century. Not only had Revd. Canon Stevenette become the fourth longest serving Vicar since the inauguration of Christ Church in 1851 (he would become third longest by 2020), he had become the only Vicar to have served in the role during two different centuries!

Originally proposed in 2016, Revd. Daphne Hardwick's ambitious vision to present a 'promenade play' to the people of Swindon finally

The Journey 2018.

The Journey 2018.

came to fruition in December 2018. It was felt that the real message behind the Christmas story had perhaps become sanitised and lost. The purpose of the production of *'The Journey'* was to make the Christian faith more relevant to the wider community in an inclusive, imaginative and contemporary way, bringing God's presence into the community and not just within the church building. *'The Journey'* was an ambitious attempt to retell the nativity story, via an immersive theatrical production, to those who may not know it, may have forgotten it, or indeed may have thought it irrelevant to them in the 21st century.

The project involved a hefty budget, meticulous planning and extensive fundraising. Grants were obtained and the PCC underwrote the financial risks of the project. Advertising Banners and photographers were arranged and rolling road closures were organised by Daniel Pitt to chaperone the crowd from Avenue Road, Bath Road, Wood Street and Cricklade Street, into Christ Church. A professional theatre company (Quirky Bird Theatre) and a professional producer (Liberty Rock Productions) were appointed. The cast consisted of two principal salaried actors and a remaining cast of volunteers. A combined choir from Christ Church, Immanuel United Reform

Church and Whitbourne Avenue Polish RC Church (led by Tim Eyles and The Revd. Geoff Gleed from Immanuel) provided carols, as the cast and audience halted outside Bath Road Methodist Church, and later within Christ Church. At the finale a rousing performance of the '*Hallelujah Chorus*' from Handel's '*Messiah*' brought the performance to a momentous conclusion.

The Journey, which ran for two performances, garnered enthusiastic support, despite the wet weather, and received positive reviews on BBC Points West, local radio and in the *Swindon Advertiser*.

Swindon and much of southern England suffered under a blanket of snow in early 2019, with many schools being closed, it was business as usual at Christ Church. While Prime Minister Theresa May was forced to present her Brexit 'Plan B' to the House of Commons as relationships frayed within her own party, parliament and Europe, Christ Church took part in the 'Forging Connections' Event. The event aimed to build a partnership between town-wide Christian Organisations and churches to work with each other and share the Gospel, creating pathways for the people of Swindon to find their way into the local church.

By 2019, the seventh successive Beer Festival, attendees were spoiled for choice, with more than 75 different beers and ciders on offer. Chris

An earlier meeting of the Mothers' Union in the old Leisure Centre

Smith, manager of the Christ Church Community Centre and organiser of the Beer Festival, said: *'It's a great fun festival to work. It's tiring. We start setting up on Wednesday and work all the way through to the end. It's about making use of that beautiful church for the community. We want people using that building as much as they can.'*

The 3-day festival in 2019 even included trialling a free pizza-and-pint session on Sunday lunchtime, with an informal service from 12pm, and the chance to listen to Christian singer Ishmael. Backed by Old Town businesses Los Gatos, The Hop, Falvos and Dotty's the festival was a huge success. Sadly, the Coronavirus pandemic meant the enforced cancellation of the 2020 Beer Festival.

While Christ Church volunteers were busy preparing for the Christmas Tree festival and the Christmas Market, the country went to the polls in the general election. The Conservative Party, led by Boris Johnson, achieved a majority of 80 seats. Shortly afterwards MPs voted in favour of the Brexit Withdrawal Agreement, paving the way for the UK's exit from the EU on 31st January 2020.

Another long-lasting partnership that came to an end in December 2019 was the Christ Church Mothers' Union, which decided to disband after having existed for 113 years. The closure was perhaps a sign of the changing times; however, the Union had contributed much to the life of the church since 1906.

Under the stewardship of Christine Senior and Caroline Pitt the popular Christmas Market returned for a 12th consecutive year in 2019. Sadly, thirteen proved to be an unlucky number, as the difficult decision was made to cancel the 2020 Market, due to uncertainty over the ongoing Coronavirus pandemic. Another casualty of the pandemic in 2020 was the Old Town Festival. Support for the ever-growing Festival had become another important part of the Church's outreach programme during the previous decade. Internationally famous pianist Paul Turner gave an annual lunchtime piano recital in Christ Church, at which the Friends sold lunches. In 2019 support for the Old Town Festival went one step further when the Church decided to celebrate Pentecost (and Festival 50) in a very different way - by entering a float in the Carnival procession. Bernard Oxborrow pulling Joan, his wife, in their scooters at the front of a colourful musical float, while many people gathered, young and old, dressed in bright red and waving Pentecostal flags through the streets of Old Town. At the culmination of the parade all the floats were judged, and the Old Town Church's Partnership won the Gold Trophy for the best float. It was the church's first trophy for 50 years! In the afternoon an open-air service was held in the grounds of Holy Rood, accompanied by barking from the adjacent dog show! God's presence was felt by all in Old Town that afternoon in an atmosphere of fun and togetherness.

Unfortunately, the popular event became yet another victim of the global crisis in 2020.

Christmas Tree Festival 2019.

Just before the events of 2020 would begin their stranglehold over proceedings at Christ Church, and indeed all aspects of life, the four churches of Old Town (Christ Church, Bath Road, Immanuel & St Mary's) were able to celebrate 50 years of working together in the longest active Ecumenical Partnership in the UK. The Partnership, which had begun in 1969, had been the brainchild of the three newly appointed Vicars at the time. Derek Palmer (Christ Church with St Mary's), Arthur Bott (Bath Road Methodist Church) and Norman Charlton (Immanuel United Reformed Church), all men of vision, and all ready to embrace change, pressed enthusiastically forward with the Partnership. A series of events was planned to run throughout 2019 to mark the 50th anniversary. A special 'Birthday Service' took place in January 2019 at Bath Road Methodist Church, hosted by Revd. Derek Palmer's son Martin, who as well as appearing regularly on the BBC had been appointed special advisor to the UN on climate change, the environment and the faiths. A golden pledge was signed, to mark 'Festival 50', and a slice of birthday cake shared. After a summer celebration in June and various other events, the celebrations culminated with a Partnership Christmas Tree festival in December. The Christmas Tree Festival was launched with a free guided walk between the churches on the 1st December, and an official opening by the Mayor of Swindon at the evening advent service.

The Festival offered a family friendly introduction to Christmas involving hospitality and a magical Christmas tree experience. Christ Church, St Mary's church in Commonweal Road, Bath Road Methodist Church, and Immanuel Church in Upham road all offered a display of sponsored, decorated trees as well as refreshments and a festive welcome. At Christ Church, the ground surrounding the church was transformed by the installation of more than 20 decorated Christmas trees, each sponsored by a local business or charity. Each day between 5pm – 8pm, refreshments were offered, as well as craft activities, Christmas carols, Christmas films and even a visit from Father Christmas. There was also a free family film screening and a fun treasure trail for the children inside and outside the church.

On 5th January 2020 Revd. Stevenette's father John, now diagnosed with Advanced Alzheimer's, came to live at the Vicarage. He settled in well with the enormous support of the congregation and loving the company of Rupert, the Stevenette family dog. Revd. John Stevenette much enjoys the Vicarage garden and celebrated his 90th birthday on 28th September 2020. The French tricolour was raised in honour of the Stevenettes' Huguenot ancestry. The wheel of vocation in the Stevenette family has now turned full circle with two of John's grandsons, Robert and Will Stevenette, currently exploring vocation to ordination in the Church of England. The Revd. John Stevenette's wise advice to them was to *'hold onto your vocation, God's call on the whole of your life'* and *'above all to stop, look and listen'*.

Fresh from the success of the events of 2019, it was hoped that 2020 would be equally memorable. Sadly, it would prove to be – but for all the wrong reasons. New Prime Minister Boris Johnson declared that *'2020 will be a year to remember.'* The year did indeed become one to remember. Warnings of a mysterious new virus in China, at the start of the year, were largely ignored, despite alerts from the World Health Organisation. Soon cases of the 'Wuhan Virus' reached mainland Europe, then inevitably Britain, and then Swindon. Worry and fear began to grip the population of the town. The importance of the church as a beacon of comfort was probably never more important to the community of Old Town, however traditional ways of welcoming people into the church would now be restricted. The

Resurrection Retreaded and The Crucifixion Recycled, 2020.

ambitious schedule of events for the year was first put on hold, then cancelled, as the number of coronavirus cases escalated in the UK. The government introduced a quarantine (dubbed a 'lockdown') on 23rd March, effectively putting an end to organised events, sport, and church services. The public were forced to stay at home. Swindon Town FC were awarded the Second Division Championship by virtue of being on top of the league at the point at which all fixtures were cancelled.

It would be four long months before worshippers would be cautiously allowed back inside the church. An event unique in the history of Christ Church. Meanwhile widespread cancellations were inevitable, including the Beer Festival, Jazz Festival, Swindon Music Festival, Old Town Festival, organ recitals, weddings and funerals, choir trips and services. Every Easter Day and Mothering Sunday Pam Bridgeman and her Church family group had organised flowers and tea for visitors to the graveyard. The events of 2020 meant this would no longer be possible. Even some planned maintenance on the church clock was delayed.

One imaginative initiative did manage to go ahead, nevertheless. Two unique modern sculptures were created on the green outside of

Christ Church, entitled *'Easter Regeneration 2020: The Crucifixion Recycled'* and *'Resurrection Retreaded'*. The exhibition was the work of Gervin Senior who had constructed a similar Crucifixion Recycled, from tin cans, fifty years previously, for a school project and town-wide exhibition in Didcot. When Revd. Canon Stevenette heard about this, he approached Gervin to ask if he would like to repeat the feat – this time with two pieces. The Old Town Partnership of Churches were becoming four eco–congregations, challenged by the words of Psalm 24, Verse 1, *'The earth is the Lord's, the world and all that is in it'*.

The second piece, the 'Resurrection Retreaded', was to enable the Church to tell the whole Easter story. The Garden Tomb, from which Jesus rose from the dead, was constructed primarily from old karting tyres donated by Gervin's son Alistair (a PHD student at Cambridge, who had preached 12 years earlier, as a 13 year-old at the Christ Church Carol Service). The painstaking work involved in building the sculptures took Gervin 2-3 weeks of hard work. However his endeavours were rewarded as the exhibition provided much joy, and a welcome distraction, during 'lockdown' as visitors were able to inspect the sculptures, from the start of Holy Week on 5th April until the end of Eastertide on 31st May, during their permitted daily hour of exercise.

A second uplifting initiative during the protracted period of lockdown was the raising of a flag to support the NHS. Simon Stevenette suggested the idea to Brian and Karen Harris (Brian Harris is a bellringer and Karen Harris was verger for many years. Their large collection of international flags is often borrowed by the church to make wedding couples or funeral parties from overseas feel especially welcome, or to mark special occasions. Karen carefully cut out and sewed pieces of white and blue fabric to both sides of the Church's Rainbow Flag. Once complete, the augmented flag was proudly flown during the Thursday evening 'clapping for carers' event that took place during the period of lockdown. These two morale boosting initiatives were probably unique among churches in the country.

As a footnote, the NHS flag was subsequently replaced with the Swindon Town Football Club flag, to mark the club's promotion to League One of the Football League! A sight that pleased Revd. Canon Stevenette enormously! With the Christ Church flagpole restored to its full height, by Daniel Pitt and Mike Palmer, visitors can truly appreciate the full and colourful range of flags on display. It is always worth glancing skywards the next time you pass by Christ Church. For example, you would not normally expect to see the Ethiopian flag flying proudly above the Swindon skyline. However, that was exactly the case on Sunday 27th September, when the flag was raised for the Church's Mission Giving Day, in support of the Send a Cow charity.

Church of England Covid-19 Guidelines were issued.

More than 42,000 people would die from the virus in the UK, with more than 100 of them in Swindon by the end of 2020. The crisis affected every person in the country, perhaps like no event before or since. The doors of the church were locked. Revd. Canon Simon Stevenette and his staff were now only able to communicate via social media, telephone and internet. The crisis proved a challenge for all; however, a new strength and determination was found, enabling everyone in Christ Church and Old Town to emerge with a sense of community spirit perhaps not seen since the Blitz.

Finally, in July, as cases of the virus appeared to ease, the country began the long and careful process of tentatively emerging, blinking in the sunshine, from their enforced quarantine. The doors of Christ Church were permitted to open once again; but only to limited numbers and with special social distancing measures in place. New policies, procedures and risk assessments would be needed, and would become a commonplace precursor to the planning of any event or function. Choirs and the singing of hymns was not permitted, although this restriction was eased in September for choirs. The congregation were seated in alternate rows of pews.

Numbers attending services gradually rose, although communion could not take place in its usual form and the wearing of masks was

2020 VJ Day

made compulsory in indoor spaces. The Parish office also remained closed. The Coronavirus crisis saw many thousands infected or killed and life changed, probably for ever, and certainly for the foreseeable future. Yet the spirit of those within Christ Church remained undimmed and the determination for life to return to normal (or as the newspapers would dub it *'the new normal'*) remained undaunted. Despite continuing infections, pupils returned to school and it felt as if life was slowly returning to its pre-virus days. However, outdoors became the safer option and indoor numbers remained subject to limitations, and the dreaded new phrase *'social distancing'*. New guidelines and policies were issued by every Diocese in the country to their parish churches. Despite the obvious restrictions, some services and events could, at last, take place. The Cumbria Clock Company were, at last, able to complete the reinstallation of the church clock as soon as the travel restrictions were lifted.

Daniel Pitt represented the Old Town Partnership of Churches at a celebration on 15th August 2020 to mark the 75th anniversary of VJ day, the end of the Second World War in the Far East. The celebration was hosted by South Swindon Parish Council in the Rose Garden in Queen's Park. Attending were the Chair of the South Swindon Parish Council, Councillor Chris Watts, other Parish Councillors and officials, the Mayor of Swindon, Councillor Garry Perkins, Deputy Lord Lieutenant Shirley Ludford, together with around 100 invited guests representing a cross section of Swindon communities. Speeches emphasized the importance of community and the need to remember those who suffered for our freedom. The Mayor and Chair unveiled the memorial, a sculpture by Mike Pringle, which represented a civilian rather than a military theme. Behind the memorial, adjacent to the lake, is a new mural featuring the words of the song *'We'll Meet Again'.*

Although the legacy of the Coronavirus pandemic remains, there is much to be positive about for Christ Church and its place in the hearts of Swindonians. The outlook of the church in the new millennium had been a much broader one. Although the turn of the century had brought with it the imperative need to restore, re-order and renovate the fabric of the buildings, the work of the church reached out as never before into the community of Old Town. Revd. Canon Simon Stevenette's ambitious vision of the church as a beacon for the people of Swindon had been achieved as Christ Church prepared for its 170th anniversary in 2021. Innovative and imaginative outreach projects had been undertaken. The new flexibility of the Community Centre and the re-ordering of the church seating now allows for exciting and imaginative events to be held, bringing many people into the church for the first time, and renewing an old acquaintance for many others.

There was a tangible feeling that the members of 'The Old Lady on the Hill' had grown, matured and developed as a worshipping community since the dawn of the new century. Thanks to the tireless efforts of the clergy, staff, friends and congregation, and the outreach programme envisaged by Revd. Canon Simon Stevenette and Brian Bridgeman (the author of *The Old Lady on the Hill*, on which this book is based) the message, heartbeat and vision of Christ Church has never been stronger. The development of the church community as an asset, there to support and enrich the lives of the people of Swindon, can be aptly summed up in a quote from Revd. Canon Simon Stevenette, who (while nominating the Building Project Team in 2018) noted that everyone at Christ Church has worked *'tirelessly in a voluntary capacity living out their Christian faith in a variety of practical ways.'*

Christ Church is also justifiably proud to be known as a church for all nations. The Church has been hugely blessed to have been joined by new members from across the world. All of whom have become valued members of the Christ Church family. Steve and Milly Dumba, who fled Uganda under Idi Amin and settled in Swindon to raise their family, have become valued members of the congregation, along with the Shinde family, Nitin and Nikita, who came from Mumbai in 2002 and settled in with their 2 sons Steven and Shalom, mother Manda, Father Madam (a retired priest) and their relatives the Patole family. Christ Church has benefited hugely from their Christian spirituality and warm hospitality. The influx of cricketing talent has also help support the Church's sterling efforts in the inter church's 6-a- side tournament at Sevenhampton, helping to revive the great sporting tradition discussed in chapter 10.

The physical and spiritual challenges of the 21st century have been met head on, and everyone had played their part in helping to cement Christ Church's place, not only at the very heart of Old Town life, but as both a spiritual and physical beacon shining Christ's love and light over the whole community of Swindon.

'What does the church have to offer? I believe that at its best we can be like bridge-builders. I passionately believe Jesus loves every-body and is out and about. Our purpose as a church is connecting the community with Christ, and that's not just done with words but with actions. Together we are Swindonians.'

Revd. Canon Simon Stevenette, April 2014

9

The Musical Life of the Church

Christ Church Organ

The organ at Holy Rood is briefly described in William Morris' book where we learn it stood in the middle of the little western gallery, leaving a space on either side where the vocalists and instrumentalists took their places. It was of small dimensions and very little tone. No doubt with the building of a new church the provision of a fine new organ was discussed and planned whilst early building works progressed.

Christ Church employed Messrs. Gray and Davison to build a new organ for the new church. There is no record of the original cost, but the firm had an excellent reputation at that time and the instrument they built was in all likelihood superior to many organs of that period. It was undoubtedly a coup for such a prestigious company to agree to construct the new organ for Christ Church. Gray and Davison would continue in business for many years until eventually being wound up in 1975. The Great Organ in particular had a magnificent range of stops. Shortly before building the Christ Church instrument the same firm built an organ for the Great Exhibition of 1851, held at the Crystal Palace in Hyde Park, London. This organ has now been restored to its original condition and moved to St. Anne, Limehouse, London. It provides the closest surviving approximation to how the Christ Church organ would have sounded at its installation in 1851.

It is hard now to imagine the impact that The Great Exhibition had on the people of Victorian Britain. The purpose-built Crystal Palace was one of the largest structures yet built by man and contained more glass than any other building in the world. The exhibition was carefully designed to display the best of British innovation and to showcase the glories of the British Empire.

In 1851 the Christ Church organ was located where the present instrument stands, on the north side of the chancel, facing west down the north aisle. The organist sat in the north transept and had before him two manuals (keyboards) and a pedal board controlling the pipes by direct mechanical action. The air for the pipes would have been pumped by hand through bellows, by a member of the congregation, or perhaps a young chorister. The original specification is shown at the end of this chapter. There are by necessity some technical terms in the following pages: an explanation of these for the interested but puzzled reader may be found in a musical dictionary such as *The Oxford Companion to Music*, visiting an organ manufacturer's website, or by enquiry of the present Director of Music at Christ Church.

Gray and Davison were renowned for the quality of the sound of their organs, and although one can only speculate, the sound of the full organ as heard in the new church at the opening services with a congregation of 950 must have been thrilling. The hushed expectation of that moment was beautifully captured by the *Devizes and Wiltshire Gazette*:

'*A hushed heart-generated stillness pervaded the place; till at length the magnificent organ rolled its thunder of harmonious sound through the arched roof of the building, and the pent feelings of the congregation burst forth with a glow of religious exultation – Oh God of Hosts, the mighty Lord,*
How lovely is the place
Where Thou, enthroned in glory, shew'st
The brightness of Thy face.'

However, there has been a tendency in England, far more than in continental Europe, for churches and organists to add stops and generally to meddle with the work of the original builder. Christ Church has been no exception and no doubt well-intentioned changes and additions to the instrument throughout its life have not always had musical merit. Although it is not known if Mr T.B. Richardson (a Professor of Music and the first organist at the church) undertook any changes. Mr Richardson stayed at the church until he moved to a parish in Preston, Lancashire in May 1858.

In 1866 the bellows were repaired, and the instrument tuned

and cleaned throughout. This fairly extensive piece of work cost just £18, money well spent at the time. In 1880 a 16' Bourdon pedal stop was added, together with Celestes to the Swell Organ. The whole instrument was at this time turned around to face the chancel, probably as part of a movement throughout the country in the late 19th century to install surpliced choirs. The organist now sat in the chancel behind the choir. Unfortunately, an effect of this was to hide the pipes of the Great Organ behind heavy masonry, so reducing the sound. Church records show the cost of this work to have been £245 (approximately £30,000 today).

In 1899 a series of seven organ recitals were held in the church, with Mr H.J. Davis as organist and the well known singer Miss Gertrude Crewe as soprano.

A second Open Diapason was placed on the Great Organ in 1908 and though it was a fine specimen of its type it unfortunately swamped the rest of the Great, reducing the clarity of the upper voices. Together with other changes and thorough cleaning the cost amounted to £354 (approximately £42,000 today). Also, during the Edwardian era, a Clarinet stop was donated to the church and replaced the original Mixture stop thus depriving the Great Organ of any brilliance remaining from the 1851 instrument. An electric blower to power the bellows was added in 1931. However, there were indications that additional investment would be soon be needed. The war years meant, of course, that there was little money, or interest, in undertaking a lengthy refurbishment, but by 1948, the organ was showing unmistakable signs that a thorough overhaul was required. To mark the approaching 100th anniversary of the consecration of the church in 1951, the Parish decided to raise funds to entirely rebuild and enlarge the organ. The Centenary Souvenir Booklet and Parish Magazines of the time record the high hopes of the church community in providing this fitting 'birthday present' for the church.

The contract was placed with Gray and Davison, the same firm who built the original instrument a century before. However, by this time the firm had lost its enviable reputation gained in the 19th century, and the work, despite costing nearly £3,000 (more than £90,000 today) was not of the hoped-for quality. Instead of accurately diagnosing the problem and correcting it, the builders used the available money to provide a third manual (the Choir Organ). Apart from removing two stops from the Great, the Great and Swell organs were left almost as before. The Great remained facing the chancel and the box for the added Choir Organ was placed in the vacant space in the transept arch, effectively blocking much of the sound which came from this aperture. The rebuild was generally unsatisfactory and there was constant trouble from the tubular-pneumatic action which was immediately outdated and susceptible to the slightest change in weather. The large congregations of the 1950's and 1960's had no choice but to accept an instrument that lacked power at full organ and suffered frequently from stuck notes. The organist contended with stops that refused to go in or come out and winced at dumb notes and others that ran into one another. Gordon Crabbe remembered it as an *'awful thing to play'* and felt that the Centenary rebuild was, unfortunately, doomed from the beginning.

In 1964 the maintenance and tuning contract was transferred to Messrs. Percy Daniel & Co. of Clevedon and planning started soon after for a further rebuild of the organ to be undertaken as soon as possible. The perennial problem was funding. Happily, a generous bequest from Arthur Button (a former tenor in the choir) in 1970 made it possible for Percy Daniel & Co. to undertake a high quality rebuild of the organ. Percy Daniel & Co. survive to this day, as part of Clevedon Organs. This time the scheme was drawn up in consultation with both the organist, Gordon Crabbe and Graham Hooper the organ consultant. Funds would not permit retaining the three-manual arrangement, but Gordon Crabbe realised it would be preferable to revert to the two-manual arrangement and use the money available to include as many registration aids as possible and recreate, instead, an excellent two-manual instrument.

The Mixture was restored to the Great Organ, adding some brilliance of tone, while on the Swell the addition of a new Sifflöte 1' stop brightened this manual considerably. The old Sesquialtera became a 3-rank Mixture on the Swell Organ and the Cornopean was extended as a 16' Fagotto, which is also very useful on the Pedal.

The Pedal Organ was greatly improved from 4 to 10 stops including Bass Flute, Octave Flute and 4' Clarion. Although three of the four ranks of pipes available to the Pedal are extension ranks, it still makes for a very firm foundation tone to the whole organ, and reduces the shortcomings of having only two manuals.

The 1970 rebuild returned the rows of pipes to a north-south axis, as they had been in the original instrument, allowing them to sing out down the north aisle and into the body of the church once more. The pedal pipes now speak into the chancel, but as lower frequency sound carries better, the effect is satisfactory. Whilst the lack of a third manual is sometimes limiting, the provision of six adjustable combination pistons to each division (Great, Swell and Pedal), meant that the majority of the organ repertoire was possible. The specification of the organ after the Percy Daniel rebuild is also shown at the end of this chapter.

The work took some five months to complete at a cost of £6,000 and the organ was re-dedicated at a special service on 31st October 1970.

In 1995 Gordon Crabbe retired as organist after 40 years-service to Christ Church, 50 years including his time at St Mary's. He was succeeded by Tim Eyles, who had himself been a member of the choir since 1993. A full list of the Organists at Christ Church can be found in Appendix B.

Following the 1970 rebuild the instrument proved remarkably reliable, giving 28 years of intensive use with only annual tuning and maintenance being required. In 1998, however, the organ started ciphering regularly; that is, notes would continue to sound after the key was released. Meakin Organs were contracted to complete a thorough overhaul, repairing the electro-pneumatic action and at the same time revoicing and remodelling the Mixtures.

The organ console, following the 1970 rebuild.

The work was completed just in time for Revd. Simon Stevenette's induction service in October 1998.

In 2013, the thumb pistons (which control a selection of pre-set stops) started to become increasingly unreliable. There was still some money available in the Button Fund and this was used to install a computer-controlled capture system, giving two extra pistons on each Division and eight general pistons. A system of 96 general channels, with a stepper and 16 divisional channels, gave unprecedented control over the stops on the organ. At this time the drawstop solenoids were replaced, giving a more reliable action when stops were drawn using the pistons. New LED lighting was also provided at the console.

In 2014 a generous donation in memory of Bill Ruck was given by his daughter Angela, a soprano in the choir, and son Nigel. The Director of Music, Tim Eyles, decided to use the money to add a 4 foot flute stop on the Swell division. The firm JW Walker procured and installed a brand new metal Open Flute from the Dutch pipe makers, Stinkens. This stop has proved a highly valuable addition to the organ in quieter music.

In 2018 the replacing of all the slates on the church roof was planned. As a consequence of the inevitable dust that this would create, the opportunity was taken to undertake a major cleaning and overhaul of the organ. This was only made possible by two generous legacies from basses in the choir: Peter Ford and John Sondermann. The Friends of Christ Church were also beneficiaries of these legacies and so some £80,000 was made available for the work on the organ. The Diocesan Organ Adviser, Dr John Henderson, visited the organ prior to the start of this work and said he had never seen an organ so dirty inside!

Quotes were obtained from Clevedon Organs and from JW Walker with the contract being awarded to the latter. The work comprised:

> Removal of all pipe work (except the largest pedal pipes) to be thoroughly cleaned and, where necessary, repaired.

> A new microprocessor transmission system to key and coupler actions.

Releathering of wind reservoirs.

New low voltage wiring to the console.

A new Great soundboard.

Removal of the Dulciana unit.

Addition of a new Viola da Gamba and a new Tierce to the Great division.

Addition of a tremulant to the Great division.

Making the 16' pedal Bourdon playable on the Great with the addition of two new pipes.

Remodelling of the old 1' Sifflöte to become a Larigot with the addition of seven new pipes.

Revoicing of the Swell Oboe to make it far louder.

Repair of the Swell tremulant, which had never worked properly.

The organ was not playable from July 2018 until April 2019, with the exception of a couple of weeks around Christmas, when the unaltered Swell division was made playable. The ten months without the organ was made more bearable by the loan from JW Walker of a 1970s 'extension' chamber organ. This meant that, although it had only two ranks of pipes, it comprised six stops and their sound was loud enough to lead the congregation in hymns. The completion of the work on the main organ was marked by a hugely successful recital on 18th May 2019 by David Halls, Director of Music at Salisbury Cathedral, which also featured the combined choirs of Christ Church and Immanuel singing *'Zadok the Priest'* and *Parry's 'I was Glad'*.

The organ now sounds better than it has for over 100 years, with a power, clarity, and brightness that it has not possessed in living memory. This is also partially due to the improved acoustics resulting from the wooden floor which replaced the carpet during the recent remodelling of the church interior. The organ is now in fine condition and should not require any major attention for several decades. The coronavirus pandemic of 2020 temporarily silenced the Church organ, however once admission to the building was permitted again, Tim Eyles planned a series of socially distanced half-hour organ recitals on Friday lunchtimes.

Whatever comes to pass, the sound of the Organ, synonymous to many with the life of the Parish Church in Swindon as elsewhere, will continue to be heard.

Specification of the Church Organ

The author is indebted to the excellent booklet published in 1970, by the late Gordon Crabbe, describing the history of the Christ Church Organ to that date. The technical specification below is taken from that publication.

Specification of the Christ Church Organ, as built in 1851

GREAT ORGAN		SWELL ORGAN	
Open Diapason	8	Bourdon	16
Stopped Diapason	8	Open Diapason	8
Clarinet Flute	8	Stopped Diapason	8
Dulciana	8	Principal	4
Principal	4	Fifteenth	2
Flute	4	Cornopean	8
Twelfth	2 2/3	Oboe	8
Fifteenth	2		
Flageolet	2		
Sesquialtera	III		
Mixture	II	PEDAL ORGAN	
Trumpet	8	Grand Open Wood	16
COUPLERS		ACCESSORIES	

Swell to Great		4 composition pedals to Great	
Great to Pedal		2 composition pedals to Swell	
Swell to Pedal		Foot pedal to Great to Pedal	
		Trigger Swell pedal	

The lowest octave on the Swell had no pipes of its own; but borrowed from the Great. The Manuals were of 54 notes, CC to F and the Pedals of 27 notes, CCC to D.

Specification of the Christ Church Organ after the Percy Daniel rebuild of 1970

GREAT ORGAN		SWELL ORGAN	
Open Diapason	8	Open Diapason	8
Stopped Diapason	8	Stopped Diapason	8
Dulciana	8	Salicional	8
Principal	4	Vox Angelica	8
Flute	4	Gemshorn	4
Twelfth	2 2/3	Fifteenth	2
Fifteenth	2	Sifflote	1
Tierce	1 3/5	Mixture (26-29-33)	III
Larigot	1 1/3	Fagotto	16
Mixture (19-22-26)	III	Cornopean	8
Trumpet	8	Oboe	8
Clarinet	8	Tremulant	
PEDAL ORGAN		COUPLERS	
Open Diapason	16	Great to Pedal	
Bourdon	16	Swell to Pedal	
Quint	10 2/3	Swell to Great	

Principal	8	Swell Octave	
Bass Flute	8	Swell Sub-Octave	
Fifteenth	4	Swell Unison Off	
Octave Flute	4		
Twenty-second	2		
Fagotto	16		
Clarion	4		
ACCESSORIES			
6 pistons to Swell – adjustable			
6 pistons to Great – adjustable			
6 pistons to Pedal – adjustable			
Swell to Great pistons			
Great to Pedal pistons			
Swell cancel pistons			

The Manuals are of 56 notes, CC to G and the Pedals of 30 notes, CCC to F. There is a Balanced Swell Pedal and the organ is of Electropneumatic action.

Specification of the Christ Church organ after the JW Walker overhaul of 2019

GREAT ORGAN		SWELL ORGAN	
Bourdon	16	Open Diapason	8
Open Diapason	8	Stopped Diapason	8
Stopped Diapason	8	Salicional	8
Viola da Gamba	8	Vox Angelica	8
Principal	4	Gemshorn	4

Flute	4	Open Flute	4
Twelfth	2 2/3	Fifteenth	2
Fifteenth	2	Larigot	1 1/3
Tierce	1 3/5	Mixture (22-26-29)	III
Mixture (15-19-22)	III	Fagotto	16
Trumpet	8	Cornopean	8
Clarinet	8	Oboe	8
Tremulant (toe piston)		Tremulant (toe piston)	
PEDAL ORGAN		COUPLERS	
Open Diapason	16	Great to Pedal	
Bourdon	16	Swell to Pedal	
Quint	10 2/3	Swell to Great	
Principal	8	Swell Octave	
Bass Flute	8	Swell Sub-Octave	
Fifteenth	4	Swell Unison Off	
Octave Flute	4	Great and Pedal combinations coupled	
Twenty-second	2	Generals on Swell Toes	
Fagotto	16		
Clarion	4		
ACCESSORIES			
8 pistons to Swell		8 General pistons	
8 pistons to Great		Swell to Pedal thumb piston	
8 pistons to Pedal		Next and Previous thumb pistons	
Swell to Great pistons		Next toe Piston	
Great to Pedal pistons		96 General channels	

General cancel thumb piston		16 Divisional channels	

Christ Church Choir

Whilst little was known of the composition of the choir during the 19th century, at the time of the original publication of *The Old Lady on the Hill*, we are now able to add some information and, more importantly, some names to the story. We do know that Henry Bizley joined the choir at the age of 9 or 10, in 1854, and remained a chorister for the rest of his life, until passing away in 1923. A memorial plaque was erected in the church by his children, following his death. It may be assumed that a body of parishioners continued, as at Holy Rood, to lead the singing of services. Around 1886 Henry Armstrong Hall introduced a surpliced choir to Christ Church, reflecting a general trend in the Anglican Church at that time. This was initially opposed within the parish, but the tradition has continued ever since.

During June 1891, under choirmaster Mr W.D. James, the Christ Church choir were asked to sing in the 'Festival of the Choirs' at St Mark's Church in Swindon. The choir proudly took their place among the seven other choirs present, and were able to show the improvements made since the arrival of W.D. James. The following year his expertise was recognized by Revd. Goddard, who said *'we should congratulate ourselves on having such a good choir and choirmaster'*.

No doubt, due to the abilities of W.D. James, a strong choir of men and boys existed, from the 1890s and into the Edwardian era. The choirboys also formed a cricket team, playing sides from other local churches. (see chapter 10). A surviving scorecard from this era does provide us with the names of 11 members of the boys' choir from 1892, which might otherwise have been forgotten.

Unfortunately, very few records of the choir remain until the second half of the century.

Gordon Crabbe took over as organist and choirmaster in 1956. His predecessor Vivian May handed over a choir some 48 strong, including women and boys, but no girls at this time. Gordon remembers that the altos had to sit on chairs near the altar and there were twelve seats in front of the choir stalls to accommodate the whole choir. However, quantity is not always an indicator of quality. It is probably true to say that the choir of the 1950's was less ambitious in its choice of music and the quality of singing now is far higher than it was seventy years ago. Anthems were not a priority and, in truth were not encouraged by the incumbents of the time. More ambitious arrangements were sung at the main festivals, but not on a regular basis. Gordon Crabbe cites an occasion of a mayoral visit at which the choir was to sing *'Lead me Lord'* by Samuel Wesley, a beautiful but simple anthem, and he was very worried as to how well it would go.

Any choirboy joining the choir in the 1950s had to endure a special form of initiation ritual. The ceremony was held outside the rear of vestry and consisted of the new choirboy standing at the foot of the lower flight of stone steps, whilst a senior choirboy stood on the stone landing at the top of steps.

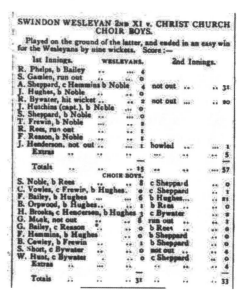

Cricket Scorecard 1892.

Christ Church Choir 1915. Revd. Charles Mayall seated centre.

The Christ Church choir in 1956. The organist and choirmaster, Gordon Crabbe, is standing at the back on the left (unsurpliced). Back row: Gordon Crabbe, J. Maunders, S. Hedges, (?), C. Morgan, Mrs Herbert White, fourth row: T. Key, Mrs Brown, Mrs Whitfield, Mrs Marsh, Mrs Herbert, (?), Mrs Taylor, J. Stevens, H. Hobbs, R. Dunstan, third row: B. Morgan, B. Cole, R. Foord, M. Tanner, M. Drinkwater, A Herbert Ferrier, (?), Miss Hughes, Mrs Jarvis, Miss Young, Mrs Hayward, N. Humphries, P, Edwards, D. Goodridge, second row: D. Hobbs, M. Williams, Glyn Calder, A. Hayward, J. Holland, P. Little, B. Wood, J. Stratford Front Row: M. Cook, S Foster-Ferrier, B. Stratford, Master Holland

He would then lean over the stone wall and tip a jug full of cold water over the incoming choirboy's head. This rite of passage was considered 'character building' and was done with the full knowledge of Gordon Crabbe and the Vicar!

There were perks for choirboys during that period too. If chosen to sing at a wedding, each boy would receive 2 shilling and Sixpence from Mrs Jones the Verger, as payment. Handsome reward indeed!

Although the choir sang Evensong at Bristol Cathedral for the first time in the 1960's it was not a great success though much was learnt from the experience. The annual Diocesan Festival was a great help and the choir always enjoyed singing with other choirs under the cathedral organist. When Canon Jackson took over as Vicar in 1964 he was keen for the choir to sing an anthem every week and this led to the realisation that higher standards and a larger repertoire were possible and indeed desirable.

Christ Church Choir 1960s. Gordon Crabbe in the centre.

Charles Vince joined the choir as a youth in 1962 and shared his memories especially for this publication:

'I can recall going on the annual choir outings to Portsmouth or Weymouth. From Portsmouth it was possible to watch the, then, new Hovercraft travelling between Portsmouth and the Isle of Wight. These carried passengers only, as the car carrying ones were developed later. The choir outings carried on as I remember well into the 1970's.

Other things that I remember. It was always the custom on Whit Sunday to process to Holy Rood on the Lawns from Christ Church, as a robed choir. We walked in the road as the traffic was stopped by the police for that occasion. It was always hoped of course that the weather would be fine, if not the service was held in Christ Church.

At Harvest Festival the church was always fully decorated with a lot of apples along the top of the screens by the altar. They were removed on a Monday and as choirboys we fought over the two buckets of apples to see who could carry the most home and to see how many we could get in our pockets.

The choirboys party was an annual event in the old Church

Hall. After tea it was time to play some games and watch some cartoons or other short films shown by a man who used to come every year and set up film projecting equipment in the hall.

At one time St Andrew's church in Walcot was part of the parish of Christ Church. They separated from Christ Church some years ago. We did have a procession down to there with cross and robed choir. I honestly cannot remember what the purpose of this procession was, as it took place I think before 1967. In my early days, the two main services that we were required to sing at were the 11am Matins and 6.30pm Evensong. (The 9.30am service was always sung by the now defunct Church of England Mens' Society). Before the 6.30pm service began, the choir always sung one verse (unaccompanied) of the hymn 'We Love Thy Place O God' in the vestry before we entered church for the service. With the vestry door open, this could be heard by the assembled congregation.

On one Monday night during the year a fair was held in the High Street so it was completely shut, (something you could not do today with the volume of traffic). As choirboys we used to visit this fair after our choir practice, which was always on a Monday night between 6.30pm and 7.30pm. There was a lawn outside the church where the Vicar's vestry is now. As choirboys we used to play on this lawn in the summer until the start of choir practice. The vestry was dedicated in 1967 by Archdeacon Bowles.' (Cyril Bowles was Archdeacon of Swindon during the 1960s, before becoming Bishop of Derby from 1969 – 1988. He passed away in 1999).

The standards achieved by the choir gradually rose until by 1975 they were able to sing evensong at Bristol Cathedral with much greater assurance. Singing in cathedrals undoubtedly gives a tremendous boost to any choir and Gordon had long held the ambition for Christ Church to sing a service in Salisbury Cathedral. By persisting in writing to Canon Moxon, the precentor there, he and the choir were finally offered the chance to sing all services for a week during August 1976. This was really quite a tall order, but with a lot of hard work and some assistance from experienced singers in other Swindon churches, the week proved a success and was the spur to raising standards ever higher.

There is no doubt that Gordon Crabbe was a perfectionist, and Christ Church had a choir of a very high standard between 1976 and 1986. The association with Salisbury was maintained for 10 years, singing a week of services each year. During this period the Choir also sang services at the Cathedrals in Bristol, Gloucester and Wells, as well as Magdalen College, Oxford. They were accompanied on the organ on these occasions by such distinguished organists as Geoffrey Morgan (now the Organist at Christchurch Priory), Ian Crabbe (retired head of keyboard studies at Marlborough College) and Clifton Graham. Whilst the latter was and is a superb organist, even the best of us can make mistakes under pressure. At the beginning of one service at Bristol Cathedral, Clifton Graham was looking over the rail at proceedings in the chancel when he suddenly realised he had to give a note for the choir to sing the introit. Gordon recounts that it was *'Nolo Mortem Pecatoris'* which starts on an E. Clifton gave a G instead and Gordon realised something was amiss as soon as the choir started singing. He knew there were some top Gs for the tenors and was dreading hearing them trying to reach a top B flat as a consequence of the higher key. However, they managed to achieve it, and no one in the congregation was any the wiser!

After 1986 numbers dwindled gradually until in 1993 there were about a dozen adults, with half a dozen girls.

Gordon retired at the end of 1995, after leading the choir as organist & choirmaster for 40 years. In January 1996 Canon Barraclough asked Tim Eyles if he would take on the position of organist and asked Mike Enright, one of the basses in the choir, if he would become choirmaster. They both agreed, although it was the first time either had undertaken such a role. The choir had become gradually smaller in Gordon's later years, but several new members joined, encouraged by Mike's relaxed attitude to attendance at practices and services. Mike stated that he had no ambition to create a choir capable of singing in cathedral services, but he wanted a good, friendly, competent parish church choir. Training, conducting and leading a choir, especially one containing children is an extremely difficult thing to do well; and Mike did an excellent job considering his lack of conducting experience. He soon found that taking junior choir practices was very demanding and felt that with numbers so low it was not a viable proposition to continue with a junior choir. Mike Enright has a wonderful voice and much experience of choral singing at the highest level with the BBC Symphony Chorus; but found the pressures of being a choirmaster combined with health problems too much to manage and resigned at Easter 1998.

Two members of the choir. 1970s.

Tim Eyles then took over as choirmaster as well as organist and discovered what a difficult job it can be. In his words, *'there has been a gradual learning curve, developing conducting technique, knowledge of vocal technique, running rehearsals efficiently and enjoyably, selecting appropriate anthems, recruiting and motivating junior members of the choir, training the choir in processing, arranging carol singing at hospitals and hotels. The art of delegation is also crucial, and members of the choir contribute most welcome administrative and organisational support'.*

In 1999, with the assistance and enthusiasm of the Hon. Curate, Revd. Judy Ashby, a music group was created at Christ Church for the first time in living memory and probably for the first time ever. Several members of the robed choir join with this group to sing for services three times a month. Instruments include electronic piano, violins, guitars, bass guitar, African drum, flutes, clarinet, and oboe. Great efforts have been made to avoid an 'us and them' attitude between the music group and the choir, and overall there is remarkable tolerance and acceptance of the two styles of worship that each represents. In fact the musical styles overlap considerably with the use of Iona and Taizé music by the robed choir. A considerable boost to the robed choir at Christmas was provided, by members of the music group, for the Lessons and Carols service.

Over the past twenty years since becoming choirmaster Tim has, with the support of the clergy, been able to raise the standard and widen the repertoire of the choir, to the extent that they are able to sing cathedral-style full choral evensongs about four times a year. There have been numerous visits to sing choral evensong at cathedrals since 2000: Bristol, Salisbury, Wells, Oxford, Gloucester, Hereford, Worcester, Winchester and Llandaff, plus Bath and Tewkesbury Abbeys.

In November 1998, with the help of Simon Stevenette the new vicar, the junior choir was restarted. This continued until 2009.

The choir has recorded three CDs, entitled Skyline Sounds, containing a mixture of choral music, organ music and bells. The church's "Skyline Appeal" for funds to repair the tower and spire provided the impetus to record the first CD. Released in 2004, 2008 and 2012 these proved very popular.

Various new choral works have been commissioned by Tim Eyles for Christ Church choir: from Robert Jones a set of Preces and Responses; an introit sung at Hereford Cathedral to words by Thomas Treherne, and a setting of the evening canticles. David Bednall contributed a setting of the Jubilate for choir organ and viola which appeared on the Skyline Sounds 3 CD; and a setting of *See amid the winter's snow* by Chris Totney, for choir, organ and glockenspiel, which was performed at the Lessons and Carols service in 2016.

The choir sang carols at the De Vere Hotel, in West Swindon, for many years and continues to sing carols around the wards at the Great Western Hospital. They have also made annual appearances to sing carols at the Christmas market, held at Christ Church each November.

Choir numbers have fluctuated over the years, however 2019 saw the arrival of several new members. The Covid-19 lockdown of 2020 completely closed the church, of course. One of the final events being a Handel Messiah Come and Sing Workshop held by the Swindon Choral Society in February. Although the choir was unable to sing together during the pandemic, a sense of unity and togetherness was maintained using internet video conferencing for a weekly chat or quiz.

10

Christ Church: The Golden Era of Sport

During the early years of the twentieth century England experienced a golden era of sport. There was much public affection for football, cricket and many other pastimes. The sports stars of that era were idolized as TV and media stars are today. In a time before smart phones, social media and television, a huge percentage of the population watched, or took part, in a variety of sporting activities.

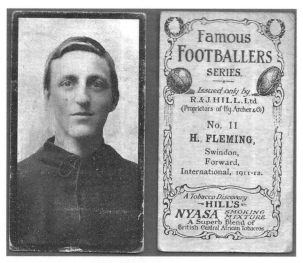

Harold Fleming.

Parishioners at Christ Church were no different and the church itself was a willing participant. During the Edwardian era, and into the 1920s and '30s, it was not unusual to see thronging crowds crammed into local parks, eager to watch a football or cricket match. Swindon Town Football Club experienced a golden period too, reaching the semi-final of the FA Cup twice in three years early in the decade whilst playing in the Southern League. The team included perhaps the most famous footballer to play for Swindon Town, Harold Fleming. He was 'capped' by England in eleven internationals in which he scored nine goals. He played for Swindon from 1907-24. Fleming was a deeply religious man and would not play on Good Friday or Christmas Day, a virtue which was recognised by Revd. Mayall during a sermon at Christ Church (see below).

Christ Church's close ties with the sporting life of the town began in 1879 with the appointment of William Baker Pitt as Curate. Pitt had been born in Exeter in 1856. His father, Thomas, was a grocer of some standing in his local community and it had been hoped William would follow his father's footsteps. However, William chose to become an Anglican clergyman, rather than a grocer and attended the London College of Divinity. In 1879, after being ordained as a Deacon, he accepted the position at Christ Church. Lodgings in the town were arranged for him at 38 Bellevue Road by Frederick Osman, a grocer and business associate of his father. Pitt settled into his new parish, quickly establishing a working relationship with Revd. Baily. He became a very popular figure in Old Town, especially amongst younger members of the church, through his involvement with the YMCA.

Early in his Curacy, Pitt was recorded as being the captain of Swindon Association Football Club in their first recorded match on

Early Swindon team. William PItt is centre holding the ball.

29th November 1879 against Rovers F.C. Pitt had formed the Swindon club to provide recreation for the young men of the Parish. It was common for the church in England to be involved in the creation of many of the football clubs founded during this period, with 'Muscular Christianity' being the vogue. Muscular Christianity was a popular philosophical movement that originated in England in the mid-19th century, characterised by a belief in patriotic duty, discipline, self-sacrifice, manliness, and the moral and physical beauty of athleticism.

Pitt's involvement in the foundation of Swindon Town Football Club was recorded in a speech given later, in September 1911 –

> *'Pitt thought he might venture to say that he was the father of the Swindon Football Club. It was in the autumn of 1879 that some young fellows belonging to the Swindon factory* (Great Western Railway) *met with him in the King William Street school to organise a club. They decided to call it the Swindon Association Football Club, but they found the name rather a mouthful to shout out, so they, later, changed the name to the Spartans. They played the first game on a field not far away, it being kindly lent by Mr Hooper Deacon, who was always a friend of sport.'*

King William Street School (as mentioned above) is detailed in the chapter 'The Church Schools'. Pitt was still a member of the Spartans F.C. team when they played St. Mark's Young Men's Friendly Society on 12th November 1881. The two teams merged under the name Swindon Town Football Club shortly after this match and for many years this date of 1881 was assumed to be the officially recognised formation date of the club. However, when the above speech was unearthed, together with the discovery of archived newspaper reports of matches from 1879, the earlier date became adopted as the original, and accurate, formation date of the club.

in a ceremony at Christ Church in 1882 Pitt married Alice Mary Kinneir (Alice was the daughter of Churchwarden Henry Kinneir). The wedding was huge social occasion in Old Town and attended by many people. Two large decorated arches were placed across the drive at the Kinneir's family home. One carried the motto '*Long Life And Happiness*', the other '*Welcome The Coming, Speed The Parting Guest*'. The footpaths to the church were lined with '*an assembly of respectable people'*, according to *The Swindon Advertiser*. The wedding was covered in such detail that we have even been left with a delightful description of the bride's wedding dress:

'She was dressed in ivory silk and Moiré, trimmed with Brussels lace and orange blossom, and wore a handsome Brussels lace veil over a wreath of orange blossom, the same as worn by her mother at her wedding. In her hand she carried a handsome bouquet of flowers sent from Covent Garden'

William Pitt left the Parish to become Rector of All Saints' Church in Liddington. He was to remain at Liddington for the next 54 years; apart from a short period during the Great War, when he served with the Church Army in France.

William and Alice had five children, Alice born in 1884, William in 1886, Edith in 1887, Clifford in 1889 and Audrey in 1892. Sadly, however, two of his children met with tragic ends. Clifford died on 1st February 1915 in Baumu, British East Africa. An Oxford graduate, he had embarked on a career in the Colonial Administration and died, aged just 26, of acute sunstroke. His parents dedicated a memorial window for him in Liddington Church, in which he was poignantly depicted shading from the sun under a tree.

Alice, the eldest daughter, died in mysterious circumstances on 23rd June 1928; she was found dead at the bottom of a well amongst the farm buildings close to the Rectory in Liddington. Alice had not returned for lunch and by mid-afternoon a search was organised. The worst fears of everyone present were realised when it was noticed that the lid had been removed from the well. Following a painstaking process her body was lifted from the well shaft. It was a heart-breaking mystery. How did someone who was so familiar with the area end up at the bottom of a well? The Coroner's report stated: *'found drowned in a well, there being no evidence of her state of mind'*.

Pitt resigned as Rector in 1935, due his deteriorating health, and moved with his wife to Bournemouth, on the south coast, in the hope that the sea air might alleviate his problems. His condition gradually worsened, however, and he suffered long periods of unconsciousness. After contracting pneumonia, Pitt died at the age of 80 on 21st November 1936. He was buried in Liddington Churchyard next to his daughter Alice. His wife survived him by seven years before

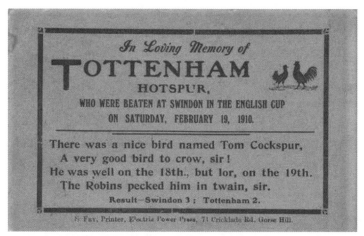

Marking one of Swindon's many achievements during the pre-war years.

passing away on 17th November 1943 in Braintree, Essex, where she had moved to live with their youngest daughter Audrey. Her body was transported back to Liddington, where she was buried alongside her husband. They lie facing the west door of the church in a grave marked by a large stone cross.

Even after Pitt's departure from Christ Church interest in sport, among the congregation, continued unabated. In 1908 the Christ Church football team even found time for an unusual 'double-header' against Cricklade Town. After a 2 – 0 defeat the church side then challenged the Cricklade players to a clay pigeon shooting competition! The following year, the St Marks' team was challenged to a 'triple-header'! This time the two teams undertook consecutive games of billiards, whist and ping-pong before Christ Church emerged as eventual winners.

As well as a wide variety of sports teams representing the church, the Choirboys even formed their own cricket and football teams (see the chapter 'The Musical Life of the Church). Bob Fulton began his football career as a member of the Christ Church Choir team. He would eventually play 22 times for Swindon Town.

Revd. Baily became patron of the Swindon Ranger Cricket & Football Club in 1880 and often assisted them in their fundraising, as did Mr Whitehead the organist.

The Great Western Railway began special excursion trains to allow spectators from the town to travel to football matches. Swindon Town

FC finished either as champions or runners up in consecutive seasons from 1908 until the commencement of the Great War. The club also managed two appearances in the FA Cup semi-finals. Large numbers attended these matches – a sight which was not lost on Revd. Mayall, who held a 'Men Only' service on 31st March 1912, the day after Swindon's FA Cup semi-final tie against Barnsley. Charles Mayall had played football in his younger days, and still took an interest in the game. However, whilst he recognised the virtues of playing the game, he spoke passionately about the dangers of over-indulgent support of the local team:

> *'Although I was fond of the game, I have no patience with those men who make the game football their god. There will be some men and young men and boys who talked of football from Satur-day mid-day to the next Saturday mid-day, and it was the only thing that seemed to be passing through their minds. It was but a pastime and there was nothing real in it. I could tell you sad stories of men who have spent their last sixpence to watch their particular team play. I have known men leave their wives and children with little food, and spend their money on that game. In the match between Swindon and Everton* (FA Cup Quarter Final, 2nd March 1912) *something like £900 (£100,000 today) was raised in an afternoon – the easiest way in the world to raise money at the present time!'*

The real object of Revd. Mayall's frustration, however, seems to have been an important local match which had been arranged for Good Friday on the fields below the church. He regretted the *'desecration of that Holy Day'* and praised one of the players involved who had refused to play for that very reason (in a similar vein to Harold Fleming).

The advent of the Great War brought an end to organised sport (both professional and amateur). However, following the armistice, the social side of life in the Parish blossomed, with Christ Church forming cricket, football, bowling, hockey and billiard teams. During the 1920s and 1930s regular football fixtures were arranged, against a variety of local sides. In January 1921 the Christ Church team were considered robust enough to provide useful opposition for two of the strongest teams in the area – Cirencester Town and Cirencester Victoria. Although a creditable draw was gained against Cirencester Town, the Christ Church team were soundly beaten 6 – 3 by the Victoria side. The management of Cirencester Town were so impressed by the side from Old Town they arranged another match for April, this time triumphing over the church team by four goals to one.

1914 Cricket Club.

Regular fixtures were arranged against many teams, including a long relationship with the Harris Bacon Factory Workers XI from Calne. Christ Church were invited regularly to Calne to play the factory team, in winter for football matches, and in summer to play cricket. The factory also extended the invite to the Christ Church ladies for regular and enjoyable ladies' hockey matches. Records still exist of a football game against Harris Calne in 1934, in which Mr Robinson and Mr Gillibrand scored for Christ Church, and of a ladies' hockey encounter in 1933, in which the score was Harris Calne Ladies 7 Christ Church Ladies 1. Sadly, the Harris Factory closed in 1984 and was a great loss to the small Wiltshire town.

In fact, during the 1930s the Hockey teams played a huge number

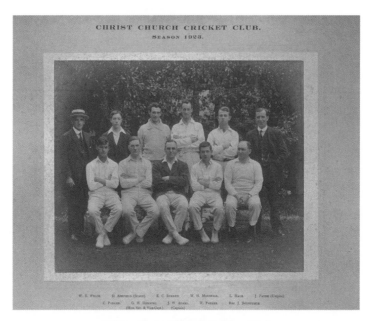

1923 - Christ Church Cricket Club.

1923 - Christ Church Football Club.

1924 cricket club.

of fixtures, with both the mens and ladies sides playing weekly from the beginning of September to the end of April every year. The teams, resplendently turned out in emerald green and black, played at Gosling's Field on the Wroughton Road. Miss J. Routledge captained the ladies' side and Mr G.T. Robinson the men's team. Matches were played against teams from the neighbouring towns, local factories and RAF bases.

The Christ Church Cricket team flourished during the inter-war years and enjoyed a packed fixture card each summer. Mr J.D. Adams captained the church side and was probably the team's best player. Reports were sent to local newspapers, who happily covered local cricket in great detail. In July 1921 Adams scored 95, from a team total of 174, against Fairford CC. It was probably the strongest performance of the era by Christ Church. The team were in a winning position too, the following weekend whilst playing at Shrivenham. After bowling the home team out for 115, Christ Church were cruising towards victory at 99-3, when it was pointed out that the charabanc driver needed to return to Swindon urgently. The team were forced to leave the field promptly and hurry back to town. Shrivenham hastily declared the game a draw!

Fixtures continued throughout the decade including memorable victories over the Cirencester Gardeners, in which Mr H. Hanson took 8 wickets, and a 20-run win over the church team from Cirencester Abbey in 1928.

Local branches of the YMCA also provided suitable opposition for more sedate games of lawn bowls and billiards, for which Christ Church joined the Wiltshire Billiards League. As well as captaining the cricket team, the obviously talented Mr J.D. Adams also took charge of the church billiards team.

The Second World War again brought a cessation to social sport in the country, as minds turned to air raids, blackouts, shortages and the threat of invasion. Following V.E Day, and the bitter winters that followed, the country entered a new era. Music, television, radio, telephones, and gradually increasing personal wealth saw the numbers willing to participate in social sport drop dramatically. The golden era of the inter-war years now seemed a lifetime away. Christ Church did manage to arrange some games during the 1950s, '60s, and '70s, however the games were less frequent and teams were often hard to raise.

Nevertheless, Christ Church's link with Swindon Town FC, which began over 140 years ago, continues to this day. Simon Stevenette

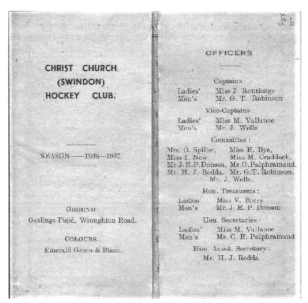

1936 - Hockey Club Office Bearers.

LADIES' FIXTURES.					MEN'S FIXTURES.			
Date	Opponents.	Result	Goals For	Ag.	Date	Opponents.	Result	Goals For	Ag.
Sep. 19		a			Sep. 19	Garrards	a		
26	Wills	a			26	Wills	h		
Oct. 3	Bedford Stragglers	a			Oct. 3	Bedford Stragglers	a		
10	Whitley	a			10	Cirencester	h		
17	Marlborough	a			17	Calne	h		
24	Ashton Keynes	a			24	Devizes & Erlestoke	a		
31	O.E.S.	a			31	Marlborough	h		
Nov. 7		a			Nov. 7	Morris Motors	h		
14	Cope Chat	h			14	R.A.F. Upavon	a		
21	Faringdon	a			21	Calne	a		
28	Purton	h			28	R.A.F. Netheravon	a		
Dec. 5	Holloway L.	a			Dec. 5	R.A. College	h		
12	Ashton Keynes	h			12	Cirencester	a		
19	Swindon Ladies	a			19	Wills	h		
26					26	G.W.R.	h		
Jan. 2	Harris	a			Jan. 2	Swindon	a		
9	Cope Chat	a			9	Pressed Steel	h		
16		h			16	Milton	a		
23	Purton	a			23	Tetbury	h		
30	Holloway L.	h			30	G.W.R.	a		
Feb. 6	G.W.R.	a			Feb. 6	Devizes & Erlestoke	h		
13		h			13				
20	Bedford Stragglers	h			20	Bedford Stragglers	h		
27	Wills	h			27	Pressed Steel	a		
Mar. 6	Marlborough	h			Mar. 6	R.A.F. Netheravon	h		
13	Faringdon	h			13	Marlborough	a		
20	Swindon Ladies	h			20	R.A. College	a		
27	Whitley	h			27	Morris Motors	a		
Apl. 3	O.E.S.	h			pl. 3	Swindon	h		
10	G.W.R.	h			10	R.A.F. Upavon	h		
17					17				
24	Harris	a			24				

Hockey Club - Fixtures

became Club Chaplain for the football team and a lifelong fan of the Robins too. When he was admitted into the Great Western Hospital, in 2016, with a serious infection, Town Head Coach Luke Williams visited him on the ward. Simon even released a statement revealing exactly what he was wearing in hospital!

'I was admitted to hospital with a serious infection on Monday 5th September. I am wearing the Swindon Town shirt given to me as part of the Football Fans in Training course.'

The church's links with Swindon Town continue to this day, with Revd. Canon Simon Stevenette remaining Chaplain to the club and an enthusiastic and vocal supporter of 'The Robins'! In 2011 Simon Stevenette attended a memorial service to mark the 75th anniversary of the death of William Pitt. The connection between the local football club and Christ Church remain as strong as ever.

It is perhaps difficult today to understand the importance of organised sport to parishioners during the early part of the last century. For many, it was their only outlet from a mundane working life. The church actively encouraged involvement, recognising the benefits to physical and mental well-being. It will be interesting to see if sport makes a resurgence again in church life during the 21st century.

11

St. Mary's Church 1926-2021

In the early 1920's, the planners of Swindon believed that Old Town's future development would be to the West, around and beyond The Mall and Goddard Avenue. Building was already progressing along Okus Road, and Canon Mayall wanted to provide Sunday School accommodation for the children in the area. In April 1925, it was announced that Major Fitzroy Pleydell Goddard had presented a site in the Mall for a *'temporary or semi-permanent'* church to be put up immediately, plus £100 towards the building costs. The site was originally part of the Great Field of the ancient Westcott Manor of High Swindon. St Mary's church was built initially from only timber and asbestos, costing £1,200, but the site was large enough for a permanent church at some future date. The remainder of the land was let out as allotment gardens.

Money flowed in and the new church was completed and furnished by December 1925 – becoming the third church in Swindon to go under the name St Mary's (four, including St Mary's at Lydiard). The second-hand organ from the Church Hall was transferred to the new church. It was unable to open, however, due to the illness and subsequent departure of Canon Mayall's one curate, the Revd. John Bodycombe. Those living in the western part of Old Town were forced to wait until July 1926, when his successor, the Revd. Frederick J. Hirst, was able to start work in the Parish. The building was dedicated by the Lord Bishop of Bristol on 6 October 1926, who quoted the unusual verse from Ezra Chapter VII, Verse 22; *'Salt without prescribing how much.'* The passage emphasising the influence that a truly Christian community can have on the world around it.

On the first Sunday of services there were sixty-six communicants at the 8am service and the church was full for Matins and Evensong. More than fifty children were enrolled at the Children's Service in

Name board outside St Mary's.j

the afternoon. The spare ground round the church was let out for members to use as allotments.

It is believed that the first Christening took place at St. Mary's in January 1927.

Over the years the original St. Mary's developed its own unique friendly atmosphere and lively congregation, Sunday School, Women's Fellowship and a successful choir. Mr Edward George (Ted) Taylor had been appointed Choirmaster in 1926 and the choir in the years prior to the Second World War included Mrs. Freda Taylor (his wife), Mrs Street, Mrs Done, Mr Brearly and Mr Cavilla. Organist was Mr. Reg Perrett who held the position until 1942. Mrs. Taylor then became the organist until she was tragically killed in the bombing of Drove Road in August 1942 (see Chapter 5). After this tragedy Mr Ted Taylor remained as choirmaster for a short period but found himself unable to continue in the task. Mr George Taylor stepped into the breach for a while before Gordon Crabbe took over in 1946 (at the age of 15). Gordon built up a first-class choir before taking over the duties of organist at Christ Church in 1956. Amongst the stalwarts at this time were William R. 'Dicky' Bird, who read the lessons, Fred Wilkins, Charles Matthews and Mr G.F. Ashworth. In 1944 another 'second-hand' organ was purchased for St. Mary's after being located near Tunbridge Wells.

Despite the planners' original predictions, the expansion of Swindon occurred in the east of the town when Walcot was developed in the 1930's and 1950's, most of the area for housing to the west of Okus Road being taken up by Princess Margaret Hospital. In 1954, Glyn Calder took over as Priest-in-Charge of St. Mary's and the Church became revitalized with much-increased congregations and a

Interior of St Mary's 1960s.

St Marys Sunday School 1960s.

renewed atmosphere of fellowship. Deputy Wardens were instituted for the first time with Dr. Robinson, John Masters, Rowland Low and John King holding these positions for many years. Rowland Low retired as Churchwarden in 1976; he and his wife Hilda being stalwarts of the church for a long time. Various organists followed Gordon Crabbe including Mr. A.R. Budd, Stan Jury, Sidney Jones, Charles Vince, Eddie Carter and Louis Curzon. Mr. John Chandler became 'temporary' choirmaster for ten years. Miss Majorie Hiscock was a regular, and longstanding, worshipper at St. Mary's from 1937, singing in the choir until it ceased in 1992, after the death of Nora Gill. She eventually passed away in 2012 at the age of 97. Trevor Summerhayes was also a loyal member of the church, playing the organ for many years, from 1988, until moving away from Swindon to be nearer his family. Trevor has sadly since passed away.

Glyn Calder left St. Mary's in 1956 and was followed as Priest-in-Charge by many different curates from Christ Church over the next forty years (see Staff listing, Appendix B). The majority stayed only three or four years before leaving but Edgar Newton remained in charge from 1971-78. One of the features of the late 1950's, and well into the 1960's, was the formation and operation of a men's working party under Dennis Biggar. Large amounts of maintenance and decoration within St Mary's was undertaken, and when Dennis Biggar left in 1961, Rowland Hill became the 'gaffer'. The Honorary Assistant Clergy, in particular George Foster, Canon Samuel Christelow and Canon Lewis Thomas, carried out much spiritual work in the area during the years and stood in when necessary for the services. In September 1971, the clergy, choir and church officials of Christ Church attended Choral Communion at St. Mary's to celebrate Canon Cristelow's 60th anniversary of the Priesthood.

In 1959, the Church Commissioners built two bungalows, Holway Cottages, on the spare land facing the Mall, for the use of retired clergy or church workers from the Bristol Diocese. A booklet produced in 1969 by Christ Church, entitled The Old Parish Church of Swindon, celebrated the work of St Mary's. Costing half a crown, the booklet was put together by Vicar, Derek Palmer, and parishioners Rosemary Stephens and Dennis Bird and described St Mary's as:

'...catering for residents in the western part of the parish. There is no hall, so Sunday School must be held in the church.'

Its existence more than justified over the previous 50 years, it was decided to commence work on replaced the original temporary structure. Before work could begin however, the original building had to be sold. In 1976, the original wooden building was put up for sale at £1,000 to anybody willing to dismantle it and take the parts away. Work on a new church finally began in August 1977. Church Army Housing paid £13,000 (today's equivalent of £90,000) for the site, and a new permanent brick church was built on the site. The structure was independent but attached to a two-story block of 18 self-contained flats, which was called 'Goddard House'. Meetings of the congregation took place in the Vicarage Room in Bath Road until the new church was ready. After completion, it was dedicated by the Bishop of Malmesbury, the Rt. Revd. Freddy Temple, on 22 March 1978. Revd. Eddy Newton shepherded St. Mary's through this difficult transition period. The new church was much smaller than the old building, but the latter was not demolished until the new one was actually in use. Most of the furnishings were transferred to the new church, altar, communion rails, seating, font and lectern etc. The old organ and pulpit were too large for the new building so new ones were obtained. 'Goddard House' was officially opened by Lord Margadale, Lord Lieutenant of Wiltshire, in June 1979.

In 1982 Olive King took over duties at the church. She had trained at Greyladies' College in London, gaining the Academic Diploma in Theology and Certificate of Pastoral Theology in 1949. After three years in West Dulwich, Olive spent five years in Cape Town and, on returning to England, worked with Derek Palmer in Bristol. She came to Swindon and worked at Penhill, Wroughton and Toothill, before officially retiring in 1981. After 1982, Olive took services, worked hard for Christian Aid and took communion to the housebound. In October 1999, she celebrated 50 years in the Ministry. The Rt. Revd. Michael Doe (The Bishop of Swindon), the Revd. Derek Palmer, the Revd. Owen Barraclough and Canon Michael Johnson (Area Dean of Swindon) joined St. Mary's to celebrate the event.

In September 1996, St. Mary's celebrated 70 years of worship on the site in the Mall with a special Holy Communion. The vestry at St. Mary's became a radio studio in May-June 2000, when Swindon Churches Together and FLAME FM ran a Christian radio station over Pentecost, as part of the national FLAME FM project. The project was repeated in 2002. St Mary's also held its first Garden Party in 2000 and the Christ Church Parish office moved into St Mary's from January until October 2000.

By the mid-1990's, the flats at 'Goddard House' were in a bad

St Marys up for sale 1976.

St Mary's 1977 During Demolition.

state of repair. The building was closed, and the residents moved elsewhere. However, the English Churches Housing Association took on the task of renovating the building and this commenced in June 2000. It now contains 15 flats and was officially opened by the Mayor of Swindon, Councillor Arthur Archer, on 1 March 2001.

In 2000 the St Mary's Fellowship began its regular Monday afternoon meetings and – in the days before internet shopping -were told about 'Shopperphone'. The Fellowship ran until the death of Maggie Bird in 2013.

Some refurbishment of the church was carried out between 2014 - 2018. Norma McKemey and Lynda Fisher painted the brick walls of the lounge area of St. Mary's and made new curtains. A new kitchen was then fitted and new flooring laid throughout the building.

St Mary's 70th Anniversary service 1996.

The worldwide Coronavirus pandemic, of course, forced St Mary's to close its door in March 2020. The multi church use of the building also presented unique logistical problems when the 'lockdown' was finally eased in the summer of 2020. In addition to St Mary's Congregation the church hosts a cosmopolitan group of worshippers - New Apostolic, Pentecost and a Brazilian Church. Just how so many groups would be able to use the limited space, while remaining safe, created a headache for everyone. With restrictions likely to be in place well in 2021, the situation may prove challenging for some time to come. Although services were finally able to resume on 18th October.

St. Mary's still offers a unique family atmosphere all of its own and its effect on the life of the Parish far outweighs its actual size.

St Mary's Church.

12

Old Swindon Charities and Anderson's Hostel

In the days before Social Security, to be poor, old or ill could literally be looking at the difference between life and death. Before the Dissolution of the Monasteries, many looked to the monastic houses for some form of relief, or to the personal benevolence of the wealthy – *'the rich man at his table, and the poor man at the gate.'*

Such piecemeal assistance was regularised by the passing of the first Poor Law Acts in 1552. Justices of the Peace were given overall responsibility for monitoring the system of relief; Overseers of the Poor were appointed annually within individual parishes. The system was based upon relieving the poor in their own homes, and a complicated set of rules governing entitlement to relief within each particular parish developed. Under this system, therefore, the homeless and wandering poor became marginalised, and the concept of 'deserving' and 'undeserving' poor evolved. This view of the poor became entrenched in Victorian times and still affects attitudes today.

By 1834, the system was starting to crumble in the face of rising costs, and the Poor Law Amendment Act of that year was implemented; it was widely regarded as one of the most important pieces of social legislation ever enacted. Under the new arrangements, Poor Law Unions were formed in each parish, each with its own board of guardians. These Poor Law Unions then became responsible for testing applicants for relief; only the most 'deserving' were helped. That assistance took the form of entry into the Workhouse, a system of establishments which were deliberately designed to be *'uninviting places of unwholesome restraint'*.[1]

---

1   Edwin Chadwick, principal architect and enactor of the Poor Law Amendment Act.

The Workhouse was nonetheless a means of survival for some, but was regarded as the last resort, and universally feared. The only other means of help open to the poorer in society was to depend upon the charity of individual members of the community. This is difficult to comprehend in the more egalitarian society of the 21st century, but in an age when everyone knew their place, to be wealthy, or even comfortably well-off, imposed a set of moral standards and obligations. Thus, it became the 'duty' of leading townspeople to give, in as practical a way as possible, to help the less advantaged. This duty was regulated not by any code of law, but by individual and collective conscience.

The image of 'Lady Bountiful' dispensing hot broth and doing good works is a powerful one, but by no means the only one in practice. The bequest of sums of money to be used for charitable purposes after the donor's death ensured that the donor was commemorated as much as the suffering of the poor was relieved.

A number of such charitable bequests are known in the Old Parish of Swindon. An enquiry by the Charities Commission in 1903 documented 13 charities which were administered by the Vicar and Churchwardens of Christ Church (although no account was taken of religious denomination when the benefits were distributed). [2]

The details of the following charities are summarised according the *Victoria County History.*

1. Burges Charity

John Burges(s), Vicar of Manningford Bruce, directed in his will, made before 1559, that 7s 5d should be distributed annually on the feast of St. Gregory among the poor, of which 1s 2d was to be paid to the five most deserving cases. The charity was paid regularly until 1782, when it was included by mistake in the Church Account. It was not paid at all between 1795 and 1826, after which Ambrose Goddard paid the arrears.

---

2   It should be noted that at that time potential beneficiaries could come from both Old and New Swindon, but the charities were advertised in Old Town only. The explanation given was that there was less regular employment in Old Town than New Town, as the latter was based on the thriving GWR works.

2. Charities of Hutchins, Lord and Cuss

Eleanor Hutchins, James Lord and Henry Cuss each gave £20 to be invested for the benefit of the poor at Easter. The income appears to have come from land; and amounted to £3 in 1737. By 1903, it was represented by the sum of £2 10s from a rent-charge from West Swindon Mead. The money was to be *'yearly distributed at Easter to the poor for ever'*.

3. Edmund Goddard's Charity

Before 1701 Edmund Goddard devised an annual rent-charge of 20s (£1) from North Laines Farm to be paid on Shrove Tuesday to the poor.

4. Richard Goddard's Charity

By his will of 1650, Richard Goddard devised a tenement in Wroughton, known as Arnold's Estate, for the benefit of the poor. The gift was overlooked until 1730, when the arrears were paid by his grandson, Richard Goddard. Churchwardens then managed the estate and rent. In 1834 the total rent was £11, the property being let to Amos Austin. It was noted at the time that this was considered to be a low rent,

5. Brind's Charity

Margaret Brind, in her will of 1740, bequeathed £100 (approximately £20,000 today) for the poor, with the interest distributed yearly on 20th July. Occasionally the dividend was used to purchase property or tenements for the use of the poor, or to protect the investment. A note in Margaret Brind's will instructed the Overseer of the Poor to *'think proper'* in his distribution of the money.

6. Broadway's Charity

Mary Broadway's will, also dated 1740, bequeathed £20 to be invested for the benefit of poor widows, with the interest distributed annually on 13th April.

Charities 4,5 and 6 were later amalgamated and the capital used to purchase three acres of land in Stratton St Margaret, called Canon's Close. The land was subsequently enclosed, and a share or 'allotment' made to Swindon church (at that time Holy Rood). In

1831 the land was let to Richard Blunsden, producing a dividend of £9 (less 6 shillings in land tax). The charities then became known as the **Poor's Allotment**. The land was sold in 1884, and the money invested as two funds, the second one for widows. In 1903 the funds produced an annual income of £30 and £5 respectively

7. Gray's Charity
Richard Gray's will of 1807 gave £400 for the benefit of the Second Poor[3]. The annualinterest of 3% was to be distributed each March to widows, widowers and single men and women aged over 60.

8. Evans' Charity
Elizabeth Evans bequeathed £70 to provide 6 poor women over 60 years of age with new gowns on the feast of St. Thomas every year. The capital was invested in 1787. It was noted in 1834 that, due to a reduction in the cost of materials, 8 gowns rather than 6 could be distributed. By 1903, the number of gowns had reverted to 6, at a cost of £2 10s.

9. Horne and Cooper's Charity - The Free School
Mary Horne gave £100 for poor householders not receiving relief from the parish, as well as £100 for the Free School. This was augmented by Joseph and Elizabeth Cooper, who settled land upon the trusts of Mary Horne's will. Nine acres given in 1796 were used to provide half the schoolmaster's income. In 1896 all the associated property was sold and income from the invested capital split between the Free School and the poor.

10. The Vilett Charity
Harriet Rolleston, by her will proved in 1870, settled £300 in trust to provide, under the name of the Vilett Charity,[4] coal and blankets for the poor at Christmas.

11. Sheppard's Dole
John Harding Sheppard, by his will proved in 1877, gave £200 to be invested *'for the benefit of 12 aged poor persons at Christmas'*. The distribution was known as Sheppard's Dole, and in 1904 the sum of £5 2s 6d benefited 12 people.

---

3   The Second Poor were those who were in receipt of occasional, rather than regular, relief from the Parish.
4   Harriet Rolleston was Harriet Vilett before her marriage.

12. Richard Bowly's Charity

Richard Bowly, by his will proved in 1885, gave £200 to distribute blankets at Christmas. In 1903, 22 recipients benefited.

13. Anderson's Institute

Alexander Anderson, by his will dated 1865, bequeathed about £1,636 for the benefit of the poor. This money, with £32 given by the local board, was used to build 4 almshouses in Cricklade Street, adjacent to Christ Church.

In 1906, all 13 charities were amalgamated under the title of the United Charities. Those of Bowly, Evans, Gray and Sheppard's Dole remained in their original form; the remainder were joined to form the Almshouse and Nursing Charities, to cover the increasing costs of the Anderson's Institute, now called Anderson's Hostel.

The almshouses were built in 1877 by W.H. Read, of stone with slate roofs. The windows face north and overlook the churchyard. An inscription was set up near the entrance, which can still be seen today, and reads:

Anderson's Hostel, A.D. 1877
From a bequest by the late Mr. Anderson of this town for the benefit of the second poor of Swindon the trustees have erected this hostel; they have also invested five hundred pounds to provide an endowment and one hundred pounds for a repairing fund for same.

Under Clause 9 of the Scheme, which was set up to administer the Almshouses, it was directed that:

The number of almspeople shall be four, who shall be poor persons of good character, being single men or single women, widowers or widows of 60 years of age and upwards who shall have resided in the parish of Swindon for not less than three years next preceding the time of their appointment, who shall not during that period have received Poor Relief, and who from age, ill-health, accident, or infirmity shall be unable to maintain themselves by their own exertions, with a preference for those persons who, being otherwise qualified as aforesaid, shall have become reduced by misfortune from better circumstances.

Clause 10 went on to detail the pensions payable out of the income of the charity – but only the occupants of Almshouses Nos. 1 and 2 were eligible. However, in 1897 John Chandler set up a trust of £100 to provide a pension for the occupant of No. 3.

The Charity Commissioners of 1903 reported on the Anderson's Hostel thus:

> *'The houses are stone built, the windows, which face north, overlooking the parish churchyard. There is a small garden with a wash-house and conveniences for the inmates. The houses are substantially built and are in a good state of repair. The entrance is badly lighted. Each house has a good-sized living room and pantry on the ground floor and a large bedroom over. There are four inmates, all women, who were all qualified for election as directed by the Scheme. The trustees are the vicar and the churchwardens.*
>
> *The inmates of the Almshouses numbered 1 and 2 are paid 2s 6d a week each, and the inmate of No. 3 12s 3d per quarter. The inmate in No. 4 has no pension. The inmates have no other special allowances, but share in the gifts of coal, blankets, etc. If there is a vacancy in Almshouse No. 1 or No. 2 the inmate in No. 3 is moved into the vacant house, and the inmate in No. 4 to No. 3. Notice of every vacancy is placed near the entrance to the Almshouses. Owing to the fact that the newly-elected inmate is placed in No. 4 and has no pension, there is not a large demand for admission.'*

The Charity Commissioners further record that in 1902 one of the 'inmates' (a not particularly flattering Victorian term for tenants!) was dismissed for disorderly conduct. No further details were given, and one can only speculate as to the nature of the offence. In 1912, a further income towards the hostel was provided from the will of J.E.G. Bradford.

The pensions payable to the occupants ceased in 1954, being replaced by grants from the National Assistance Board. By 1960 the occupants were themselves expected to pay 7s 6d towards the maintenance of the Almshouses. By the 1980s work was needed on the buildings (especially the replacement of the windows) and the accommodation was also re-arranged as four flats (rather than houses)

The Inscription Stone from the Street side of the Almshouse.

during 1991.

The process of replacing the windows was a long, drawn out and arduous one. The grade II listed status of the buildings meant that any replacement windows must appear identical, to meet the requirements of the Planning Officer. Eventually, after failed fundraising appeals to English Heritage and the Almshouse Association, and a temporary refurbishment in 2003, an appeal to the Big Lottery Fund enabled the project to be completed by the architect Edward Tucker and Cotswold Casements in June 2010.

A certificate displayed in the church commemorates a conservation award given by the Borough of Thamesdown (as was) to the Swindon United Charities in respect of the Almshouses, 27-30, Cricklade Street. The judges considered the scheme to be: *'A project which successfully combines the preservation of this important historical building with the need to provide elderly residents with modern facilities.'*

No more apt description can be found to end this chapter.

The Anderson's Almhouses.

13

The Church Schools

The origin of the present Church of England school in Old Town lay in the founding of a 'Free School' in 1764, one of the first in the country. In fact the decision by the Church of England to offer free education to every parish in the land did not officially begin until the founding of the Church of England National Society for the Promotion of Free Education in 1811 (50 years before free education became Government policy). The new school in Swindon was sited in Newport Street, and was formed for the purpose of educating twenty boys (and from 1796, five girls). Education was to be based on the principles of the Christian religion (although it was not strictly a church school), the reading and writing of English, and common arithmetic. However, the teaching of science, or any language other than English, was not encouraged.

The money to endow the school was raised by voluntary subscription, principally from grants and bequests from Thomas Goddard (the Lord of the Manor), William Nash, Mary Horne and Joseph and Elizabeth Cooper. One of the first trustees was the Vicar, William Nicholls, and Mr House one of the first teachers.

In 1836 the school was considered too small and was pulled down, a new one being erected on the same site. This was known as the National School, named after the National Society, an Anglican association which promoted education. The school now taught about 80 pupils, both boys and girls. Admissions registers from the period show that the occupations of the pupils' parents remained predominantly agricultural in nature. They included shepherds, cowmen, blacksmiths, saddlers and ostlers, a toll-bar keeper, a tripe dresser and a water seller! Also among the pupils was Swindon author Richard Jefferies, who attended the school during the 1860s. The standard of education was high, with the school receiving an exemplary report from Government Inspectors.

However, Swindon was changing fast however and by 1871 a

The original National School name stone.

new and larger site was found for the school in King William Street, nearer to the thriving industry of the New Town. Mr Jenkins, the school's headmaster, opened his own private school at Sandhill House in the town. The old National School building continued to be used by Christ Church for various functions, until it was demolished during the widening of Newport Street in the early 1960s. Money from the sale of the land was used to partly fund the building of the Leisure Centre adjacent to Christ Church in September 1969. The name stone from the school, which weighed almost one ton, was removed and restored by the Council. It was then installed as a monument next to the petrol station on Newport Street, where the school once stood. However, in 1990 it was noticed that this very large name stone was missing; it has never been located, despite extensive enquiries within the Council and further afield.

In 2002 Swindon mayor David Cox unveiled a 12-inch plaque on the side wall of Monahans Chartered Accountants in Newport Street, Old Town. The plaque reads:

'Near here stood Swindon's first free school, opened circa 1764. In 1836 it was replaced on the same site by the National School, itself closed in 1870 and demolished in 1962.'

The new King William Street School was instigated by the industrious Revd. Henry Baily. However, it was not officially known as a Church of England School until 1902, after it came under the control of the local education authority of the newly formed Borough of Swindon.

Land for the new school was purchased for the sum of £310 (approximately £37,000 today), at a plot known as Tucker's Piece in New Road, Eastcott. This subsequently became King William Street. Well known Swindon architect Thomas Lansdown (who has a street named after him in Old Town) designed the building at a cost of £1,784 -today's equivalent of more than £200,000. King William Street School was opened by the Bishop of Gloucester and Bristol on 17th August 1871.

The building was of Swindon stone, with Bath stone dressing. Boys, girls, and infants each had separate entrances, classrooms and playgrounds, taking approximately 340 pupils (170 boys and 140 girls) in total. Accommodation was provided on site for the schoolmaster. Basic heating was provided by two heating chambers feeding pipes

Girls' class at the school, c. 1890.

into the classrooms, however they were not lit until early November every year! Gas lighting was not installed until the following year.

The popularity of the school soon began to create problems, however. In 1890 the management of the school wrote to the Education Department to inquire about the possibility of a £4,500 loan to extend the school buildings, to help alleviate the acute shortage of school places in the ever-growing town. An 1889 report from the Education Board listed Swindon as having a *'deficiency of 580 school places'*, despite King William Street School having places for 256 boys, 229 girls and 187 infants!

By 1904 Revd. Estcourt was forced to report to the Bishop, stating difficulties in the payment and employment of teachers. Several had left their posts at the school, and the local authority seemed to be ineffective in finding replacements. *'Warm and spirited discussions'* followed in which Revd. Estcourt and the Education Board debated the relevant merits of church involvement in the selection of new teaching staff.

In 1914 Mary Slade, the first Headmistress of the school, was instrumental in leading the efforts to send Red Cross parcels to the troops on the Western Front.

By the 1920's, overcrowding in the school had become a serious problem, and further alterations were made, including the conversion of the schoolmaster's accommodation into classrooms. Despite other minor upgrades and improvements, the building today remains substantially the same as it did when it was first built.

Lessons at the school in the nineteenth century still concentrated on the '3 R's' – reading, 'riting and 'rithmetic. In addition to this, boys studied singing, geography and mechanics, whilst the girls were taught singing, needlework and domestic economy. All pupils were examined annually in Religious Instruction by the Diocesan Inspector. Because of the school's associations with the Church, denominational teaching featured at the start of every school day. The range of subjects studied gradually broadened over the years, and today the school is fully integrated into the National Curriculum.

The original eighteenth century endowment continued to offer free places for 20 boys and 5 girls, but all other pupils were expected to pay weekly fees until all children were given free, but compulsory, school places following the Education Acts of 1880 and 1881. In 1872 the fees cost 2d for infants, 3d for boys and girls, and 4d for the children of tradesmen. Finding the fees often caused a problem for some of the poorer families in the town, and the remedy was simple absence. Truancy was endemic for other reasons too – the school logs record excuses such as blackberrying, planting potatoes, Band of Hope and Sunday School treats, visiting menageries, fairs and circuses, steeple-chases and cattle markets! In 1893, the Headmaster recorded *'the oddest excuse for absence I have ever heard has been given – "To oil the bedstead"'!'*

Children were often absent because they were required to work, in order to supplement their family's income. Full-time working under the age of 13 was not allowed by law, but the school could issue a certificate to allow certain pupils to work part-time – a bizarre concept to our modern sensitivities! Another practice which is condemned today, but was commonplace, was that of physical punishment. Many children were beaten or caned at school for the slightest misdemeanour, with the full approval of their parents. In 1874, the Headmaster recorded in the log: *'Two fathers called to ask me to thrash their sons for robbing a garden – declined'.* This did not prevent him two years later from obtaining a birch especially for use on truants – on the first day alone it was used on three boys.

Further evidence of the hard nature of people's lives at the time can be found in references to illness and death in the school logbooks. In 1879 it was recorded; *'Of the 12 boys absent, 1 was dead, 8 had left the neighbourhood, 1 was ill of scarlet fever, 1 was visiting, and 1 refused to come.'* In 1884, a pupil named A. Ponting died – the first for four years. In 1886, another pupil, Daniel Hoare had his right arm amputated as a result of 'meddling with machinery'. In 1905 a scarlatina epidemic necessitated disinfecting the whole school, including the books; a measles epidemic in 1915 allowed children to be exempted from school.

School lessons started at 9 a.m. and ended at 4:15 p.m., with a break for lunch. School holidays were much shorter than they are today – only 3 weeks in the summer, for example (increased to 4 weeks in 1892). The school was divided into 6 'standards' (7 from 1882), but these were not necessarily composed of children of the same age. School leaving age was originally 13, raised to 14 in 1901. The school was officially listed as a Primary School in 1946, after which time older children were expected to attend a separate senior school. The boys' and girls' schools were amalgamated in 1932, and the infants school ceased to be a separate school from 1937.

The first Headmaster of the school was Mr Arthur Stote, who served in that capacity from 1871 until his retirement in 1899 (he later became Churchwarden of Christ Church from 1898-1901). He was initially assisted by Pupil Teachers (youngsters aged 13 ½ or 14, who could subsequently qualify as Assistant Masters). Later, certificated teachers and qualified Assistant Masters were required as well, as by 1888 pupil numbers had increased to 941.

Both World Wars had an impact on the school, as former pupils and masters were called up to serve in the armed forces. Several were killed in action or became Prisoners-of-War. During the Second World War in particular, civilian life was affected in several ways, not least with rationing and air raid alarms. Up to 450 evacuees from London were temporarily billeted in the school in August 1939. At the end of the year, 124 pupils from St. John's Church of England School in East London were amalgamated with their Swindon compatriots, who numbered 334 at the time.

The Bostock & Wombwell Menagerie was a popular treat for the boys.

School life had its compensations, however, as well as its trials and tribulations. To celebrate Queen Victoria's Jubilee in 1887, the children were given a holiday and joined other schools at a Fete in Faringdon Road Park. In 1892, 192 boys (no girls!) were allowed an afternoon off to visit Bostock & Wombwell's Travelling Menagerie (a popular Victorian travelling animal show, founded by George Wombwell), and in 1900 an extra half hour's play was allowed to celebrate the relief of Ladysmith. In 1905, there was an eclipse of the sun, and the school encouraged pupils to observe this (through smoked glass) and discuss the phenomenon as reported in the press. Extra time off was allowed for the deaths, weddings and coronations of monarchs. A day off was allowed when King George V and Queen Mary visited the GWR Works in Swindon in 1924, when the Duke of Gloucester visited the Civic Offices in 1938, and in 1950 when the (then) Princess Elizabeth visited the town.

Pupils at King William Street School during the 125th anniversary celebrations, March 1996.

In 1964 a pageant was staged by staff and pupils to celebrate the bicentenary of the founding of the Free School, and in 1996, the school held events to celebrate its 125th anniversary.

In 2006 Alan Voyce stood down as Headteacher of King William Street School, after 24 years in the role. During his tenure the school modernised considerably, including the construction of a new kitchen (in the old boys' toilets!), music room, IT Suite and staffroom. Carpets replaced the wooden floors, a Dynamic Parent Working Party was formed, and blackboards were swapped for interactive whiteboards.

Funds were raised in 2010 for the purchase of 80 bibles for Key Stage 1 children at the school. This event was repeated in May 2013, and again in 2014, courtesy of money raised by the Mothers' Union. A presentation and thank you service was held to mark the occasion.

New Head Teacher Simon Burrell then organised several events during the noughties including a Bollywood themed evening, Parents Aloud sessions, and even a bushcraft day – in which the children learnt to build a fire and gut a fish! Simon Burrell left at Easter 2010 and was replaced by new Head Mrs Margaret Clark. Pupils from the school regularly perform Nativity

King William Street School 2007.

Services at Christ Church, to packed congregations, in which the children present, a variety of Christmas songs, dancing and, of course, the traditional Christmas story.

At Easter 2014 pupils from the school performed a moving Easter service at the school, involving a powerful dance with a voiceover narration telling the story of Jesus on the cross and the resurrection, with the Year 4 class reminding the audience that *'it's not all about the chocolate, it's all about Jesus'*. A useful confirmation of the school's careful blend of traditional values and modern outlook.

The school still flourishes, serving children in Old Town and maintaining its links with the parish church. King William Street celebrates its 150th anniversary in 2021.

14

The Church Bells

Church bells are a part of life we take for granted, and which sum up a feeling of continuity and stability. We are aware of Sunday bells, wedding bells, and perhaps weekday practice bells, and their clear loud notes rise above even the noise of traffic and machinery which dominates our lives today.

In earlier times, before the advent of radio, television and smart phones, church bells were a vital form of mass communication. Bells were rung not just to summon the faithful to church on Sunday, but for a variety of other reasons too. In times of trouble or war, they gave urgent warning to take refuge. In times of celebration they joyfully proclaimed battle victories, royal births, weddings, and coronations. Other public and civic events, both national and local, have been commemorated by the pealing of the bells.

More morbidly, a single tolling bell reminded the living of their mortality as it rang for the newly dead. Traditionally, it rang nine times for a man, six for a woman and three for a child, followed by a stroke for each year of their age.

Holy Rood Bells

The original parish bells of Swindon were, of course, housed in Holy Rood. Church bells, wherever possible, are accommodated in the church tower, which has the dual purpose of practicality (the sound of the bells carried further) and psychology (it gave an air of monumentalism to the church). Other churches without the benefit of tower or spire, would have made do with a small bellcote. Holy Rood acquired a bellcote during the eighteenth century when it housed just a single small bell. This would have been rung as a 'minute bell', for latecomers on Sundays to warn them that the service would start in literally a minute's time.

The main peal hung in the belfry 30 feet above the ground floor and consisted of six bells, installed in 1741. These were cast by Abel Rudhall, from Rudhalls of Gloucester, a long standing foundry who had cast bells for Tewkesbury Abbey, Christ Church Cathedral in Dublin, and the *'first bells for the British Empire'* (those for the the the Old North Church in Boston, USA). In 1851 a new tenor bell was added, cast by Messrs. Mears and Stainbank, of the famous Whitechapel Bell Foundry. The extremely prestigious business was in existence for 450 years, only finally closing its doors in 2017. Ironically Mears and Stainbank had purchased Rudhalls of Gloucester when that company had ceased trading in 1838. It is also interesting to note that Holy Rood's original tenor bell was cast by the same company who created the Liberty Bell in Philadelphia, Big Ben, the bells at Canterbury Cathedral and St James's Church in Sydney, Australia, and in more recent times, commissioned the Olympic Bell for the 2012 games in London and the table bells for the TV show Downton Abbey!

When the parishioners of Holy Rood moved to the new church at Christ Church in 1851, the bells moved with them. At the same time, the clock, dating from 1843, was also moved to the new tower at Christ Church. In 1881, two new treble bells, cast by Llewellins and James of Bristol, were added to take the total to eight.

The Church clock mechanism.

Llewellins & James who cast two new bells for Christ Church in 1881.

New Ring of 1924

By the early 1920's, the bells had notched up a minimum of 40 years and a maximum of 180 years service – a total of over 1,000 years between them! Not surprisingly, their fittings were worn out and had become unsafe. A fundraising appeal was launched in October 1923 to raise money for a new ring of ten bells.

The new bells outside the West Door, prior to their installation in 1924 (2).

By early 1924, £1,154 (today's equivalent of £70,000) had been raised in the parish; the Sunday School alone had raised enough to pay for one of the bells in its entirety, which subsequently became known as 'The Children's Bell'. The Freemasons paid for the ninth bell, in memory of John Campbell Maclean. A tenor bell, weighing 22 cwt, was paid for by the ringers, including a substantial bequest from a former ringer, O.W. Layng. The total cost of the new bells was £1,487, with the balance being made up from a credit given by the foundry when the old bells were melted down. The new bells

SWINDON PARISH CHURCH.

ORDER OF SERVICE
AT THE
DEDICATION of
A NEW PEAL OF BELLS.

FRIDAY, APRIL 11th, 1924, at 7 p.m.

Order of service for the dedication of the new bells, 1924.

were cast by the John Taylor & Co. Bellfoundry, at Loughborough, and were dedicated by the Bishop of Bristol on 11th April 1924, being only the second ring of ten in Wiltshire (Trowbridge beat Christ Church by one year). This set of bells has rung at Christ Church ever since; and are regarded by many as among the finest 'ring of ten' for their weight in the country. Thanks to a succession of devoted and skilled steeple keepers, they are still in almost perfect ringing order. A full list of inscriptions on the bells is shown at the end of this chapter.

Bellringing and special peals

Bellringing as we understand it today dates from the seventeenth century, when mechanical developments in the way bells were hung enabled the ringers to control the bell in such a way as to ring 'changes' or a series of sequences. Like any complex activity, bellringing has developed its own arcane language and methods. There is no music as such, but a diagrammatic representation of the changes, based on mathematical principles. The way in which an individual bell is rung during these changes is shown as a blue line running through the diagram.

A 'peal' means something very particular to a bellringer. A 'full peal' indicates a minimum of 5,000 changes without stopping over a period of at least 3 hours – not something to be undertaken by the faint-hearted or the unfit. With over 7 bells, no repeats are needed in working out the changes. Currently, up to eight peals a year are rung at Christ Church, plus numerous quarter peals (1200 – 1300 changes, lasting 45 – 50 minutes).

Special peals have always been rung to mark special events. Of national importance, the victories of Trafalgar and Waterloo were marked in this way, as were the death of the sovereign and the coronation of his or her successor. It is a salutary thought that when all ten bells ring at once, there is a combined weight of 5 tons swinging overhead! The peals rung at Christ Church are all recorded in the archive in the ringing chamber; in addition, some of the special peals are recorded on individual peal boards or plaques, mounted on the walls around the room. The earliest peal recorded in such a way dates from 1896. Two years later, a board recorded the first peal to be rung in Christ Church by ringers who were all railwaymen from the GWR

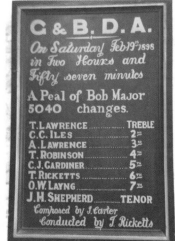

The earliest Peal Boards in the   1898.
Ringing Chamber 1896.

works. In 1923, the Christ Church ringers were the first Wiltshire band to ring a peal in a Surprise method. This was Superlative Surprise Major with 5,088 changes in 3 hours and 12 minutes, rung not at Christ Church itself, but at the Church of All Saints in Wootton Bassett. The band was led by Charlie Gardiner, who was determined that this particular record would be set by Swindon, not by Chippenham, who were proposing to do the same thing!

The first peal to be rung on the new 10 bells was appropriately enough in honour of their dedication, although this was not achieved until 24th January 1925, nine months after the dedication service. The peal was led by the 'Master of the Tower', Mr Ernest Bishop, who was first Captain, and then Master, for 35 years from 1900 to 1935 and had taken a leading part in the re-casting and re-hanging of the new bells. Mr Bishop's name was inscribed on number 6 bell. The peal consisted of 5,037 Stedman Caters in 3 hours, 21 minutes. The term 're-casting' is not strictly accurate. It implies that the original, individual bells were broken up and their metal kept separate, then melted individually and poured into the moulds for the new bells. In other words, casting direct replacements using the same metal for each original, individual bell. In reality, the old bells are much more likely to have been

The bellringers of 1919.

broken up and thrown into the furnace all together, before the new ones were poured from their mixed metal.

During October 1934 the Swindon Guild of Bellringers entertained the Wincanton Guild, as Christ Church was used to help celebrate Mr F. Wilson's 40th anniversary as a bell-ringer, with a quarter peal of the ten bells at Christ Church. The 1,263 changes taking 53 minutes.

In 1918, the end of the First World War was marked by the Allied Victory Peal of 5,040 Stedman Caters in 3 hours, 5 minutes. A peal of 5,014 Stedman Caters (3 hours 14 minutes) was rung on 5th January 1952 to mark the centenary of Christ Church, and a further peal on 9th June 1953 to mark the Coronation of Queen Elizabeth II, and again in 2013 to mark the 60th anniversary of her Coronation. Remarkably, two of the ringers, Brian Bladon and Enid Roberts, rang on both occasions! Enid, who had returned from Australia for the 60th anniversary peal, subsequently offered to pay for a new peal board to record it. The 1953 peal board appears to have been painted in the GWR carriage livery colours of 'chocolate and cream', perhaps using paint left over from the Railway Works following nationalisation in 1948. Indeed, it seemed at one point in the 1950s and '60s, that half of the properties in Swindon had been painted with supplies liberated from the Railway Works!

Quarter peals have been rung on very many occasions, far too

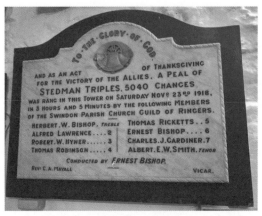

WW1 victory peal board 23 Nov 1918.

*Peal board for the first peal rung on the
new bells, 1925.*

numerous to mention. For example, the 60th anniversary of the re-hanging of the bells on 11th April 1984 and the 70th anniversary on 17th April 1994 (also broadcast on BBC Radio 4). The bells also rang in the new Millennium, as Swindon celebrated with a beacon in the grounds of Christ Church, overlooking the urban sprawl of the new town.

In 1951 the BBC (Western Region) recorded the bells, and again in 1978 for the 'Christmas Day Bells' broadcast. A permanent recording of the bells was made by HMV on a 10-inch record, which sold at a profit for a number of years at a cost of £1-11s (£1.55). But perhaps the most famous advertisement for the bells was the poem written by

Sir John Betjeman – *'On Hearing the Full Peal of Ten Bells from Christ Church, Swindon, Wilts'* – which is reproduced at the beginning of this book.

However, thanks to modern technology, and for those unable to make the steep 46 step climb into the bell ringing chamber, a digital recording of the bells can be listened to on the Christ Church website by visiting:

http://www.christchurchswindon.co.uk/bellringer.php
or https://www.youtube.com/watch?v=68KUEUwD3jI

Bellringers

The relationship of bellringers to the church itself is not as straightforward as it might first appear, and ranges from extremely close to extremely tenuous. Some hold offices within the church such as churchwardens, sidesmen, PCC members, choristers; some worship at one church but ring at others; others do not attend church at all, but ring as a passionate hobbyist. In earlier times, the ringing band had great autonomy from the Vicar, although this did begin to change by the end of the nineteenth century. However, records show that even in the early twentieth century there was a strong reflection of the class structure of society within the band. The ringing master was afforded great respect, even if he was not a regular participant and the office could be more honorary than actual. In contrast, the rank and file who formed the backbone of the band were often not even accorded the privilege of having their names recorded in official reports!

There is little written record of the bellringers at Holy Rood and at Christ Church before 1900, but it is assumed they were active since the bells were augmented to six and then to eight during the course of the nineteenth century. We do know that the Christ Church bellringers, led by Mr Colbron, agreed to perform a special handbell ringing display in 1877, to help raise funds for the church. Mr F.S. Wilson also began his bellringing career at Christ Church in 1894, staying several years, before moving to Somerset. He returned to Christ Church in 1934 to celebrate his 40th anniversary as a ringer. Thankfully, however, Minute books and attendance records do exist from 1901 to the present day, giving a continuous record over the past 120 years.

In Swindon, it is assumed that many of the ringing band were originally local traders; but in time the majority were GWR workers. These men lived and worked in New Swindon, but were attracted by the sound of the bells from Christ Church on the hill in Old Swindon. The ringers were exclusively male until the Second World War, when the first ladies were admitted. The current band is equally divided between the sexes.

Given the high quality of the bells themselves, the standard of ringing has always been similarly ambitious. Christ Church has always attracted and welcomed visiting bands of ringers". Similarly, the home ringers are also dedicated visitors to other towers. There was traditionally an annual outing, dedicated to 'ringing away from home' which has not changed in spirit if it has in cost – the hire of the charabanc for the 1912 outing, for example, cost the grand sum of £5, with 14 suppers at 2 shillings each, coming to a grand total of £1 8s!

Some brief biographical sketches of some of the ringers over the past century are provided below.

Ernest Bishop

Ernest Bishop was born in Horton, near Ilminster, where he first learned to ring. He came to Swindon about 1887 via Bury (Lancashire) and Reading. His first peal in Swindon was Grandsire Triples, rung on 27 September 1890. In his business life, he was an estate agent in the firm of Bishop & Edgington, which still survives today. In his private life he was also a Freemason, and took part in the first peal by a band of Freemasons. Bishop was the Captain at Christ Church Tower from 1900 (and Master when that title was introduced in 1920) until 1935, and well respected as a Ringer. The Minute Books however record the reality of the situation, whereby Bishop was hardly ever present for practices, and the day-to-day running of the Tower was delegated to the Deputy Captain (Captain from 1920), Robert Hyner and then Charlie Gardiner. Nevertheless, Bishop was instrumental in bringing about the new ring of 1924, and is commemorated in the inscription on bell number 6. In May 1927 Bishop was asked to take part in an attempt to ring a full peal of Grandsire Cinques at Exeter Cathedral. Unfortunately, the attempt had to be stopped when one of the ringers fell ill, probably as a result of the extremely hot weather. He rang his last peal at Christ Church on 3rd February 1934. This was followed in March 1935 by a peal on the twelve bells at Cheltenham. The Minute book records the following, for the practice of 4th June of that year: *'no ringing, Mr Bishop passed away'*. Ernest Bishop is buried in Christ Church graveyard, next to the illustrious GWR Chief Mechanical Engineer G. J. Churchward.

Bert Bishop
No relation to Ernest, Bert Bishop was a monumental mason. His down-to-earth approach to his trade was typified by his saying about his customers *'catch 'em with tears in their eyes!'*. He was a great friend of the photographer from the 'Adver' (*Evening Advertiser*), who would come on tower outings and use his professional skills to record the day. As a pair, they would usually be last out of the pub and onto the 'bus. Bert Bert Bishop made two fine marble peal boards recording the 1918 Victory peal on the old eight bells and the first on the new ten. The plaques still hang in the Ringing Chamber today.

John Odey
After moving from Bath to Stanley Street in Swindon in 1912, John Odey, an upholsterer with Chandler Bros, began his time as a bellringer here. Such was his diligence that he soon became 'Tower Keeper'. Sadly, it was to be cut short. Tower records show his exemplary attendance until 18th September 1916, when the register shows he *'left on His Majesty's Service'*. He was mobilised in early 1917 and posted with the 13th Battalion, Durham Light Infantry to the Western Front. By early June 1917 Odey was based in the Ypres Salient around (what would become the infamous) Hill 60. The Battle of Messines started early in the morning of 7th June 1917. Allied forces had employed a new tactic of tunnelling and burying high explosives under enemy lines. Just a few hours before the detonation British General Charles Harington uttered these infamous words, *'Gentlemen, we may not make history*

tomorrow, but we shall certainly change the geography'. At 3.10am the largest non-nuclear explosion in history obliterated the hillside. The Germans responded too, with mining operations and a heavy artillery barrage of their own. The Battle of Messines was considered a British success that greatly boosted moral eamong the Allies, although the cost was high: 25,000 German soldiers and 17,000 Allied troops. The shattered hillside still remains today, the disturbed earth still probably containing the remains of hundreds

John Odey and his family.

of missing men. John Odey's body was never recovered and he was named as one of the missing, presumed dead.

When news of John's death at the Battle of Messines reached Christ Church in June 1917, his fellow ringers rang the bells half-muffled as a final mark of respect. An obituary in the bell ringers' newspaper *The Ringing World* reported that *'Odey's services will be missed by his fellow ringers, his unassuming disposition made him very popular'*.

John Odey's name was added to the 54,000 names of unknown soldiers on the Menin Gate at Ypres. His name appears on four war memorials in Bath – the civic memorial at the entrance to Victoria Park, parish memorials at Widcombe and Bathwick and the memorial in the Abbey to ringers from the Diocese of Bath and Wells. He has no known grave. John Odey's service medals were sold at an auction in 1996 to an anonymous buyer for £20.

John Berry

A quiet, gentle man, he learnt to ring as part of a group that started soon after the 1924 installation. He held several offices in the Tower over his ringing career.

J. Lewis Cockey

Cockey came from a family of bellfounders in Frome in Somerset. His unmarried sisters ran a private school in Bath Road until the 1950's. Cockey worked abroad and in London for many years. His office in London was in Victoria Street near Westminster Abbey, where he was a supernumerary in the ringing band until his retirement to Swindon.

Bill Daniel

A much-loved and respected ringing teacher. His teaching skills were honed by his job at the Garrards factory, where as a Toolroom supervisor he oversaw the progress of raw apprentices to skilled craftsmen. On his death, Bill left the tower a sum of money to go towards an automatic clock winder (installed in 1996); highly appropriate, as Bill had been personally responsible for turning the big, heavy winding handle once a week for many years.

Nancy Davis

Along with Pearl Townsend, Nancy was the first lady ringer recorded at Christ Church, in 1944. Nancy left a legacy of £1,000 in her will that was used to fund the set of glass doors engraved with bell motifs in the south door of the church, as well as the GWR stained glass window in the south porch.

Charlie Gardiner

Charlie was a mainstay of the band in the first half of the twentieth century, with a ringing career which spanned the 1890's to the 1950's. He learned to ring at Beenham, near Newbury, before arriving in Swindon in 1895 to work for the GWR. He was noted for his ringing as part of a number of peals, including the Railwaymen's Peal of 1898. In 1920, he rang at Painswick in a peal of 13,001 Grandsire Cinques, a record which still stands today. A gentleman of the 'old school', he never raised his voice, and always spoke with great dignity. His last peal was for the 1953 Coronation, when he was still able to ring for the full three hours non-stop without a fault. He died on 6th October 1957.

Robert W. Hyner

He was born in Ledbury in Herefordshire, where he learned to ring, despite a deformed hand. Hyner worked for Swindon Press Ltd for 40 years, and joined Christ Church in 1902, when he was resident at The Knoll. He died on the 20th January 1937.

Bert Kynaston

Bert moved to Swindon from Oswestry following the 1923 amalgamation of several railways into the GWR. He was a member of an established ringing family and probably the most accomplished ringer of his day in the southwest of England. He set standards which ringers today still aspire to. Although he moved to Rodbourne before the War, and became a stalwart of the church there, he seldom missed a Tuesday night practice at Christ Church.

Alfred Lawrence

Lawrence learned to ring at Christ Church at the tender age of 13. He worked for the GWR for 54 years and was one of 80 veterans with more than 50 years service who were presented to King George V and Queen Mary in 1924. Lawrence lived at Little London in the last thatched cottage in Swindon. He died in 1945 at the age of 89.

Margaret Richards

A skilled lady ringer who joined the band in 1945 (Nancy Davis and Pearl Townsend had joined the year before).

Thomas Ricketts

Born and learned to ring at Kempsford. He came to Swindon at the age of 20 and took part in the Railwayman's Peal of 1898. He died in 1932.

James H. Sheppard.

A native of Ilminster, he was educated at Bristol University and came to Swindon at the age of 19 as a GWR apprentice, retiring in 1935 as assistant out-station manager. Another Freemason, he was remembered as a great ringing character. He was particularly interested in the tenor bells of the various towers that the band visited. He travelled widely, thanks to the free rail travel provided with his job, but was also a great cyclist in pursuit of new towers to visit. His plus fours, big moustache and racing bike made him a familiar sight in Swindon. He died at his home in Gloucester Street in March 1950 at the age of 80.

Thomas Robinson
One of the band who took up change ringing under O. W. Layng, he died in 1922 at the age of 57.

The Townsend Family – George, Reg, Tom and Pearl
All the Townsend family were in the licensed trade, as well as being bellringers. Tom (Thomas) was born and learnt to ring at St Neots, in Cambridgeshire. He came to Swindon in 1923, and died in 1959 at the age of 60. Tom was licensee of the Victoria Arms. A big man in a brown suit and boots, often sucking a peppermint, he always ensured that there were fresh flowers on the tower table. Pearl was his daughter, who along with Nancy Davis was one of the first lady ringers at Christ Church. George was the publican at the White House, near the station, until he retired. Always smartly dressed, he sported a dapper diamond tiepin. His son Reg ran the Old Town Station refreshment rooms, even after the rail traffic ceased there – inevitably it became known as the 'Ghost Train'. Reg was a well-known personality in the town as well, running a 1920's Bentley Tourer, complete with 'dicky seat'.

Walter Trueman.
Although not a full-time Christ Church ringer, he was associated with the tower. He was invited to ring by Charlie Gardiner in 1920 at the age of 17. Firstly for practices and then for services. Walter had the distinction to ring in the last peal on the old eight, and the tenor on the first peal of the new ten.

He established a strong band of ringers at Blunsdon before the war. Eventually back trouble caused Walter to retire from ringing in 1975. He subsequently retired to Romsey. He remained as enthusiastic as ever about ringing right up until his death in 2002 at the age of 99.

Eli Vincent

A GWR employee and a quiet, modest man, he could ring the tenor with the accuracy of a metronome.

George Wells

Known as 'Long George', as he was nearly six and a half feet tall! A gentle giant, he is remembered in the tower by the gift of a beautiful bookcase donated by his niece. George was buried at Christ Church, very close to Eli Vincent.

Modern Times

The ringers of Christ Church continue to be active. A number of the current band have been dedicated ringers at Christ Church for many years, some for over half a century. Regular Sunday ringing took place without fail throughout the 20th century, apart from the war years when ringing was banned between June 1940 and January 1944. The ban had been imposed by the Government, because of the fear of a German invasion. Had such an attack occurred, church bells were to be rung as a warning to the population. The ringers' attendance records for 1940 show an entry in purple ink, written on 9th June – '*All Ringing Suspended*'. In the weeks that followed an '*A*', for absent, was marked against many of the ringers' names, as they had either joined up or were engaged on essential work. The ringers used handbells during this period to keep in practice. Ringing was also suspended between August 1959 and February 1960 when work was carried out on the steeple and again between May and December 2005. Since 1901, (and possibly before) regular practice has always taken place on Tuesday nights, when newcomers can be 'shown the ropes'! The perennial problem of attracting and retaining enough youngsters to keep the band going is no different to 50 years ago.

Regular maintenance ensures that the bells are kept in first class order, and new ropes are purchased every 8 to 10 years. In addition, the belfry contains a small library of ringing publications, including every issue of *The Ringing World* since it was first published in 1911, and a set of handbells, all donated by past and present ringers. Previously the bellringers also had one other duty – to wind the church clock by hand once a week which they had done for 150 years since it was removed from Holy Rood. This task came to an end in 1996, when an automatic winding mechanism was finally installed. The adjustment to and from British Summer Time, however, remained a manual operation until October 2020 when this too became automated thanks to a device installed in 2020 by the Cumbria Clock Company and paid for by a legacy from John Plaister, an eminent horologist, member of the congregation and trustee of the Friends of Christ Church.

Because of the essential work carried out to the stonework of the tower and spire, the bells fell silent again, after ringing for the 6.30 evening service on Sunday 1st May 2005. During this period of enforced abstinence the ringers continued to hold weekly practices and rang regularly at other churches in the area. The bells themselves also received some attention during this period. The clappers were refaced and lined at the Loughborough foundry of John Taylor Ltd – the foundry at which they were originally cast in 1924. The clappers were then displayed in the church to give everyone the opportunity to witness the size and weight of each one. Finally, on 17th December, a team comprising Daniel Pitt, Brian Harris, James Harris and Mike Palmer began the reassembly project. Eric Sutton and Michael Stanley having first cleared up the worst of the mess made by the builders in the Ringing Room.

The bells' wooden pulley wheels were also refurbished by Bernard Oxborrow and replaced in their housings in the run up to Christmas. Finally, the bells were able to ring again in time for New Year's Day 2006, and (according to many Swindonians) could be heard from even further away than before!

During July of 2011, as part of the centenary celebrations of The Gloucester & Bristol Diocesan Association of Church Bell Ringers, the Swindon branch held an open day, with members visiting 19 'ringable' towers throughout the town and in other locations ranging from

Christ Church, to Ashton Keynes and across the M4 to Wroughton. This event reflected the social side of ringing, which has seen ringers from Christ Church welcomed all across the world to church towers as far away as Australia, New Zealand, and the USA – including Hawaii.

At the Church's Christmas Market in 2017 the rare opportunity to climb the 46 steep stairs to the belfry was given to visitors, giving them the unique opportunity to witness the history of the bell tower first-hand. One guest, however, used the stairs as a special way of entering the church and surprising all the children present – Father Christmas!

In November 2018 a special event saw the band from Christ Church ring a special three-and-a-half-hour peal as part of the commemoration marking 100 years since the Armistice. The ringing was a 'full peal, rung half muffled', and an especially poignant occasion, as it gave an opportunity to remember all the fallen from Christ Church, particularly John Odey (mentioned above) and William 'Harry' Thomas, the son of Swindon pub owner Henry. A new peal board has also been designed to mark the occasion, incorporating a ropework moulding against a white background, and will be completed by early 2021.

Harry Thomas was born in 1888, and volunteered to fight in the Great War, alongside many other Swindonians. However, just before his 30th birthday he was badly wounded during the push on German defences at Arras in April 1917 and died shortly afterwards.

Harry's Bell.

What is less well known is that Harry, who was a talented artist, could have avoided his call-up to the army call-up on medical grounds. However, he voluntarily chose to undergo a painful hernia operation enabling him to be declared fit for duty in 1915. Harry's poignant letters home tell us of soldiers battling both the Germans and the terrible conditions in the trenches: *'I have not had a change of clothes for weeks, nor a wash or shave for days and my feet have been wet for a week, but I am not especially uncomfortable in spite of it all.'*

William 'Harry' Thomas.

Following the war, Harry's father Henry (a wealthy local businessman and pub owner) paid for his son's name to be added to the second of Christ Church's ring of 10 bells. Henry Thomas was a member of the Old Town committee that organised the recasting of the church bells in 1924.

The public were invited to climb the 46 steps and experience the ringing room in the tower for themselves, during the Heritage Open Day and Autumn Fayre in 2019. Sadly, the impending events of 2020 would preclude a repeat of this popular experience.

As the coronavirus crisis impacted the Church in 2020 it also affected the bellringers too. Eventually, some ringing was allowed to resume, but with significant restrictions, including the use of just five of the bells to maintain social distancing between the ringers. Like all parts of the Church, and of society, the ringers wait in nervous anticipation, wondering what developments 2021 will bring.

Details of Christ Church Bells

The bells began as a ring of six at Holy Rood church, cast by Abel Rudhall of Gloucester in 1741. The tenor was replaced with one cast by the Whitechapel Foundry in 1851, at the time the bells were moved to Christ Church. Two additional bells were supplied by Llewellins & James of Bristol in 1881 to make a ring of eight. In 1924, those eight bells were replaced with the present ring of ten by John Taylor & Co. of Loughborough. Most of the inscriptions of the previous bells were reproduced on the new ones, along with additional inscriptions, as detailed below. It is interesting to note that some of the weights of the bells supplied in 1924 have recently been discovered to be incorrect. The bell foundry admitted in 2005 that most of the bells are, in fact, smaller than claimed when originally supplied in 1924. The correct weights are listed here:

BELL	ORIGINAL WEIGHT	OLD INSCRIPTION	ADDITIONAL NEW INSCRIPTION	CURRENT WEIGHT
1 Treble	4:3:9	Henry G. Baily MA Vicar John Chandler (Churchwardens) William Reynolds	William Dean (Parish Clerk) 1883 – 1923	5:0:13
2	5:1:14	Presented by J.E.G. Bradford in memory of his Mother, 1881	In memory of my son Private W.H. Thomas, HAC. Killed in action in France in 1917. H.W.T	4:3:15
3	6:2:12	Peace and Good Neighbourhood A R 1741	Suffer little children to come Unto Me. Given by Children	5:1:19
4	7:1:4	Prosperity to this Parish A R 1741		5:2:16
5	7:3:13	Prosperity to the Church of England A R 1741		6:3:2

6	8:0:8	Wm. Nichols. Vicar A R 1741	Canon C.A. Mayall, Vicar F. Pleydell Goddard Churchwardens F.W. Marilliar (CBE) E. Bishop Secretary	7:3:19
7	9:2:8	Richard Wayt & Wm Lawrence Church Wardens A R 1741	F. Pleydell Goddard E. Kathleen Goddard 1895	9:2:12
8	13:0:11	(Tenor Bell 1851)	In loving memory of my Father and Mother S.V.R.	11:0:23
9			Given by Freemasons in memory of Brother John Campbell Maclean	15:1:13
10 Tenor			Given by the Ringers	21:3:9

Peal Boards in the Ringing Chamber.

Peal board to commemorate the 60th anniversary of Her Majesty's Coronation, 2013

Hastings stays. These were invented by former engineer Revd. Edward Hastings Horne in 1892.

Remembered with Honour

Their Name Liveth   for Evermore

On Saturday 10th November 2018, a peal of
5039 Grandsire Caters in 3 hours 23 minutes

Cynthia E. Howell	Treble	Simon W. Edwards	6
Lucy H. Eyles	2	Brian Harris	7
Hilda C. Ridley	3	Richard L. Thumwood	8
John R. Ridley	4	Mark Edwards	9
Jeremy A. H. Samson	5	Alan M. Eyles	Tenor

Composed by George F. Williams   Conducted by Simon W. Edwards

Rung half-muffled before a Festival of Commemoration of Swindon's role in
World War I, remembering especially Pte. John H. Odey of this tower
and Pte. William H. Thomas in whose memory the second bell was given.

Rev'd Canon Simon M. Stevenette, Vicar

The agreed design of the newly commissioned Peal Board, to be in place by 2021.

15

A Hidden Story

Within the grounds of Christ Church lie many graves, some old and worn, some fallen and damaged, some new and pristine. Each one bears a simple epitaph that conceals a life's story, obscured from the casual passer-by; perhaps only known to a few family members, who are themselves now gone. The 170-year old churchyard conceals many remarkable stories, perhaps of devotion, sacrifice, bravery, or tragedy. To recount all of those tales would require an entirely new book, and it would be an injustice to abbreviate them all, in a foolhardy attempt to squeeze them into this one. Instead, I have selected one story from among those memories laid to rest within the churchyard, which – although relatively unknown – is so remarkable it would be remiss of me not to include it.

Joyce Garraway was born in Old Town, Swindon during the summer of 1922. Britain was at the height at of its Imperial power. The 'sun never set on the British Empire', and it certainly shined down over 71 Prospect Place, in Old Town, as George Garraway introduced his neighbours to the family's newly born daughter Joyce. Meanwhile trams still clattered down Victoria Hill into the town, lucky owners of the new Austin 7 motored along Swindon's streets. Families wanting to listen to the new BBC Radio service on the family wireless set where forced to pay the newly introduced Licence Fee of 10 shillings, while men drank in the many public houses discussing the impending General Election.

Joyce enjoyed a happy and uneventful childhood. She attended Prospect Place Methodist Church as a child, then, later, Sunday School at Christ Church. Her family regularly attended services at the church too. Joyce, like many other young girls, grew up through the hardships of the depression in the 1930s, leading a mundane and sheltered existence. Finally, as the future seemed a little rosier, and she reached adulthood, war was declared; and, virtually overnight, the town became a very different place. Swindon placed itself on a war footing. The large GWR factory made Swindon a target for the Germany Heinkel bombers, and well within their range. The church bells fell silent, gasmasks were issued, blackout blinds and blast tape were placed over the windows of the houses, and the streets were plunged into darkness at nights. Swindon filled with servicemen all looking for entertainment before being shipped off on their next posting. At one such dance in 1940 Joyce met a handsome and dashing young flyer named Edwin Cyril Graham. He was an experienced wireless operator and air gunner with the Royal Air Force, and newly promoted to Sergeant. Then aged 25, and seven years Joyce's senior, Edwin Graham (known as Ed) was interesting and well travelled. Born in Saharanphur in Bengal, India in September 1914, his parents Arthur and Muriel then moved to London. After receiving a good education, Ed Graham then joined the RAF prior to the outbreak of war. By the time the Blitz arrived, and he had met Joyce, Graham was already an experienced flyer. Stationed near to Swindon, the couple found time to see each and soon fell in love. While awaiting his next posting Graham proposed and Joyce accepted. A June day in 1941 was selected for the wedding and the couple chose Christ Church for the ceremony. Graham's leave was extended by a few days to enable the marriage to take place and the marriage licence was hurried through. The government's regulations on weddings, caused by rationing and shortages, meant the young couple were restricted to a 'war wedding'. A car to bring Joyce to Christ Church was governed by distance, petrol consumed and a time limit of two hours. Luckily, someone managed to obtain camera film to record the big event. In spite of the wartime restrictions, family and friends rallied around to chip in with clothing coupons for the wedding dress. Sufficient material was scraped together for bridesmaids' outfits. Her mother's sewing machine was kept busy as the preparations intensified.

Regardless of the number of guests, the only thing allowed 'on the ration' for a wedding was two pounds of cooked ham, and nothing more. Again, family and friends came to the rescue, donating their valuable rations of butter, tea and sugar. Some gave up their precious bottles of preserves and those with gardens raided their winter stores of potatoes, beetroot and swede. A wedding cake was created, using whatever ingredients had been donated, and decorated with any trimmings that could be found. Flowers were strictly rationed too. The bride's bouquet was also limited by the regulations. A dozen red roses was an entire month's ration for the florist!

George Garraway gave his daughter away and the wedding was attended by family and friends. Revd. Gilbert performed the service.

Shortly after the wedding, and a few days together, Sergeant Graham's posting came through and he was ordered back to his squadron. Graham was attached to 210 Squadron, based at Oban, on the west coast of Scotland, and tasked with protecting the Atlantic convoys, by patrolling the grey ocean waters in search of German U-Boats.

On July 14th, just four weeks after his marriage, Sergeant Graham and the rest of his crew were ordered to fly to the Marine Aircraft Experimental Establishment at RAF Helensburgh, near Greenock, to collect their Catalina Seaplane, which had been sent for an overhaul. An overnight stay in Helensburgh in 1941 would have seemed a very welcome contrast to spending countless hours in Catalina seaplanes combing the Atlantic for U-Boats. Visiting RAF crews hosted by the MAEE stayed at Rhu, usually in the Officers' Mess (the requisitioned Royal Northern Yacht Club headquarters, which retained its opulent surroundings previously enjoyed by yacht club members). The off-duty pilots and aircrew drank in the Rhu Inn while the flying boats were serviced and repaired at the Rhu Hangars, or on the slipway. Catalina patrols of the Atlantic searching for U-Boats took a toll on both aircrew and aircraft. In contrast RAF Helensburgh was generally regarded as a 'good place to be at' during the war.

The crew of Catalina AH 533 consisted of 27-year-old Squadron Leader Patrick Hutchinson, co-pilot Edward Ruxton Pinches, Sergeant Wireless Operator Edwin Cyril Graham, Corporal James Calder Kinniard, Corporal Tudor Simner-Jones, Leading Aircraftman Charles Arthur Kew, Aircraftman First Class Ronald Feamley, and Aircraftman John Kelly.

There is no record of what Squadron Leader Hutchinson and his crew did during their short stay at Helensburgh — no doubt they had time on their hands before taking off the following day. It is also

Catalina Mk 1.

not known if Ed Graham was even able to tell his new bride Joyce exactly where he had been stationed. Restrictions were placed on what information could be divulged, even to spouses, to prevent vital knowledge ending up in the enemy's hands. Had he told her, she may well have been pleased, imagining that an obscure posting on the west coast of Scotland would be far away from the dangers of the south coast or of flying missions over occupied Europe.

It was the morning of Tuesday 15th July 1941. Consolidated Catalina Mk 1 AH533 was overhauled, serviced and checked. After being signed off, and marked in the log, as *'ready to fly'* by the Squadron Leader the seaplane took off along the Gareloch. Another Catalina seaplane flown by Pilot Officer Ted Southwell, whose seaplane had also been at Helensburgh for overhaul, took off first. His Catalina arrived safely at Oban, Ed Graham's plane did not.

A search was mounted. Pilots (including the famous Percy Hatfield, who had tracked the fleeing German battleship Bismarck during a record 27-hour flight in a Catalina) fruitlessly scoured the Atlantic, following the supposed route taken by Graham's plane. Percy Hatfield reported 'nothing seen'. The search was widened to cover the coastline and the mist covered islands of the Inner Hebrides. Other pilots, anxious to locate their lost colleagues, reported 'nothing spotted'. Finally, at 4.37 pm, the burnt-out wreckage of the crashed Catalina AH 533 was spotted by Aircraftman Don Campbell, scattered on high ground known as Cruach na Seilcheigh on the northern tip of the Isle of Jura. The island lies 20 miles south of Mull and approximately 70 miles west of Helensburgh.

The rescue seaplane landed nearby on the water and the crew went ashore to the crash scene to find just one survivor, John Kelly, who had dragged himself from the wreckage, despite a badly damaged leg. The remains of the rest of the crew were taken back to Oban by pinnace.

It seems that after Ed Graham's Catalina had taken off from Helensburgh it approached Oban by a different route to Southwell's plane. In bad weather the crew of AH 533 had attempted to land, but were forced to take off again, damaging the aircraft in the process. Squadron Leader Hutchinson decided to either re-try at their earlier landing site, or to land out at sea, awaiting better inshore conditions. Either way, the pilot turned onto a southerly course from Oban and while flying in low cloud the aircraft crashed into the north east face of Cruach na Seilcheigh, where it burst into flames. Pieces of the wreckage are still visible to this day.

Tragically, if AH 533 had followed Southwell's plane and flown via the Sound of Bute, at an altitude of 3,000 – 4,000 feet, the journey would have been accomplished with visibility of three miles and in relative ease.

There seems to be some confusion as to whether Sergeant Graham (who was the aircraft's wireless operator) contacted Oban by radio to report any problems. Maybe Squadron

Crash wreckage is still visible today. The view towards the Gulf of Corryvreckan.

Leader Hutchinson thought it not necessary as they had almost 'made it home', or perhaps there simply was not enough time in the few seconds before tragedy struck.

Ironically, AH 533 has been wrongly recorded in national records

MILITARY HONOURS

Swindon Funeral of Sergt. E. C. Graham

The death has taken place under exceptionally tragic circumstances of Sergt. Edwin Cyril Graham, R.A.F., of Oban, Scotland, aged 24 years. Sergt. Graham was born in India, but came to England with his parents when a youth, and lived in London. He joined the R.A.F. before the war broke out in September, 1939, and became a wireless operator air gunner.

It was only a month or five weeks ago that Sergt. Graham was married at the Parish Church, Swindon, to Miss Joyce Garraway, youngest daughter of Mr. and Mrs. George Garraway, of 71, Prospect-place, Swindon.

The body was brought to Swindon under the direction of a sergeant of the R.A.F., and the funeral, which was military, took place from 71, Prospect-place, on Tuesday afternoon. The coffin, which was covered with the Air Force Standard, was borne on a tender. Over 20 young men of the R.A.F. acted as a Guard of Honour, aid six sergeants were the bearers.

The service, which was very impressive, was conducted by the Vicar, Canon John Gilbert, and "Reveille" and "Last Post" were sounded at the graveside. There was a large congregation in church.

The family mourners were: Mrs. Joyce Graham (widow), Mr. and Mrs. Graham (father and mother), Mr. Douglas Graham and Mr. Clarence Graham (brothers), Mrs. D. Graham (sister-in-law), Squadron Leader Hammond and Mrs. Hammond (uncle and aunt), Mr. Jones (uncle), Miss Heather Hammond (cousin), Mr. George Garraway (father-in-law), Mr and Mrs. Mead (brother-in-law and sister-in-law), Mrs. Nulty and Mrs. J. Garraway (sister-in-law), Mr. and Mrs. R. Lambert (uncle and aunt), Mr. and Mrs. Cryer (uncle and aunt), Mrs. Smith and Miss Molly Smith (friends).

3Sgt. Graham's Funeral (Evening Advertiser 1941).

as having taken part in the capture of U-570 and the Enigma cipher machine on August 27th 1941. That dramatic event was the stuff that films are made of, sadly it was not Swindon's own Edwin Graham and his Catalina AH 533 that was involved in that tide-turning event, but Catalina AH 553. AH 533 was by that date no more.

Lone survivor John Kelly was treated in hospital for his injuries. He recovered but with a slightly shortened leg. The body of Edwin Graham was returned to Swindon, where he was to be given a full military funeral, with honours, at Christ Church.

The funeral took place from Joyce's home in Prospect Place on Tuesday 22nd July. Sergeant Graham's body was brought to Christ Church borne on a tender and draped with the RAF Standard. Twenty RAF serviceman formed a guard of honour and six sergeants acted as pall bearers. Revd. Gilbert conducted '*a moving and impressive service*', in front of a large congregation, and *The Last Post* was sounded at the graveside. As well as Graham's widow and family members, a large number of friends and colleagues attended. Joyce returned to her mundane life at her parents' home in Prospect Place. The brief marriage was over in the cruellest possible way. Her

271

husband's body had been interred at Christ Church and Joyce often visited the graveside. The grave would be eventually be marked with an official Commonwealth War Grave, which reads as follows:

IN FOND REMEMBRANCE OF
EDWIN CYRIL GRAHAM (SN 648550) SERGT 210
SQUADRON R.A.F. KILLED ON ACTIVE SERVICE15TH JULY
1941. AGED 26 YEARS
MEMORY – LINGERS – STILL

If one visits Christ Church now, the neat, and understated, official Commonwealth War Grave of Sergeant Graham sits gracefully in the gently sloping churchyard, hiding its tragic story from the world. Strangely, next to Graham's final resting place lies an even simpler official war grave to another RAF flyer. The men never knew each other, but their stories are tragically intertwined.

The unassuming stone plaque rests on the ground next to Graham's grave and reads simply:

IN LOVING MEMORY OF
IVOR JOHN SANSUM
DIED OCT 7TH 1946 AGED 25

This is his story.

Ivor Sansum came from the large and well known Sansum family in South Marston, near Swindon. His mother had been of Irish and Gypsy descent. Born on 26th March 1921, Ivor had lived with his parents in Oxford Road, Stratton-St-Margaret, Swindon, and had started as a machine apprentice at a Swindon factory, after leaving school. Sansum joined the RAF in early 1941 and trained as a wireless operator with the Operational Training Unit at Abingdon. His knowledge gained working with machinery during his apprenticeship no doubt proved useful. After training he was posted to 78 Squadron, Bomber Command, tasked with flying bombing raids over occupied Europe.

Early in 1943 Ivor Sansum, while on leave from his squadron's base at RAF Breighton in Yorkshire, returned to Swindon. While out drinking with colleagues one evening he met Joyce Graham

(Garraway), who had now been widowed for almost two years. The couple struck up an immediate understanding and saw each other socially. When Sansum returned to his squadron he promised to write to Joyce.

On the 15th July 1943 (coincidentally, the second anniversary of Ed Graham's death), Ivor Sansum and the rest of the crew of Halifax bomber DT768 EY-W took off as part of a mission to bomb Montbéliard , a city in the Bourgogne-Franche-Comté region of eastern France. The Peugeot motor-car factory close to the town had been converted to make tank turrets for the German army and Focke-Wulf engine parts for the German air force; and was an important target for Bomber Command. At approximately 12.20am, in pitch darkness, the Halifax Bomber developed engine failure, possibly from German anti-aircraft fire and started to lose altitude as well as flying speed. Pilot Officer Oswald Marshall, ordered the remaining crew of six to bale out over Nogent-le-Rotrou in northern France, approximately 110 miles southwest of Paris. It would be the final time Ivor Sansum would see any of his fellow crew again as they bravely jumped from the bomber's doors into the blackness. Pilot Oswald Marshall was unable to bring the plane under control and it crashed into the French countryside, lighting up the skyline. He was killed instantly. Second in command, Flying Officer Norman Reid, was also killed. Both men were buried in the nearby village. The remaining five flyers, scattered by the wind, landed safely but were separated and in darkness somewhere in the French countryside. Navigator D. Gibson, and gunners Stevenson and Lee, were all betrayed while trying to seek help, and captured, eventually being sent to German Prisoner of War camp Stalag Luft III (now immortalised on film as the locations of *'The Great Escape'* and *'The Wooden Horse'*). That left Flight Engineer Peter Ablett and Wireless Operator Ivor Sansum. Ablett managed to escape capture by patrolling German soldiers and was put in touch with one of the many escape lines, who were able to smuggle him close to the border with neutral Spain, until he was taken ill crossing the mountains, and was captured by a German patrol. That left just Ivor Sansum. RAF flyers were briefed in evading capture and taught some words of French, as well as being kitted out with maps and compass hidden in the lining of their clothing. Sansum's incredible story follows now, in his own words, and is taken from his classified interrogation given to Military Intelligence following his return to England. The document was marked 'Most Secret' by M19 (the covert department tasked with supporting the resistance movement in occupied Europe) and was classified 'Secret', under the Official Secrets Act, for many years following the war. Now declassified and available in the National Archives in Kew this is the first time the document has been published in its entirety:

M19 CLASSIFIED - **MOST SECRET**
EVADED CAPTURE IN FRANCE
Statement by 1311760 Sgt, Sansum, Ivor James, 78 Sqd
Bomber Command
The information in this report is to be treated as
MOST SECRET

'I took off from Breighton (Yorkshire) in a Halifax aircraft about 2200 hours on 15 Jul 1943 to bomb Montbéliard. About 0020 hrs (16 Jul) the aircraft lost flying speed and went into a dive and the captain gave the order to bail out. I came down in wooded country close to Nogent-le-Rotrou. My pilot and bombardier were buried in the village. I sprained my ankle on landing but I hid my parachute and Mae West (lifejacket) *in a ditch and started to walk south, hoping to find some of the other members of my crew. I stopped at two houses trying to get help, but did not meet with any success. About 0230 hrs I lay down on a straw stack in a farmyard and went to sleep. In the morning I was discovered by a young lad. I spoke only a few words of French, but I managed to explain who I was. He went to fetch his mother who brought me some milk and told me to move on as a gendarme would soon be arriving. I walked on a little further, but as my ankle was giving me a great deal of pain, I lay down in a field. While I was there a woman let some cows into the field and she saw me. She did not offer to help, but told me to shut the gate when I left.*

Half an hour later a man arrived. He told me to hide, as there were many Germans in the vicinity. He then put me on his back and carried me to a wood nearby. He returned a little later bringing me food and wine. Some time after this he came back again and gave me a note. This note, written in bad English, asked me if I had any friends or any other means of helping myself. I wrote back saying I had 2000 francs and a map. A reply came back saying this was not much use and I had best give myself up.

I told my unknown helper the contents of this last note, and he went away again returning with a horse and cart. He carried me into the cart, hid me under some straw and drove into Nogent-le-Rotrou. Here he took me into a back yard and I was taken out of the cart, put into a basket chair and given some food. I also met the girl who had been sending me notes. She went away and returned with a man who spoke good English. He told me that it would not be safe for me to remain where I was, as there was a German garrison in the town. I spent the night at this house and about 1000 hrs (17 Jul) I was given a civilian mackintosh, put in a horse-drawn cart and taken by another man to his farm about two kilometres away. I do not remember his name or address. I remained there for three weeks. My RAF uniform was taken away and destroyed and I was given a set of civilian clothes. During this time I was constantly visited by the girl who written the note to me. She brought me English books and told me she was trying to get in touch with someone who would help me. After two weeks this girl managed to contact someone called Jacqueline Frelat, in Paris. From this point the journey was arranged for me. About the beginning of Aug '43, Jacqueline Frelat, got in touch with a member of an organisation in Paris. This man was known to me as Axel. He then sent a lady called Helene Gill to see me.'

Jacqueline Frelat, who lived locally in Nogent-le-Rotrou helped a great number of evading flyers during the war and would eventually be arrested by the Gestapo on 1ˢᵗ June 1944. She was tortured by the Gestapo for two months in Chartres Jail, in an attempt to find out the location of Mme. Helene Gill. Jacqueline never divulged any information and survived the war when the Germans fled suddenly in August, as the American Army arrived, leaving the prison gates open.

Despite a price on her head and the Germans threatening to 'cut

Helene Gill, who survived the war,
but kept her escape work secret for
the remainder of her life.

off her head', Helene Gill survived the war. She was a Russian woman, living in France and married to an Englishman, at the beginning of the war. When the Germans invaded France, her English husband was interned in a concentration camp. She, however, was allowed to remain free (partly because she had a three-year-old son), although the Germans were suspicious of her activities and she was forced to routinely report her movements to the local Police Station. Despite this, she bravely continued to help the escape lines, evading capture herself and eventually settled in Australia. Helene Gill died in 2011 at the age of 94. She never spoke of her wartime heroics and her family only discovered her secret after her death.

> 'On 4th Aug I met Mlle. Carmen, a member of Axel's organisa-
> tion. This was the first time she had guided an evader, and it was
> decided that Mme. Gill should also accompany us for part of the
> journey.'

Ivor Sansum was taken to the Railway Station by the farmer and Mlle. Carmen. Here he met Helene Gill and her young son. They waited on the platform for about five minutes then boarded the train. Mlle. Carmen sat with the child and Sansum and Helene Gill stood in the corridor. However, as Sansum's ankle was hurting they managed to find a seat. They were forced to change trains at Le Maur, at which time Sansum was forced to walk through a crowd of German soldiers on the platform. He managed to remain calm and was not challenged. Eventually they arrived at Mortree, where Sansum was delivered to Mr Chevreuil the Mayor (and leader of the local resistance).

'In Mortree I was taken to the house of the Mayor. He took me to his sister's house and I remained there for two weeks. At 1700 hrs on 19ᵗʰ Aug, Sergeant Mankowitz (an escaping United States Airforce pilot whom Sansum had met in Mortree), *Jacqueline and I, left for Lyon by car. We went first to Le Mans and there met Mme. Helene Gill again. She told us we must not wait in Le Mans, as a British plane had crashed in the vicinity the night before and the Germans were searching for survivors. We drove on to Ecommoy and spent the night in the woods. At 630 hrs (20 Aug) we drove to the station and caught a train for Tours. We waited for two hours at Tours and then got another train to Bourges, arriving in the evening. From Bourges we took a taxi and went to a farm, about 3km north of a village that I believe was called St. Florent.*

Next morning we crossed the old line of Demarcation without any trouble (the Demarcation line marked the divide between occupied and Vichy 'Free' France up until 1942). *We then boarded a train for Lyon going via Montlucon. At Lyon there was a hitch in the arrangements and we were not met at the station. Jacqueline tried to telephone M. Bonamour, but could not contact him, and we spent the night on the platform. Next day at 730 hrs we went by taxi to M. Bonamour's house at 8 Avenue Marechal Foch, Lyon. He gave us a meal and then contacted a man whom we were told was a British agent. That afternoon M. Jules and a girl called Annie came to see us. We were taken back to Annie's flat in the Rue Vendome. We told them our story, and M. Jules said this would be checked with London. He told us that all his communications had to go through Geneva, and after about two weeks word came through from Geneva that he was to use his own method of evacuating us. M. Jules told us that he had previously had an organisation which had been picked up by the Germans and that he was the only surviving member. He was just starting a new one and had no contacts. On 12th Sept, after we been given false identity papers Mankowitz and I were sent to stay with M. Sigot at Flurieux, about 40 km north of Lyon. We stayed there for four weeks.'*

Lyon's cafes were busy with German officers and the Gestapo patrolled the town. Despite two narrow escapes, when their false papers were checked and when Helene Gill had to hide to avoid a Gestapo check, the group were taken into the city to be handed over to another Escape Line, who would coordinate the rest of the journey.

'At 1730 hrs on 12 Oct we were taken into Lyon and handed over to a man belonging to another organisation. This man said he could only look after one of us, and it was decided that I should remain with him and Mankowitz should go back with M. Jules. I do not know my new helper's name, but his organisation went under the name of "VIC". I met Pilot Officer Brown at this address (another evading pilot).
At 1800 hrs, 25 Oct, I was collected by a man and taken to another flat where I met a Belgian Naval Officer and two British agents, one English and one Belgian, whom I was told were going to Spain with us. At 2245 hrs that night we got on the Perpignan train. The Belgian and I, accompanied by a lady guide, travelled to Carcassonne, which we reached about 0830 hrs (26 Oct). From Carcassone, the Belgian and I, our lady guide and a new guide we had just met, went by diesel train to Quillan, arriving about 1200 hrs. Here our first guide left us; and we went by motor coach to Perpignan. At Perpignan we got off the bus and walked to our rendezvous about 2 or 3 kilometres away, where we met up with the other members of our party and two new guides.
We were given a supply of sandwiches and a pair of rope-soled shoes and started off on our journey at once. It was raining hard, but we walked across country for about nine hours. We were to have rested on the way, but, as we were late, we were handed over to new guides at 0700 hrs (26 Oct) and continued walking all that day. At dusk we were taken over by another guide who took us almost up to the frontier. After walking for about three hours we stopped at a farm. We remained at this house from 27 – 29 Oct.
At 1800 hrs on 29 Oct we walked two or three kilometres down a road and were then picked up by a car and driven through Figueras to a

village south of Barcelona. We spent the night in a hotel and the next morning at 0700 hrs caught a train for Barcelona, arriving at 0900 hrs. Here we went to the British Consulate.'

Sgt. Ivor Sansum, 12 Nov 1943

Following a full 17 weeks on the run, Ivor Sansum was taken to Gibraltar and, from there, flown back to Bristol on the 11th November 1943. Following his debrief he was able to return to Swindon and was reunited with Joyce who had heard nothing for 17 weeks; and may well have presumed her new sweetheart was dead. The couple resumed their short-lived romance and married at Christ Church in 1944. Revd. Gilbert again performing the service.

Ivor Sansum survived the war and remained a Warrant Officer with 187 Squadron even after the cessation of hostilities. Joyce breathed a sigh of relief in 1945 when the bells rang again at Christ Church to celebrate the end of the conflict. The couple settled into the routine of married life, living with Joyce's family in Prospect Place. Ivor was stationed at Membury Airfield, close enough to Swindon that he could easily return home on his motorcycle after his shift at the base.

A year after the war, on Monday 7th October 1946, Ivor was returning from Membury Aerodrome after another day at work. As he passed the Spotted Cow public house, at Coate on the outskirts of Swindon, he had to manoeuvre his motorcycle around a brewer's lorry delivering to the pub. Just as he drove past the rear of the vehicle the delivery driver, failing to notice Ivor, swung open the doors at the back of the vehicle. With a sickening noise the swinging door caught Ivor and sent him flying from his motorcycle and crashing into the ground. In the days before crash helmets he stood little chance. Despite being rushed to the Victoria Hospital in Swindon he was pronounced dead on arrival.

Joyce Sansum had lost her second husband in four years.

Ivor Sansum was buried at Christ Church in the same grave as Joyce's first husband Edwin Graham. Later, both men were given official Commonwealth War Grave designation, with the stone carrying Sansum's name becoming the curb stone on Graham's grave. Their details were entered onto the War Graves' Register, along with the many thousands who served so bravely during both world wars.

Ivor Sansum's will was read in 1947. Like most servicemen, employed in a hazardous occupation, he had been encouraged to make early provision for his loved ones. He left all his worldly possessions to Joyce, some £998 (approximately £40,000 today).

Death in Motor-Cycle Crash After Surviving War Hazards

AFTER surviving the hazards of the war years, when he was missing for 17 weeks following an operational flight over enemy territory, Warrant Officer Ivor John Sansum (25) of 71, Prospect, Swindon, has met his death in a motor-cycle accident.

The fatality occurred on Monday night, when, as reported in yesterday's "Evening Advertiser," Warrant Officer Sansum's motor-cycle was involved in collision with a cattle lorry.

He was stationed at Membury Aerodrome, and had been in the R.A.F. for about six years. He was reported missing in July, 1943, when he was a sergeant wireless - operator. He came down in enemy occupied territory, but after being missing for 17 weeks, he managed to make his way back to England with the assistance of members of the underground movement on the Continent.

He was married three years ago, and by his death, Mrs. Sansum has lost her second husband in six years. Her first husband was killed during the war only three weeks after they were married. She is the daughter of Mr. G. E. Garraway, with whom she lives at 71, Prospect.

I. J. SANSUM

Report of Ivor Sansum's death 1946.

Happily, Joyce did find love again, and married a young man called Leslie Morris in 1949. Leslie, a fitter in the Railway Works, who lived in Ferndale Road, was the same age as Joyce and had also survived the war.

This truly remarkable tale required considerable detective work to unravel, the facts are not readily available. The simple and unassuming nature of the two men's graves belies their hidden story. As one passes an idle moment strolling through the graveyard at Christ Church, one cannot help wondering how many other amazing stories lie behind the few simple words etched onto the stones.

Janet French and Christine Senior undertook a considerable amount of work cataloguing the records of those who lost their lives serving their country; and are remembered at Christ Church. A copy of their war memorial booklet is available from the church, should anyone wish to examine the records. Several war memorials and war graves are available to view inside and outside the church, ranging from the elegant and impressive, to the small and understated. All are worthy of spending a moment viewing and gratefully reflecting the sacrifice of others.

Sgt. Ed Graham's grave.

Sgt. Ivor Sansum's simple gravestone.

16

The Visitors Guide to Christ Church

For one hundred and fifty years the brooding beauty of the spire of Christ Church, Swindon's parish church, has dominated the changing pattern of Swindon life. This section of the book gives, in detail, a guide to the fabric and memorials both inside and outside of the church. With a copy of *The Beacon on the Hill* in your hand, we hope this guide will help bring you even greater pleasure as you explore this wonderful building. The first part of this chapter takes the reader on a tour of the interior of Christ Church (from right to left), listing points of interest, marked on the diagram. The second part of this chapter lists further information on the windows and other memorials contained within the church.

Finally, a plan of the churchyard is included, listing some resting places of interest.

1. The Tower of three stages, with west gabled porch and corner buttresses. Broach spire and tower were based on the 13th Century church of Buckworth, near Huntingdon. The Tower stands 150 feet high. The Clock of 1843 on the west side of the tower was transferred from Holy Rood Church together with six bells. The present peal of ten bells is immortalized in a poem by Sir John Betjeman (reproduced at the beginning of this book).

2. The South Porch, 1916, erected in memory of Henry and Harriet Kinneir. The Porch contains a small window dedicated to Nancy Davis, one of the first female bellringers at Christ Church. The window contains the design of a locomotive and the coat of arms of the Great Western Railway. Although easily overlooked, this window represents an interesting comment on the history of Swindon. In the same bequest, Nancy Davis is commemorated by the doors in the porch. These are engraved with bells and the motto *'Venite Adoremus'*

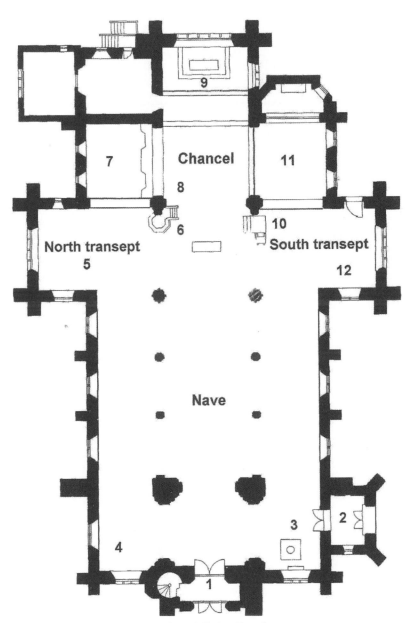

Plan of Christ Church.

(Come let us adore him). Both the doors and the window were dedicated on 7th September 1975.

The GWR Window.

3. After passing through the glass doors with the etched bells design; note, in the left corner, the marble and alabaster 1914-18 War Memorial, commemorating those from the Parish who were killed in the conflict. This was recently renovated as part of the 2018 Centenary celebrations. In front of this stands the font of the same material. It was donated in 1905 by Edward Hesketh Goddard in memory of his late wife Dulcie. The elaborate cover of wrought iron carries their initials in the decoration. DGG -

Dulcie Gwendoline Goddard. EHG – Edward Hesketh Goddard. HPG -Hesketh Pleydell Goddard.

The WWI Memorial.

4. In the north west corner is the Canon Thomas Corner, named after Canon Lewis Thomas (1894-1972). The area provides a quiet place for prayer, reflection or gathering. A bookcase here holds a selection of bibles in many different languages

5. The North Transept contains a unique stained glass window created by Martin Travers in 1931, in memory of Fitzroy Pleydell Goddard—the last Lord of the Manor to live at The Lawn (manor house of the Goddard family). It depicts the Downs and Liddington Hill through an array of hollyhocks, daisies, poppies and butterflies - the view that could be seen every day from windows of the Goddard's estate at The Lawn – and is probably the most attractive window in the building. The Coats of Arms of the Goddard Family, and of Christ Church, Oxford complete the window.

Look carefully to spot a green parrot -the favourite pet of Fitzroy Goddard!

6. The marble and alabaster pulpit, dated 1906, matches the font, war memorial and reredos. It was presented to the church by Pleydell and Jessie Goddard in memory of their parents. On the pulpit can be seen the carved figures of Christ and some of his apostles.

The Pulpit, 1906.

7. The organ is an instrument of fine quality. Significant maintenance work was carried out on it in 1951, 1970 and 1998. This was followed in 2019, when major refurbishment and rebuilding

works took place to ensure it will be working at its full potential for many years to come.

8. On the north wall of the Chancel is a memorial plaque to Henry Baily, Vicar from 1847-1885, whose drive and energy were mainly responsible for the building of Christ Church. The plaque also gives the date of the dedication of the building on 7th November 1851.

9. Behind the High Altar, below the East Window, is the marble and alabaster Reredos of 1891, erected in memory of Ambrose Ayshford Goddard (the brother of Fitzroy and Jessie). Carved in the marble are two biblical scenes- The Expulsion from the Garden of Eden and the Annunciation. The East Window was given by the widow of James Grooby, Vicar of Swindon 1823-1847, in memory of her husband and Col. Vilett, her brother. It depicts some well known scenes and parables from the Gospels of Matthew and Luke. The image of the feast to celebrate the return of the Prodigal Son has been carefully placed in a central position to give the impression of The Last Supper that Jesus shared with his disciples.

The East Window.

10. The brass eagle Lectern is dated 1881. It was a gift from Henry and Harriet Kinneir in memory of their son Henry Jnr.

The Brass Eagle Lecturn

11. The Lady Chapel was created in 1935; and designed by Harold Brakspear. Its exterior features a canopied figure of Jesus the Good Shepherd. Note the contemporary window by John Hayward (1987) depicting The Annunciation –when the Angel Gabriel visited Mary. This window replaced one previously vandalised although the top lights remain from the original. The chapel is used for a daily service of worship and prayer and provides a place for quiet prayer and reflection throughout the day.

12. On the west wall of the South Transept is a WW2 Roll of Honour from the Boys High School in Bath Road placed here when the school closed in 1979.

Stained Glass Windows In Date Order (Where Known)

Churches have been characterised by stained or painted glass set within traceried windows from early medieval times. At first, it appeared only in great churches, but was present in parish churches from at least the fifteenth century, if not earlier. By the time Christ Church was built in the nineteenth century, stained glass windows were nearly always used as a form of memorial, and Christ Church is certainly no exception in this respect.

It appears that when the church was first built, the windows would have been of plain glass, as many of the windows were dedicated at a much later date; the first one was installed in 1855. The majority of the windows were installed as memorials to prominent parishioners, mainly between 1855-1860 and 1891-1902.

A report on the installation of the 1855 window, after giving effusive description of the detail in the window itself, goes on to say *'We are glad to learn that proposals for further embellishing the church have been favourably entertained by parties erecting memorial windows or a portion of windows, which it has been ascertained can be done at a cost not much exceeding ordinary tablets.'*

Below is a list of the windows in chronological order, giving their location, dedication and description. The list of dedications reflects the most important families in the Old Town parish at that time.

East Window, 7th November 1855

Dedicated by Catherine Mary Grooby (see below) to the memory of her husband Revd. James Grooby (died 6th March 1854) and her brother Colonel Vilett (died 3rd April 1846). Catherine Grooby had herself died earlier in the year; and left this bequest in her will.

The window was made at Newcastle by Messrs. Wailes and at the time was described at the time as *'one of the finest now erected in this county'*. It has considerable detail, including 15 depictions of parables from the gospels of SS. Matthew and Luke. The story of the Prodigal Son is not in the correct order, however. This was done so that the picture of the banquet to celebrate the return of the Prodigal Son (which appears at the end of the story) actually appears in the exact centre of the window, giving the appearance of a Last Supper immediately above the High Altar.

South Window, South Transept, 1855

Dedicated by Harriet Rolleston to her sister Catherine Mary Grooby (died 3rd January 1855), wife of Revd. James Grooby (Vicar) and daughter of Revd. T. C. Vilett.

There are 4 lights, showing the Resurrection, with the Rolleston Coat of Arms.

North Transept, 1860

Dedicated to Samuel Rolleston Esq. (died 9th April 1860) by his widow Harriet Rolleston. Harriet Rolleston was also responsible for setting up the Vilett Charity in 1870. She was a Vilett before her marriage, and the last descendant of that family in Swindon.

This is a large four-light window, showing the Nativity scene, with the Adoration of the Magi and Shepherds.

South Aisle, East Window, 1861

Dedicated to James Bradford, who died 24th August 1861. He was Churchwarden from 1846-52. The window depicts Christ with a penny and Roman Soldiers, illustrating the text *'render unto Caesar the things that are Caesar's and to God the things that are God's.'*

Lady Chapel, 1868

Dedicated to John Harding Sheppard, who died 15th April 1868 aged 90. John Harding Sheppard was a well-known Freemason in Old Town, and was a founder member of the 'Lodge of Emulation', held at the Goddard Arms Inn. He was also the benefactor of the charity known as 'Sheppard's Dole'. He is buried in Christ Church churchyard. The window shows the Children of Israel in the wilderness.

Chancel Window, South side, 1871

Dedicated to Harriet Rolleston, widow of Samuel Rolleston, by her step-daughter, also called Harriet. Mrs Rolleston had previously dedicated the window of the North Transept to her husband.

The window has three lights, with 3 trefoils above, spelling out the motto *'Fides Charitas Spes'* – Faith, Hope and Charity.

South Aisle, Centre, 1885

Dedicated to Matilda Rebecca (died 3rd September 1885), first wife of John Green.

Shows the Resurrection, with the angel and the empty tomb, based on Luke 24:5-6

South Window, Lady Chapel, 1888 and 1987

Dedicated to Annice Hilda Vere, who lived for only 2 years from 13th March 1886 to 26th March 1888, the only child of James and Charlotte Bradford (see James Bradford's dedication in the East Window).

Appropriately enough for such a poignant memorial, the window depicted heavenly children with palms in their hands, and verses taken from Psalm 8:2 and Jeremiah 31:15. Sadly, this window was vandalised during the 1980s. It was replaced in 1987 by a window designed by John Hayward, with a design appropriate to the Lady Chapel. In a subtle palette of colours, it depicts the Annunciation, with the motto *'Greetings Most Favoured One The Lord is with you'*. The memorial dedication for this window (recorded on a brass plaque mounted on wood) is far longer than any of the Victorian windows.

The names recorded are:

Ethel May Church and her husband	1904 – 1986
George Arthur Church	1897 – 1974
John Gilbert, Priest	1883 – 1962
Hon. Canon of Bristol Cathedral	
Vicar of this Parish 1929 – 1952 and his wife	
Winifred Gilbert and their son	1900 – 1968
Alan John Gilbert, Priest	1929 – 1986
William Gillespie	1912 – 1989
Principal, Swindon College of Further Education	
Queenie May Hustings and her husband	1906 – 1983
Arthur Ackland Hustings	1906 – 1983
Ruth Maude Port, Sunday School teacher	1904 – 1986

South Aisle, West End, 1891

Dedicated to Jane, wife of John Green (died 28th March 1891), and their son Percy, who died 2nd August 1891, aged 3 ½. Jane was John's second wife; his first wife is commemorated in the Centre of the South Aisle.

The window shows the story of Martha and Mary with an inscription from Luke 10: 38-42: '*Mary hath chosen that good part*'.

West Window, North Side, Easter 1892

Dedicated to Jane Reynolds, who died 12th September 1891. Jane was obviously well-loved and respected, as the window was given by members of the congregation, including many of the poor and children of the Sunday School as a token of respect and remembrance of 44 years of Parochial and Sunday School work in the parish.

The window shows Saints Cecilia, Anne, and Catherine, each carrying an appropriate object. St. Cecilia has a portable keyboard or organ (she is the Patron Saint of music); St. Anne, the mother of Mary, carries an open bible; whilst St Catherine carries a sign of her martyrdom. A wheel (the instrument traditionally, if erroneously, associated with her death) sits in the background.

West Window, South Side, Easter 1894

Dedicated to Richard and Anne Bowly, by their children. Richard left £200 in his will to distribute blankets and coal to the poor at Christmas. He is buried in the churchyard.

The window has 3 lights, with Christ in the centre, flanked by angels. The inscription is from Revelations 3:20: *'Behold / I stand at the door / and knock'*. The image of Christ shows him standing at a door, with a lantern in his hand. It is based on the popular Victorian painting *'The Light of the World'*, which was painted by William Holman Hunt (a member of the Pre-Raphaelite Brotherhood) in 1853.

North Aisle, West Window, 1900

Dedicated to John Green, who died 29th October 1900. His wives and son are commemorated in the South Aisle. All are buried on the south side of the church in the churchyard. John Green's window shows the baptism of Christ by John the Baptist. At the outer corners, it also shows plaques depicting the Masonic symbols of a crown, measure and set square.

North Aisle, Centre, 1902

Dedicated by children to their parents, William Hall (8th September 1815 to 30th August 1898) and Martha Hall (12th July 1818 to 22nd January 1902), 4th daughter of the late John Jefferies of Swindon. William Hall was the founder of the Swindon Permanent Building Society and lived in Longford Villa in Bath Road. William and Martha are both buried near the Southwest corner of the church, and their grave bears a Celtic cross.

The window shows SS Patrick and George (for Ireland and England), Hall being from County Longford, and Jefferies from England. At the top, a quatrefoil light shows two animal heads of stylised form, with the motto *'Fumus et Erimus'*. ('We are')

North Aisle, East Window, post 1918

Dedicated to the men of the Wiltshire Regiment and to Lt. Sydney G. H. Reed of 104th Battalion MGC, who died in the Great War (1914 – 1918).

Appropriately enough, the window shows two soldiers in ancient armour, depicting Justice and Peace. The top trefoil light shows an angel with the motto *'Fight the Good Fight'*.

North Transept, East Window, 1922

Dedicated to Jessie H. Goddard, by her brother Fitzroy Pleydell Goddard. The window, although small (a single light), is beautifully made, showing an angel carrying blue irises. She stands on clouds with the earth beneath (lake, mountains, rocks, trees etc), along with the Goddard Coat of Arms.

North Transept, West Side, 1931

Dedicated to Fitzroy Pleydell Goddard, last Lord of the Manor of Swindon, who died on 12th August 1927, aged 76. See number 5 above.

Lady Chapel, to the right of the alter, 1944

Dedicated to Ambrose Michael Andrew Goddard, eldest son of Lieutenant Colonel Ambrose William Goddard, M.C., who died on active service 16th July 1944.

The single light shows Mary with the infant Jesus, and Madonna lilies.

South Porch, 1975

Dedicated to Nancy Davis, the first female bellringers at Christ Church. See number 2 above.

Other windows in the church do not have a dedication, and little is known about them. These include the following:

West Window

A small, trefoil light, placed high on the wall over the door.

Chancel Window, North Side

Three trefoil lights, which echo the 'Faith Hope and Charity' window the other side of the chancel. These are decorated with foliage and flowers, with three inscriptions:

'*Let thy priests be clothed / with righteousness and let / Thy saints sing with* Joyfulness'

Chancel, small window to the east of the organ recess

This small trefoil window can barely be seen, placed high up on the wall and obscured by the organ pipes. It clearly shows Masonic symbols; and may have been hidden for this reason (the other two windows with Masonic associations are the John Harding Sheppard window in the Lady Chapel and the John Green window in the North Aisle). The windows behind the organ are also obscured, but they are plain glazed.

Other Church Memorials

As well as the window to Sydney Reed and the Wiltshire Regiment, there are four general war memorials, and two individual plaques.

World War I Memorial 'In Memory of our Glorious Dead 1914 –1918'; there are 51 names inscribed on the marble plaque. The top centre shows a Christian soldier, flanked by cannons. To each side are symbols of the Army and Navy (crossed rifles and an anchor). Lower down is the emblem and motto of the RAF, plus the emblem of the Wiltshire Regiment, and the Three Crowns crest of the Bristol Diocese. The Memorial was renovated in 2018 as part of the Armistice Centenary commemorations.

World War II Memorial A wooden plaque, on the shelf in front of the WWI Memorial

World War II Far East Memorial Presented to the Church by the Burma Star and Far East P.O.W Associations, 15th August 1995

Roll of Honour, of the Old Boys of Bath Road School. The wooden memorial was removed from the school when it was demolished in 1979.

Brass Tablet, in memory of **Lt William Henry Walker Moore,** of the 9th Wiltshire Regiment, who was killed in action in France on 25th September 1915.

Plaque with the emblem of 22nd Special Air Services Regiment, in memory of **S/SGT Vincent Phillips, SAS,** who died on active service in the Gulf War in January 1991.

There are also a number of other tablets scattered throughout the church, dedicated to individuals, both clergy and parishioners. These include:

Ambrose Lethbridge Goddard (1819 – 1899) and his wife Charlotte (1824 – 1904)

Ambrose Ayshford Goddard, eldest son and presumptive heir of Ambrose Lethbridge Goddard. He died in 1885 on board *HMS Tyne*

Henry George Baily, MA, Vicar of Christ Church from 1847 to 1885

Henry Bizley (1846 – 1923), chorister for 67 years

Edward Timms (1855 – 1928), Warden for 4 years and Sidesman for 21 years

Edward Bays (1848 – 1922), Churchwarden for 13 years and Justice of the Peace

William Reynolds (1845 – 1913), Warden for 14 years and his wife Lucy Lane (1845 – 1928)

Arthur Stote (1834 – 1921), Headmaster at King William Street School, and his wife Annie (1834 – 1902)

Arthur William Deacon, his wife Martha and their daughter Alice

Matilda (the floodlighting of the church was installed in their memory in August 1939).

Olive Marjory Deacon, died 9 April 1950

Revd. Charles Frederick Goddard (1863-1942), youngest son of Ambrose and Charlotte Goddard, and Curate at Christ Church.

Mr W. H. and Mrs E. E. Eggins, '*devout members of this church*'

Miss Jessie Elizabeth Handley, whose bequest contributed to the rebuild of the organ in 1970

Margaret Denise Waite (died 1982), in whose memory the choir lights were made by her father, John Bremner

Ernest Drew, in whose memory the chancel loudspeaker was dedicated in September 1975

Gordon Crabbe, ARCO, FTCL. Organist of St. Mary's 1946 – 55, Organist and Choirmaster of Christ Church 1956 – 1995

H. J. Edmonds, choirmaster 1914 – 27

A. E. Forsey, in whose memory the Vestry improvements were made in 1966

John Wirdnam (died 1985), Churchwarden 1979 – 1980

Harold and Gladys Woodman (pews in Lady Chapel, dedicated October 1960)

Jill Rosemary Holbrook Smith (died September 1953) and the mistresses and girls of Gardenhurst

Some Interesting Memorials in Christ Church Churchyard

The numbers below correspond to the numbers on the Plan of the Churchyard shown here:

1.TURNER, Thomas. Died 7th April 1911 at Brighton. Builder and brickmaker. He was also a director of the Wilts & Berks Canal Company. His clay pits were in Drove Road where Queen's Park is today. Turner lived in Grove House adjacent to the brickworks, now a steak bar/restaurant called The Grove. His ornate terracotta plaques and distinctive bricks can still be seen in many houses in Swindon, notably in Turner Street, Westcott Place, Hunt Street, Belle Vue Road, Lansdown Road, Kingshill Road, Avening Street and The Rangers'

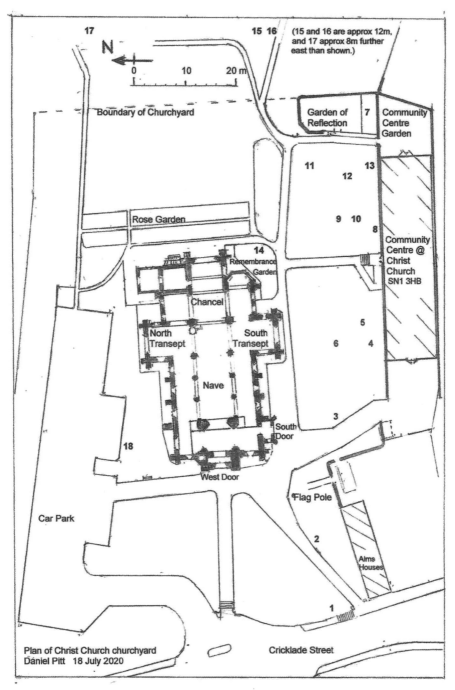

Plan of Christ Church Churchyard (2020 by Damiel PItt).

Centre at Coate Water. Adjacent to his home in Drove Road he built three small cottages, which are adorned with many motifs, including pottery pineapples, as a catalogue of pottery available at the nearby works.

2. AFFLECK, William. Died 29th July 1894. A well known local ironworker. His engineering firm began in the 1850s with premises at the Prospect Works. At one time he occupied the Corn Exchange in the Market Square as a show room for his goods: implements, small engines and machines of every description used in agriculture.

3. HALL, William and Martha. Died 30th August 1898 and 22nd January 1902 respectively. William was born in Longford, Ireland, and his home in Bath Road was called 'Longford Villa' (symbolised by the Celtic cross on the memorial). The Halls were well-known Victorian citizens of Swindon who also have a stained glass window dedicated to them in the north wall of Christ Church. Martha Hall was daughter of John Jefferies (grandfather of author and poet, Richard Jefferies).

4. BOWLY, Richard. Died Easter Day, 1885 at the early age of 49. Originally from Cirencester, Bowly, a draper by trade came to Swindon in 1865 and acquired the North Wilts Brewery in High Street after the death of John Harding Sheppard (see below). The brewery finally closed in 1945 but the offices were utilized as an area office for Courage until 1978. The premises then became a branch of Barclays Bank, but the name 'Bowly Brewer' may still be seen engraved over the central arch in High Street.

5. SHEPPARD, John Harding. Died 2nd March 1877. From Stoke-on-Trent. Brewer, farmer and landowner. Sheppard left £200 in his will to be invested for the benefit of twelve elderly persons every Christmas. In 1904 the income, known as 'Sheppard's Dole' was £5 2s 6d. Sheppard Street and Harding Street are named after him.

6. NEW, Frederick J. A railwayman, he was killed on the Great Western Railway on 19th February 1878.

7. MORRIS, William. Died 15th June 1891. Morris was Swindon's first historian and founder of the *Swindon Advertiser* in 1854. His book *Swindon: Reminiscences Notes & Relics of Ye Old Wiltshire Towne*, published in 1885 and reprinted in 1970, gives a most interesting view of pre-railway Swindon. Dr Desmond Morris, the well-known zoologist and author of *The Human Zoo* and *The*

Naked Ape is William Morris's great-grandson.

8. PIPER, Joshua H. Died 16th June 1885 at the early age of 48. A newspaperman, Piper was the Editor and Proprietor of the *North Wilts Herald* in Victorian days.

9. KEYLOCK, Edward J. Died 18th May 1912. A butcher, his business was at 17 Wood Street, on Old Town, for many years. The building is currently the sight of Youngs the gift shop.

10. TOWNSEND, John Coplestone. Died 25th March 1885. From Whimple, near Coldridge in Devon. Born in 1825, he became a solicitor in 1847. A prominent Freemason, sometime Clerk to the Local Boards of Old Swindon and New Swindon, Registrar of the County Court, Solicitor to the Wilts & Berks Canal Company, the Swindon, Marlborough & Andover Railway Company and the Goddard Estate. Townsend Solicitors occupied premises at number 42 Cricklade Street (until the property was acquired for residential development in 2007). The building still probably the finest townhouse in Swindon; and is a listed building of special architectural interest.

11, 12, 13. JEFFERIES' family memorials. Relatives to the author and poet, Richard Jefferies, 1848-1887. Only one of these memorials now remains intact and is leaning against the wall of the Community Centre.

14. BAILY, Henry George, MA. Vicar of Christ Church for 38 years and Rector of Lydiard Tregoze for 15 years. See plaque on north wall of chancel near pulpit. His energy and drive were mainly responsible for the building of Christ Church.

15. GODDARD, Fitzroy Pleydell. Died 12th August 1927, aged 74 years, and his wife, Eugenia Kathleen Goddard, widow of Mr A.G. Sutton. Major Goddard was last Lord of the Manor of Swindon and a prominent Freemason. See also many memorials of the Goddard family in Christ Church. His Christian names appear in the names of two roads off Croft Road.

16. SUTTON, Alexander, son of Mr A.G. Sutton and Mrs F.P. Goddard. Died 24th July 1945, aged 58 years, & **SUTTON, Naomi**, daughter of above, who died 2nd September 1910, aged 17.

17. CHURCHWARD, George Jackson, CBE. Born at Stoke Gabriel in Devon in 1857. Locomotive, Carriage & Wagon Superintendent / Chief Mechanical Engineer of the Great Western

Railway from 1902-1921. He was responsible for the design of a large range of locomotives during his period as Locomotive Superintendent, which were unsurpassed in performance and efficiency. These included the famous classes such as the 'Cities', 'Saints' and 'Stars'. Churchward was the first Mayor of the Borough of Swindon from 1900-1901 and made a Freeman of the Borough in 1920. He was killed on the foggy morning of 19th December 1933 when struck by a train while crossing the GWR line near his home, Newburn House.

18. TOOMER, John. Died 2nd July 1882. Coal, Coke, Hay, Straw & Corn Merchant. He lived in Apsley House, now the Museum in Bath Road.

Other Interesting Memorials not shown on the plan

BRIDGEMAN, Brian. Died 19th April 2003. The writer of the original *'The Old Lady on the Hill'*, and local historian and author, who died two years after its publication. Brian's son, Mark, is the author of this book (follow the path to the south east corner, near the fence).

GRAHAM, Edwin & SANSUM, Ivor. As featured in Chapter 15. From the Churchyard, continue down the sloping path that leads into the Burial Ground. Take the first left turn and approximately half way down on the left, against the hedge, is the Graham/Sansum grave.

The Graveyard at Christ Church.

DUNN, Raymond. 2nd Battalion Parachute Regiment. Raymond Dunn was killed in the Warren Point Bombing, Northern Ireland 27th August 1979. From the location of the Graham/Sansum grave, continue down to the area called Lower Lawn, close to the willow trees at the boundary - there is a small circular bed - the Dunn grave is on the left corner by the side of the path.

Afterword
by Reverend Canon Simon Stevenette

In recent times Christ Church, our PCC and staff team have worked hard, with Phil Mansfield, on developing a revitalised vision and mission underpinned by clear values. Our vision is to be Christ's church in the Community. We will do this through our mission goals which are:

by proclaiming Christ through teaching and example,

by welcoming and serving all through hospitality

by encouraging people to find God through worship, faith and prayer

by providing a spiritual home and resources for the local community

by transforming Swindon and beyond with God's hope and compassion.

We will do this through our values living with humility, grace and respect listening prayerfully to God and our neighbour.

Each year, during my Incumbency, we have based our Christian ministry on a Bible verse. In 2020 our verse is Psalm 24 verse 1:

'The earth is the Lord's, and everything in it, the world and all who live in it'.

Being an eco-congregation proclaiming generosity and love of God in the Good News of Jesus, in the power of the Spirit is all about teamwork.

Legacy is also really important. We are all life-long learners and we are all on this earth to live, love, learn, listen and leave a legacy. As I pray each day, I thank God for those who have gone before us and for those who will come after us including the next Vicar of Christ Church whoever that might be and whenever that might be. God knows and we trust that he will lead us forward.

I use this Celtic Blessing at every Baptism, Wedding and Funeral I take. It reminds me that as much as I love our churches God is to be found out and about in his amazing creation and in his wonderful people. May God bless us all and all who will read this book as we journey on with him radiating God's love from the Beacon on the hill, looking upwards to God, outwards to our Old Town Swindon parish community he has called us to serve, remembering Jesus's work, 'love one another as I have loved you'.

May the road rise to meet you
May the wind be always at your back
The rain fall soft upon your fields
And until we meet again
May God hold you in the palm of his hand
May God hold you and all you love and pray for in the hollow
of his hand
Now and forever,
Amen.

Appendix A

VICARS OF SWINDON

1301	Richard de Haghemaz
1319	Nicholas de Haghemaz
1361	Richard de Taillour
1361	John de Wotton
1381	John Brok
1388	Richard Suggeworth
1440	John Stockbrygg
1481	William Camell
1486	William Brown
1527	John Unthanke
1560	Aristoteles Webb
1575	William Wattes
1579	Richard Powell
1580	Thomas Painter
1580	John Bestpich
1584	Milo (Miles) Kendall
1623	William Gallimore
1662	Narcissus Marshe
1663	Henry Thompson
1703	John Neate
1719	Gilbert Cowper
1728	John Broadway
1737	William Nichol(l)s
1758	Thomas Smyth
1790	Edmund Goodenough
1809	Matthew Surtees
1823	James Grooby
1847	Henry G. Baily
1885	Henry Armstrong Hall
1887	Newton Ebenezer Howe
1901	Edmund Estcourt
1910	Charles A. Mayall

1929	John Gilbert
1953	Francis W. Thomas
1964	John W. Jackson
1968	Derek Palmer
1977	Owen Barraclough
1998	Simon Stevenette

Appendix B

CLERGY STAFF

E.H. Jones	1874-80
S. Rogers	1877-78
William B. Pitt	1879-82
John Samuel	1882
C.R. Greaves	1883
Frederick J. Sloan	1884-85
A.H.F. Barder	1887
Jonathan S. Puckeridge	1885-88
M.L. Eaton	1889
John Colmer Godwin	1885-87,1920
R.L. Atkinson	1889-90
Charles E. Hutchinson	1890-92
Ernest.J. Houghton (Curate in Charge of Parish)	1890-91
Charles F. Goddard (Curate in Charge of Parish)	1892-95
Allen E. Dams	1892-94
William Scott (Curate in Charge of Parish)	1899-1901
W. Singleton (Curate in Charge of Parish)	1900
George J.S. Bowyear	1901-04
J.H.O. Every	1902
Charles S. Jones	1902-04
Edgar F. Hornsby	1904-06
C. Dams	1905-08
T. Astin	1907
Cyril Aston	1908-10
Robert W. Philipson	1911-16
E.H.H. Lough	1911-12
K.G. Mortimer	1914-15
Eric V. Rees	1916-18
John Bodycombe	1919-25
S.M. Atkinson	1919
Frederick J. Hirst	1926-29
Ralph S. Mundy	1926-29
J. C. Field	1929

C.S.R. Atkins	1929-30
Harold Spence	1930-33
Bernard F. Ritson	1933-34
Francis W. Thomas	1931-36
Harold G. Wood	1934-37
Leonard Golledge	1936-39
Edward Shannon	1937-40
Philip H. Scott	1940-43
Clifford A.G. Saunders	1942-46
Donald Hillman	1943-48
Albert S. Thorne DFM	1948-53
John Homer Green (Hon. Assistant)	1948-52
Glyn M. Calder	1954-56
Michael Wilkinson	1953-57
Clifford Halstead	1957-59
John C. Poarch	1956-59
Dennis A. Biggar	1957-61
Royston G. Bryant	1959-61
Hector G. Dorrington	1961-62
Robert L. Parker	1961-63
Ernest G.F. Swinnerton	1961-67
Peter A. Tanton DFM	1963-64
Michael O. West	1963-66
Samuel A. Adebayo	1964
George Foster (Hon. Assistant)	1961-62
Canon Samuel. J. Christelow (Hon. Assistant)	1957-71
Edward A. Farley	1965-68
Brian W.E. Banks	1965-68
Michael B.G. Pain	1967-70
Ronald J. Lucas	1967-71
A. John Stephens	1968-71
Ronald A.K. Loxley	1968-71
Beryl Morgan (Hospital Church Sister)	1969-79
Judith Thomas (Hospital Church Sister)	1979-81
Barbara Richards (Hospital Church Sister)	1981-87
Lewis L. Thomas (Hon. Assistant)	1964-72
Archdeacon Cyril W.J. Bowles (temporary)	1964, 1968

John Hewitson	1971-73
David Goldie	1970-73
Edgar J. Newton	1971-78
Stanley Whale (Hon. Assistant)	1972-81
Richard Taylor	1973-76
Alex George	1974-76
Lloyd Scott	1976-79
Alan K. Knight	1976-80
Anthony Lynett	1978-81
Philip Slade	1978-79
James Dott (Hon. Assistant)	1978-79
Peter Down	1979-82
Peter Dyson	1981-84
Roger Salter	1982-84
Leonard Colton (Non-Stipendiary Minister)	1984-90
James Fisher	1984-87
Alastair Stevenson	1984-87
Paul Firmin	1987-91
Colin Mee	1988-90
Andrew Hake (Hon. Assistant)	1978-92
John Beall (Hon. Assistant)	1983-90
Duncan Hannam (Hon. Assistant)	1985-90
Dr. John Gosling	1991, 1995
Robert Sanday	1991-94
Annis Fessey	1995
Olive King (Licenced Stipendiary Lay Worker)	1985-2003
Peter Dawes (Hon. Assistant)	1993-2005
Janet House	1995-99
Ruth Walker	1999-2000
Guy Donegan-Cross	1999-2003
Judy Ashby (Hon. Curate)	1999-2003
Judy Ashby (Associate Minister)	2003-2005
John Stevenette	2002-2014
Paul Rush	2006-2013
Ray Lowe	2006-2008
David Howell	2010-2020
Jo Northey	2009-2011

Trudie Wigley	2011-2014
Norma McKemey (Curate)	2010-2013
Norma McKemey (Associate Minister)	2013-
Daphne Hardwick	2012-

ST. MARY'S IN THE MALL

Frederick J. Hirst	1926-29
Glyn M. Calder	1954-56
Dennis A. Biggar	1957
John C. Poarch	1959
Royston G. Bryant	1959-61
Clifford Halstead	1957-58
Michael Wilkinson	1956-57
Hector Dorrington	1961-62
Robert L. Parker	1962-63
Peter A. Tanton DFM	1963-4
Edward A. Farley	1965-8
A. John Stephens	1968-71
Canon Samuel J. Christelow (Hon. Assistant)	1958-60, 1970
Edgar Newton	1971-78
Alan K. Knight	1978-80
Roger Salter	1983-84
James Fisher	1984-87
Colin Mee	1988-90
Dr. John Gosling	1991-95

ST. ANDREW'S (1958-1967)

Clifford Halstead	1957
Denis A. Biggar	1957-61
Ernest G.F. Swinnerton	1961-76

ORGANISTS AT CHRIST CHURCH

T. B Richardson	1851-1858
J. Ainsworth	1860-61
Thomas Simpson Camidge	1863, 1889
W. Jenkins	1866-68
H.G. Baily, Jun.	1871-72

J.T. Mew	1874-75
H. Vaughan	1876
G. Whitehead	1877-89
W.H. Painter	1890-1929
W.A. Vivian May	1929-55
Gordon Crabbe	1956-95
Timothy Eyles (Director of Music)	1996-

CHURCHWARDENS AT CHRIST CHURCH/HOLY ROOD

Richard Wayt	1741
William Lawrence	1741
John Goolding	1770
William Heath	1770
Richard Farmer	1781
Wm Kemble	1781
? Freeman	1805
William Farmer	1807-25
? Gray	1806
? Maisey	1806-07
John Harding Sheppard	1825
William Jenner	1846-48
Robert Reynolds	1847-55
James Bradford	1846-52
Richard Read	1852- ?
Edmond Sheppard	1854-64
J.L. Hawkins	1861-63
J.H. Browne	1856
William A. Barnes	1864-67
John Chandler	1864-85
Henry Kinneir	1868-70
William Dore	1871-72
Robert S. Edmonds	1873-79
William Reynolds	1880-90, 1892-96,1902-06
Alfred Plummer	1886-89
Robert Croome	1890
William J. Smith	1890-1901

William H. Kinneir	1893-94,1911-16
John Holland	1895-96
Captain Martin	1894-95
J. Holland	1895-96
Arthur Stote	1898-1901
Henry J. Scotton	1896-97
Edward Bays	1902-14
Edward Timms	1907-10
George Brooks	1915
R. Reynolds	1916-20
Major F.P. Goddard	1891, 1918-26
F.W. Marillier, CBE	1921-26
A.E. Dean	1926-27,1930-46
Dr R.P. Beatty	1926-30
E.C. Beard	1927-42
K.J. Cook. OBE	1943-51
G.V. Smith	1946-52
Edgar J. Baish	1952-72
A. Jack Turner	1951-63
Denis R. Winslow	1963-72
A. John. Wright	1972-76
Edgar R. Harvey	1972-75
Peter Jones	1975-77
John Britt	1976-78
John Woodruffe	1977-79
Fred Hazell	1978-80
John Wirdnam	1979-80
George Clubley	1980-82
John Bremner	1980-82
Anthony Dale	1982-84
Philip Chapman	1984-85
Eddie Slade	1985-87
Bill Griffiths	1986-88
Lawrence Trowbridge	1987-89
Enid Sheldrake	1989-91
Stanley Jonathan	1990-91
Malcolm Wallace	1991-93

Alice French	1983-85,1988-92
Ivan Cotton	1994-96
Brian Stratford	1993-95
Freda Troughton	1992-97
Bernard Oxborrow	1996-99
Mary Trickett	1997-2002
Harry East	1999-2000
John Little	2001
Martin Hiscock	2002-2005
Daphne Hardwick	2002-2006
John Michaux	2005-2009
Pam Bridgeman	2006-2012, 2017-
Gareth Hutchinson	2012-2015
Lynda Fisher	2009-2013
Daniel Pitt	2013-2018
Mike Ranstead	2015-2017
Jim D'Avila	2018-

PARISH CLERKS

Isaac Ann	1851-71
F. Saunders	1871-72
J.W. Painter	1875-83
William Dean	1883-1923
F. Foss	1923-32
W.A. Jones	1933-39
Mrs Edith E. Jones	1940-66
Squire Shackleton	1966-74
Hilda Newton	1974-77
Ruth Haddrell	1978-2006
Ailsa Palmer (Parish Secretary)	1993-1997
Ailsa Palmer (Parish Administrator)	1997-2016
Carol Simmons	2007-
Helen Parker-Drabble (Parish Administrator)	2016-

DIOCESAN LAY READERS

E. Hewins	1911 - ?
Capt. H. Richardson	1916-18

W.E. Welch	1918-20
J.S. Witchell	1925
J. Allen	1925
J. Payne	1926-40
William J. Law	1940, 1954-72
H. Field	1955-58
Norman A. Herbert	1958-63
H. W. Pettitt	1960-63
Ernest R. Herbert	1963-91
H. P. Chapman	1964-72
Margaret Williams MBE	1974-
Noreen Bint	1981-86
John Britt	1987-96
Dianna Firmin	1990-91
John Seacombe	1996-99
Sue Vaughan	2004-2008
Teresa Michaux	2005-2012
Trevor Day	2007-2012
Norma McKemey	2007-2010
Daphne Hardwick	2007-2012
Anne MacMillan	2007-
Genny Williams	2007-2019
Carol Simmons	2009-2020
Ailsa Palmer	2010-
Kevin Penfold	2020-

ECUMENICAL PARTNERSHIP OF SWINDON OLD TOWN CHAIRS

The Revd. Derek Palmer	1969-74
The Revd. Norman Charlton	1974-76
A. John Wright	1976-79
Eric Holloway	1979-82
Alan S. Peck	1982-83
Margaret Williams	1984-86
Avril Cozens	1987-89
Norman Sedgwick	1990-91
Eric Sparkes	1992-94

Norman Goodall   1995-97
Ivy Wilkins   1998-2001

(RENAMED IN 2002 SWINDON OLD TOWN PARTNERSHIP OF CHURCHES)

Colin Smith (Bath Road)   2001-2003
Revd. Geoff Gleed (Immanuel)   2003-2006, 2009-2013
Martin Hiscock (Christ Church)   2006-2009
Godfrey Room (Bath Road)   2013-2018
Daniel Pitt (Christ Church)   2018-

Appendix C

ALLOCATION OF PEWS AT HOLY ROOD

Pews in the Middle Aisle (at the Pulpit)
1. Reading Desk and Pulpit
2. Broom Farm (Goulding)
3. The Vicar of Swindon
4. Sundry Persons (Men)
5. Sundry Persons (Men)
6. Sundry Persons (Men)
7. Catherine Hopkins
8. John King
9. Sundry Persons (Women)
10. Sundry Persons (Women)
11. Sundry Persons (Women)
12. Joseph Cooper (Hornes)
Coats 13. A. Goddard Esq
14. William Harding Esq
15. William Buy (Eastcott)
16. A. Goddard Esq (Haysey)
17. Sundry Persons (Women)
18. Sundry Persons (Women)
19. John Kemble
20. Sundry Persons (Men)
21. Thomas Strange (Coventry)
22. Mrs Jones (Hornes)
23. Ambrose Goddard (Manor Seat)
24. Ambrose Goddard (Men Servants)

25. Chancel Seats 1,2,3,4 Rev T. Goddard Villet

Pews in the South Aisle (the West End)
1. A. Goddard Esq (Marsh)
2. Richard Farmer (Bell Inn)
3. Ambrose Goddard (Women)
4. Josh Heath (Gentleman)
5. Sundry Persons (Men)
6. Sundry Persons (Men)
7. Sundry Persons (Men)
8. Sundry Persons (Men)
9. Sundry Persons (Men)
10. Elizabeth Gosling
11. John Gosling
12. Jasper Coates & Roger
13. William Farmer (Eastcott)
14. Thomas Hatt
15. John Rogers
16. James Strange
17. Sundry Persons (Mixed)
18. Sundry Persons (Mixed)
19. Sundry Persons (Mixed)
20. James Phelps
21. John Cook
22. Rev. D. Villet (Eastcott)
23. Thomas Coventry
24. Sundry Persons (Women)
25. Sundry Persons (Women)
26. James Crowdy
27. William Farmer
28. Josh. Woodham

Pews in the North Aisle (at the North Entrance)

1. John Handell
2. Richard Farmer
3. A. Goddard Esq (Walcott)
4. James Bradford Esq
5. Sundry Persons (Women)
6. Sundry Persons (Women)
7. Sundry Persons (Women)
8. R.D. King & Others
9. Stephen King (Lawrence)
10. Josh Heath (Servants)
11. Sarah Humphries

12. Hannah Herring
13. Richard Jefferies
14. A.Goddard Esq
15. The Crown Inn
16. William Bradford (Gentleman)

17. A. Goddard Esq (Okus)
18. James Bradford (Servants)
19. William Harding Esq (Servants)
20. Sundry Persons (Men)
21. Sundry Persons (Men)
22. Sundry Persons (Men)
23. W. Farmer & J. Shepherd
24. The Vicar's Servants
25. Richard Gray (Brewery)
26. William Nobes
27. Josh Woodham
 (King of Prussia Inn)
28. Stephen King (Goolding)
29. Richard Farmer's Servants
30. Josh Cooper (Tarrant's)
31. Mrs Jones (Woodruffs)

32. Samuel Shepherd

Appendix D

'List of Subscribers towards the erection of the new Parish Church for Swindon 1849' (Originally published in 1849)

The list of subscribers was published in the Wiltshire newspapers in 1849. Below are some of the interesting names, with a brief biography and an index linked equivalent showing the value of their contribution today.

Name	Amount	Today's Equivalent
Ambrose L. Goddard MP for Cricklade and North Wiltshire	£1,000	£127,000
Sarah Goddard wife of Ambrose Goddard	£100	£12,700
Rev. Henry Baily The first Vicar of Christ Church	£50	£6,350
William Pinnegar Well known Swindon family	£10	£1,270
Edward Wackerbath Wealthy Wiltshire business family	£10	£1,270
James Crowdy Famous London solicitor, who also served the British Empire as a Colonial Secretary	£5	£635
Rev. John Prower Canon of Purton Church	£15	£1,905
Rev. S.W. Warneford Founder of the Warneford Asylum Hospital in Oxford.	£20	£2,540
1st Viscount Walter Long, MP Secretary of State for the Colonies and First Lord of the Admiralty	£20	£2,540

Joseph Neeld, MP   £20   £2,540
Wealthy MP for Chippenham who purchased
Grittleton Estate, near Chippenham in 1831. He was a successful
and generous philanthropist who married Lady Caroline Cooper,
who then filed for divorce on discovering he had an illegimate child
by a French woman. Despite being an MP for 24years, he never
spoke once in parliament!

Captain Horsell   £1   £127
From the famous army family, who fought with Wellington at the
Battle of Trafalgar

Cornelius Bradford   £1   £127
Married into the Pinnegar family, buried at Lydiard

Thomas Southeron Estcourt MP   £20   £2,540
MP for Devizes and related to future Vicar Edmond Estcourt. His
statue stands in Devizes

Robert Holford   £10   £1,270
The owner and creator of Westonbirt, near Tetbury

Sir Walter Farquahar   £2   £254
An MP and son of Robert Farquahar, who, while Governor of
Mauritius attempted to free all the slaves and replace them with paid
Chinese labour

Mr & Mrs Coulston   £2   £254
Owners of the Roundway Park estate in Devizes. The family lived at
the estate until 1949, when it was broken up and sold off.

Lady Elizabeth Baker   £2   £254
The Baler family owned the Ranston estate in Dorset and were one
of the richest and most influential families in Britain at that time

A. Churchman   £1   £127
An alias, we assume!

Major-General John Whetham   £2   £254
Owned the Kirklington Estate in Nottinghamshire and was wounded
fighting against the Spanishduring the assault on Montevideo

Captain William Cole, R.N   £1   £127
From Lechlade, served in the Royal Navy

Henry Hussey Vivian   £20   £2,540
Wealthy Welsh businessman and industrialist. Later became an MP
and 1st Baron of Swansea

Rev. Henry Hamilton   £2   £254
Author, Mathematician and Dean of Salisbury Cathedral from 1850-
1880

Oliver Codrington   £1   £127
Builder of the Dean House Estate in Hampshire

The Hon. G.D. Ryder, MP   £1   £127
Helped found the British and Foreign Bible Society

Colonel Samuel Swinhoe   £5   £635
Served in the East India Company and is remembered in Dorchester
Museum

R. Parry Nesbit, Esq   £5   £635
High Sheriff of Wiltshire

Edward Warner   £1   £127
Philanthropist from Loughborough who founded a school and a
charitable trust that still exists today

Acknowledgements (2001)

Thanks must go to the staff at Swindon Reference Library and the Swindon and Wiltshire Records Office at Trowbridge, for making available publications relating to Christ Church, plus answering the many queries which inevitably arose during the course of research for this book.

John Murray Publishers kindly gave permission to quote in full the John Betjeman Poem '*On Hearing the Full Peal of Ten Bells from Christ Church, Swindon, Wilts.*'

The Swindon Society made available photographs from its extensive collection. Permission to use copyright photographs was also given by Shirley Matthias on behalf of Newsquest (Wiltshire) Ltd.

Many individuals both within and outside the parish of Christ Church gave freely of their time and knowledge to supply information, literature and photographs. Without their help this book could not have been published in its present form, and we are deeply grateful to them all. We acknowledge them here, and apologise to any we have inadvertently left out:

Jean Allen; Mandy and Duncan Ball; Revd. Canon Owen Barraclough; David Bedford; Pamela Bevan (Luckington); Denis Bird; Maggie Bird; Brian and Lesley Bladon; Revd. Canon Brian Carne; Gordon Crabbe; John English; Suzanne M. Eward (Cathedral Library, Salisbury); Tim Eyles; Revd. Paul and Mrs Dianna Firmin; Mrs. A. Fitzsimmons (Assistant Librarian, Magdalene College, Cambridge); Alice French; Janet French; Sarah Finch-Crisp; Pat Gilbert; Ruth Haddrell; Brian Harris; Myra Hartshorn; Katherine Henly; Marjorie Hiscock; Revd. Canon John Jackson; John Jarvis; Ailsa Palmer; Revd. Canon Derek Palmer; Ron Palphramand; Revd. Robert Parker; Anthony Peake; Lew Pedler; Revd. Canon John Poarch; Bill Ruck; John Sondermann; Dr. M.N.N. Stansfield (College archivist, Merton College, Oxford); Revd. Canon John Stephens; Rosemary Stephens; Revd. Simon Stevenette; Norma and Trevor Summerhayes; Eric Sutton; Revd. Ernest Swinnerton; Ken Trennery; Walter Truman; Ivor Truman; Jenny Vowles; Brian Way; Ivy Wilkins; Revd. Michael Wilkinson; Margaret Williams; Gwen and Graham Wirdnam.

Finally, special thanks to Pam Bridgeman and Paul Squires for unfailing love and support during the writing of this book.

Acknowledgements (2020)

In addition to those who helped with *The Old Lady on the Hill*, or who granted permission for the use of material, my thanks go to Revd. Simon Stevenette for his guidance and vision in the direction the book should take, Pam Bridgeman for granting permission for the update or the use of material from the archives of Brian Bridgeman, Caroline Pitt for coordinating the efforts of the FOCC, Helen Parker-Drabble for her advice, Daniel Pitt for all his hard work in updating vital information, Janet French for her advice, help with the cataloguing of the memorials, the supply of new photographs and permission to use existing ones, and for the background that led to the chapter *'A Hidden Story'*, Stephen Grosvenor, Andy Binks and everyone at the Swindon Society for their patience in locating several photographs for me, Noel Beauchamp, The Denis Bird Collection, Teresa Squires, Daryl Moody and the Swindon Local Studies team for their hard work in locating files, West Sussex Court, the Goddard Association, the Friends of Christ Church, Diocese of Worcester, Charles Vince, Richard Goddard, Tim Eyles for his hard work and knowledge in assisting me in updating the chapter about the Christ Church organ and choir. Brian Harris for his help with the history of the bells at Christ Church, Karen Harris, Henry Elliot, Steve Brain, Margaret Williams MBE, John Wilson, American Air Museum, RAF Command, Commonwealth War Graves Commission, Keith Janes for generously allowing me access to his research, Revd. Norma McKemey, Patricia Gemmell, Elmar Rubio Photography for permission to use photographs of *The Journey*, National Archives Kew, HM Prison Services, HMP Lewes, Dan Gill, Radical Stroud, BBC History, Wiltshire Records Office, St Mary's Church, National Library of Australia

If I have inadvertently missed anybody's name, I apologise. However, rest assured, your help was still appreciated. Any images, whose source is not mentioned in the acknowledgements above, is in the public domain and reproduced under the Creative Commons License, or the original copyright was unknown at the time of publication.

Photograph Acknowledgements

Chapter 1.
1. Public Domain
2. Pembroke Estate
3. Trinity College, Dublin
4. The Deveraux Estate
5. Mark Bridgeman
6. Cotswold Collection
7. Denis Bird Collection
8. Denis Bird Collection
9. Swindon Library Archives
10. Swindon Library
11. Swindon Society
12. Swindon Society
13. Denis Bird Collection
14. David Bedford
15. Swindon Advertiser
16. Swindon Library
17. Public Domain
18. Christ Church

Chapter 2.
1. Swindon Library
2. Gilbert Scott Archives
3. Public Domain
4. Cambridgeshire Archives
5. British Museum
6. British Museum
7. Christ Church, Southgate
8. Brian Bridgeman
9. Swindon Advertiser
10. Swindon Advertiser
11. Valentines
12. Herbert Barrauld Archive

13. Public Domain
14. Lydiard Tregoze Church
15. Janet French

Chapter 3.
1. Swindon Society
2. Swindon Society
3. Swindon Society
4. Swindon Society
5. Myra Hartshorn
6. BBC History
7. Unknown
8. Nat. Library Australia
9. Wiltshire Standard Archive
10. Unknown
11. HM Prison Services

Chapter 4.
1. Swindon Society
2. Swindon Society
3. Swindon Society
4. Swindon Society
5. Swindon Advertiser
6. Swindon Advertiser
7. Unknown
8. Swindon Society
9. Wiltshire Records Office
10. Brian Bridgeman
11. Brian Bridgeman
12. Swindon Society
13. Swindon Society
14. Unknown
15. Imperial War Museum

16. BBC History
17. Swindon Society
18. Swindon Society
19. Swindon Society
20. Swindon Society
21. Swindon Library Archives
22. Swindon Society
23. Swindon Society

Chapter 5.
1.Swindon Society
2. Andy Binks
3. Andy Binks
4. Swindon Advertiser
5. Unknown
6. Mark Bridgeman
7. Swindon Society
8. British Newspaper Archive
9. Andy Binks
10. Swindon Society
11. Mark Bridgeman
12. Mark Bridgeman
13. Mark Bridgeman
14. Swindon Society
15. Mark Bridgeman
16. Swindon Society
17. Norma Summerhayes
18. Norma Summerhayes
19. Mark Bridgeman
20. Swindon Society

Chapter 6.
1. Revd. M. Wilkinson
2. Mark Bridgeman
3. Swindon Library
4. Swindon Library
5. Denis Bird

6. Mark Bridgeman
7. Swindon Society
8. Canon John Jackson
9. Swindon Advertiser
10. Swindon Advertiser
11. Swindon Society
12. Revd. Derek Palmer
13. Steve Brain
14. Mark Bridgeman
15. Ivy Wilkins
16. Swindon Library
17. Denis Bird
18. Denis Bird
19. Denis Bird
20. Unknown
21. Mark Bridgeman
22. Mark Bridgeman
23. David Luker
24. Swindon Society

Chapter 7.
1.Swindon Advertiser
2. Caroline Pitt
3. Janet French
4. Public Domain
5. Royal Mail
6. Shutterstock
7. Caroline Pitt
8. David Bedford
9. Diana Swan
10. Brian Bridgeman
11. Mark Bridgeman
12. Swindon Advertiser
13. Brian Bridgeman
14. Swindon Advertiser
15. Mark Bridgeman

Chapter 8.
1. Mark Bridgeman
2. Janet French
3. Caroline Pitt
4. Caroline Pitt
5. Janet French
6. Peter Taylor
7. Swindon Advertiser
8. Unknown
9. Janet French
10. Swindon Advertiser
11. Janet French
12. Swindon Advertiser
13. Janet French
14. Janet French
15. Janet French
16. Janet French
17. Public Domain
18. Janet French
19. Janet French
20. Janet French
21. Pam Bridgeman
22. Janet French
23. Janet French
24. Janet French
25. Janet French
26. Swindon Advertiser
27. Janet French
28. Janet French
29. Janet French
30. Mark Bridgeman
31. Janet French
32. Janet French
33. Janet French
34. Janet French
35. Janet French
36. Elmar Rubio
37. Elmar Rubio
38. Elmar Rubio
39. Elmar Rubio
40. Elmar Rubio
41. Janet French
42. Pam Bridgeman

Chapter 9.
1. Swindon Society
2. Christ Church
3. British Newspaper Archive
4. Wilts. Record Office
5. Frank Foord
6. Swindon Society
7. Swindon Society

Chapter 10.
1. Public Domain
2. Public Domain
3. Swindon Library
4. Swindon Library
5. Swindon Library
6. Swindon Library
7. Swindon Library
8. Swindon Library

Chapter 11.
1. David Bedford
2. John Sondermann
3. Denis Bird
4. David Luker
5. David Luker
6. Canon Owen Barraclough
7. Mark Bridgeman
Chapter 12.

1. Janet French
2. Janet French

Chapter 13.
1. Swindon Society
2. Swindon Society
3. Swindon Society
4. Public Domain
5. Canon Owen Barraclough
6. Mark Bridgeman

Chapter 14.
1. Public Domain
2. Janet French
3. Christ Church Bellringers
4. Wilts Record Office
5. Brian Harris
6. Brian Harris
7. Swindon Society
8. Brian Harris
9. Janet French
10. Swindon Society
11. Swindon Society
12. Swindon Society
13. Janet French
14. Brian Harris
15. Brian Harris
16. Brian Harris

Chapter 15.
1. Unknown
2. John Wilson
3. John Wilson
4. Dan Gill
5. John Wilson
6. Janet French

7. Janet French

Chapter 16
1. Janet French
2. Janet French
3. Janet French
4. Janet French
5. Janet French
6. Janet French
7. Daniel Pitt
8. Mark Bridgeman

Front and back cover images by Janet French

Bibliography

Astill's Original Swindon Almanack & Trades Register (various issues),

Bavin, W.D. *Swindon's War Record* (John Drew Ltd., Swindon, for Swindon Town Council, 1922)

Bird, Denis. *The Story of Holy Rood; Old Parish Church of Swindon* (privately published, 1975. Revised edition, The Swindon Society, 1991)

Bird, Maggie. *A Brief History of St. Mary's Church, Commonweal Road, from 1926 to 2000* (published privately, Swindon, 2000)

Braun, Hugh. *Parish Churches. Their Architectural Development in England* (Faber, 1974)

Bristol Mercury (various issues)

Brian Bridgeman & Teresa Squires. *The Old Lady on the Hill* (2001)

British Newspaper Archive

Buildings of Special Architectural or Historic Interest: Swindon (Thamesdown Borough Council, 1989)

C.E.M.S.

Chandler, John. *Swindon History and Guide*

Charity Commission. *Endowed Charities (County of Wilts) Parish of Swindon* (Printed by Eyre and Spottiswoode, for HMSO, November 1904)

Child, Mark. *Swindon An Illustrated History*

Child, Mark. *Swindon Old Town Through Time*

Child, Mark. *The Swindon Book Companion*

Christ Church, Swindon 1851 – 1951 A Centenary Souvenir (Graham Cumming Ltd, Ramsgate, 1951)

Christ Church Parish Magazines

Cockbill, Trevor. Our Swindon in 1939

Crittall, Elizabeth, Rogers, K.H. and Shrimpton, Colin, with architectural descriptions prepared in collaboration with Tomlinson, Margaret. *The Victoria County History of Wiltshire, Vol. IX* (Oxford University Press, 1970)

A History of Swindon to 1965 (reprinted from above) (Wiltshire Library & Museum Service, 1983)

Crabbe, Gordon. *The Organ of Christ Church Swindon* (privately published, Swindon, 1970)

Crockford Clerical Directories (various editions)

Debrett's Peerage

Devizes and Wiltshire Gazette (various issues)

English Heritage. *Listing description of buildings and Monuments at Holy Rood and Christ Church*

Faringdon Advertiser (1912, 1915)

Fuller, Dr. Frederick. '70 years of St. Mary-in-the-Mall', *Swindon Outlook* (September 1996)

Gardiner, Juliet & Wenborn, Neil (eds). *The History Today Companion to British History* (Collins and Brown 1995)

Goddard Association Archives

Grinsell, L.V., Wells, H.B., Tallamy, H.S., Betjeman, John. *Studies in the History of Swindon* (Swindon Borough Council, 1950)

Hereford Journal (1857)

Hey, David. *The Oxford Companion to Local and Family History* (Oxford University Press 1996)

Janes, Keith. *They Came From Burgundy* (Troubador Press)

King William Street School

Laird, Lucy *A Celebration of 125 years 1871 – 1996* (King William Street C.E. School, Swindon 1996)

Large, F. *A Swindon Retrospect 1855-1930* (Borough Press, Swindon, 1932, republished 1970 by SR Publishers)

List of Buildings of Special Architectural History & Interest;

Borough of Thamesdown, Wiltshire (Area of Swindon) (Dept. Of the Environment, 1986)

List of Stained Glass Windows at Christ Church (booklet, no date or author, copy held at Swindon Reference Library)

Lupson, Peter. *Thank God For Football*

Monuments at Christ Church and Holy Rood (unpublished list transcribed by the Wiltshire Family History Society)

Morris, William. *Swindon – Reminiscences Notes and Relics of ye old Wiltshire Towne* (1885, re-issued 1970 by The Tabard Press)

North Wilts Directories (various issues)

North Wilts Herald (various issues)

Pevsner, Nicholas. *The Buildings of England : Wiltshire* (Penguin Books Ltd., 1963 & 1975)

Plowman, Paul. *Swindon Town 1879 - 2009*

Old Town Group, *Millennium Memories*

Report of Board of Health Inspector on Swindon (HMSO, 1850)

St Mark's 1845-1945, A Record written by Priests and People (St. Mark's Parochial Church Council, Swindon, 1945)

Saunders, Keith. *Notes on the History of the Old Parish Church* 1965

Sheldon, Peter. *Swindon in Camera 1850-1979*

Silto, J. *A Swindon History 1840-1901* (privately published, 1981)

Silto, J. *The Railway Town: A Description of Life and Events in Swindon from 22 January 1901 to 11 November 1918* (privately published, undated)

Smith, Edwin, Cook, Olive and Hutton, Graham. *English Parish Churches* (Thames and Hudson, 1976)

Stephens, Rosemary and Bird, Denis. *Swindon Parish Church, A short history of a Community and its Church* (British Publishing Company Ltd, Gloucester, 1969)

Swindon and *Evening Advertiser* (various issues)

Swindon Heritage Magazine

Swindon Library Services

Swindon Town Football Club

Tallamy H.S. *Studies in the History of Swindon 1950*

The Old Town Parish Church, published 1969

The Tablet Magazine (1884)

Tompkins, Richard & Sheldon, Peter. *The Changing Face of Swindon*

Walter, K. *Swindon Air Raids in World War 2: A Review of Remaining Evidence, Part Two: 1942* (published privately, Swindon, 1998)

Walters, H.B. MA, FSA. *The Church Bells of Wiltshire Their Inscriptions and History* (1929, Reprinted by Kingsmead Reprints, Bath in 1969)

Waylen, James. *The Chronicles of Devizes* (1853)

Western Advertiser

Western Gazette (1934)

Western Daily Press (1907)

West Sussex Court Archives

Wikipedia

Wilts & Glos Standard (1908)

Wiltshire Independent (1854)

www.oodwooc.f9.co.uk (Wiltshire Parish Churches and their monuments)

www.christchurchswindon.co.uk

www.tinyonline.co.uk/dandbsinclair

www.swindonweb.com

www.2013dollars.com

Index

..

Friends Of Christ Church

The Friends of Christ Church was formed in April 2001 as a registered charity. Its principal purpose being the raising of funds for the maintenance of the church, and its grounds, as a place of worship and as a community resource for the town.

Principally, the Friends support specific projects for the maintenance and enhancement of the fabric of the church and the churchyard. The scope of the organisation also includes assisting projects at St Mary's in Commonweal Road, the Community Centre, and supporting the publication of this book.

Christ Church has been a familiar and a comforting presence in Swindon for 170 years. By joining The Friends of Christ Church, you can help us to maintain, protect and improve the building for the future.

If you are interested in becoming a Friend it's very easy. You can pick up a membership from Christ Church or the Community Centre, and by visiting:

www.christchurchswindon.co.uk/friends

You can join as an individual or a family, and on either an annual or life basis. Yearly membership costs £5 per person and £10 per family. Life membership is a single payment of £75. Membership gives you the opportunity to become involved both practically and socially. Members have the opportunity to influence future developments, especially at our AGM, and also receive our occasional newsletter.

If you would like to contact the Friends of Christ Church:
The Friends of Christ Church,
c/o The Parish Office,
The Community Centre@ Christ Church,
Swindon,Wiltshire, SN1 3HB

Tel: 01793 522832
email: parishoffice@christchurchswindon.co.uk
facebook: facebook.com/Christchurchswindon

Registered Charity: No. 1088767

Other Titles By The Author

Mark Bridgeman is the son of the original author of The Old Lady on the Hill, Brian Bridgeman. Mark now lives in Aberfeldy, Scotland and is a published author who has inherited his father's passion for local history.

The River Runs Red

Nineteen true stories of murder, mystery and deception from Highland Perthshire's dark past. Read about one of Scotland's most infamous murders and the psychic who located a body.

Blood Beneath Ben Nevis

21 true stories of murder, myth and mystery from Fort William and Lochaber, covering the years 1700 – 1971. Learn about the massacre in a cave, ghosts in the High Street and take part in a £10 million treasure hunt!

Surviving In The Shadows

The surprising story of cricket in Highland Perthshire, from 1850 to the present day. Read about Breadalbane Cricket Club's links to test cricket and some of the biggest names in the history of the game.

The Lost Village of Lawers

Discover the forgotten and abandoned village in Perthshire that lies in ruins by the shores of Loch Tay. Who lived there and why did they leave? Find out about the mysterious 'Lady of Lawers'. Who was she? Did she really have special powers?

All Mark's titles are available from amazon.co.uk, Waterstone's and selected bookshops.

For further stories and information from the author why not follow him @:

www.facebook.com/markbridgemanauthor
or https://markbridgeman.wixsite.com/author/blog